ServiceNow Certified System Administrator Certification Guide

System administering ServiceNow for managing ITSM, automating workflow, and application configuration for different industries

MageshKumar G Embuswamy

www.bpbonline.com

First Edition 2026

ISBN: 978-93-65894-868

LIMITS OF LIABILITY AND DISCLAIMER OF WARRANTY

The information contained in this book is true and correct to the best of author's and publisher's knowledge. The author has made every effort to ensure the accuracy of these publications, but the publisher cannot be held responsible for any loss or damage arising from any information in this book.

All trademarks referred to in the book are acknowledged as properties of their respective owners but BPB Publications cannot guarantee the accuracy of this information.

Distributors:

BPB PUBLICATIONS
20, Ansari Road, Darya Ganj
New Delhi-110002
Ph: 23254990/23254991

DECCAN AGENCIES
4-3-329, Bank Street,
Hyderabad-500195
Ph: 24756967/24756400

MICRO MEDIA
Shop No. 5, Mahendra Chambers,
150 DN Rd. Next to Capital Cinema,
V.T. (C.S.T.) Station, MUMBAI-400 001
Ph: 22078296/22078297

Published by Manish Jain for BPB Publications, 20 Ansari Road, Darya Ganj, New Delhi-110002 and Printed by him at Repro India Ltd., Rewari.

www.bpbonline.com

Dedicated to

My dad and my mom,
Embuswamy** and **Saraladevi

My wife,
Jyothy Yadhati

My son,
Amrit Magesh

About the Author

Magesh Kumar Gopalswamy Embuswamy is working as a ServiceNow delivery lead in a reputed organization. He did his bachelor of engineering in **Government College of Technology** (**GCT**) in Coimbatore, India, and he did his MBA in **Indira Gandhi National Open University** (**IGNOU**) in New Delhi, India. He achieved the highest level in ITIL certification, ITIL 4 Master, in October 2023. He has worked for 30 years in the IT industry. He is a **Project Management Professional** (**PMP**) and **PMI Agile Certified Practitioner** (**PMI-ACP**) certified person. In ServiceNow, he is certified with **Certified System Administrator** (**CSA**) and **Certified Implementation Specialist – Human Resources** (**CIS-HR**). He is excited about reading and writing books. This is the first book he wrote in that journey. He has a vision to serve the community by providing his ideas and knowledge so that others can benefit and grow. This book is the start towards that vision.

About the Reviewer

Saaniya Chugh is an experienced IT professional with over a decade of hands-on experience across the ServiceNow platform. She is currently working at ServiceNow, where she helps organizations design, build, and optimize ServiceNow solutions that improve service delivery and operational efficiency.

Saaniya is also the author of two books on the ServiceNow ecosystem, where she focuses on making the platform more accessible to learners and early-career professionals. Her writing reflects her practical understanding of the platform, combining real-world experience with clear, structured guidance.

In addition to her consulting and writing work, Saaniya remains closely involved with the community. She started the ServiceNow Community Meetup in Montréal and frequently contributes to discussions, mentorship initiatives, and learning forums to support newcomers entering the ecosystem.

As a reviewer, Saaniya brings a balanced perspective shaped by her technical background, implementation experience, and commitment to helping professionals build strong foundations on the platform.

Acknowledgement

I would like to express my sincere gratitude to all those who contributed to the completion of this book.

First and foremost, I extend my heartfelt appreciation to my family and friends for their unwavering support and encouragement throughout this journey. Their love and encouragement have been a constant source of motivation.

I am immensely grateful to BPB Publications for their guidance and expertise in bringing this book to fruition. Their support and assistance were invaluable in navigating the complexities of the publishing process.

I would also like to acknowledge the reviewers, technical experts, and editors who provided valuable feedback and contributed to the refinement of this manuscript. Their insights and suggestions have significantly enhanced the quality of the book.

Last but not least, I want to express my gratitude to the readers who have shown interest in the book. Your support and encouragement have been deeply appreciated.

Thank you to everyone who has played a part in making this book a reality.

Preface

Understanding a tool like ServiceNow for those who start their careers and those who are experienced will place them in the perfect place in their careers.

Comprising nine insightful chapters, this book covers a range of topics towards the ServiceNow CSA certification. These chapters are designed as per the certification syllabus learning domains provided by ServiceNow, driving readers exactly towards the certification.

Chapter 7 provides case studies in which practical scenarios are discussed in which CSA system admins will play their role. Thus, this book guides the readers to understand theoretical concepts towards passing the CSA certification and applying them when readers handle those situations practically. Hence, the vision of the book is to provide a complete wholeness towards ServiceNow system admin work.

This book caters to all inspiring readers who want to be qualified as ServiceNow admins and start their journey into the ServiceNow world. All concepts are discussed and explained so that they can provide a complete picture in that journey. Readers will be able to get an idea of the usefulness of the ServiceNow tool for automation and how it effectively enables no-code or low-code solutions.

Further future trends are detailed so that readers can tie in with upcoming trends in automation and **artificial intelligence** (**AI**).

Chapter 1: CSA Platform Overview and Navigation- This chapter provides an introduction to the ServiceNow platform, detailing its capabilities and services. Details Next Experience Unified Navigation detailing navigation items. Mentions procedure to avail the **personal developer instance** (**PDI**) at no cost for use. Different products within ServiceNow are detailed in a high-level manner, providing the usefulness of ServiceNow in all these fields. ServiceNow's capabilities, such as workflow automation, customizable dashboards, and mobile app access, are mentioned in this chapter. Discusses Flow Designer, which is the latest ServiceNow tool with a visual drag-and-drop interface, enabling no-code/low-code for building business workflows. Discusses the Employee Service Portal, which is a built-in frontend web interface of ServiceNow.

Chapter 2: CSA Instance Configuration- This chapter provides details about applications and plugins in ServiceNow. Applications are a set of functionalities or features. Plugins add additional functionalities to the installed applications. This chapter talks about how to configure the context menu and its submenus for each of the components, such as business rules and tables. In general, as soon as the application is enabled as per the user's license, default applications and their functionalities appear. After that, based on the customer's needs, an instance is configured for the needed functionality, such as adding a new field in the incident form.

Chapter 3: Configuring Applications for Collaboration- This chapter details configuring ServiceNow applications components, such as lists, forms, and tags. In classic list view, configuration is done by a context menu, which appears by right-clicking on a column header. In the form context menu, the configuration appears when right-clicking the breadcrumb at the top of the form.

Context menu for configuration consists of ServiceNow elements such as UI policies, table, data policies, UI action, and notification. This chapter details configuring dashboards and reports. ServiceNow provides a set of reports and dashboards as out-of-the-box and available as the application is enabled. This chapter focuses on details regarding configuring notifications.

Chapter 4: Self-service and Automation- This chapter focuses on self-service capabilities and automating workflows. Details about the component Flow Designer, which is used to automate workflows. Details about Flow Designer, which is a **graphical user interface** (**GUI**) component with drag-and-drop elements in a palette. Flow Designer has elements that enable integration with external systems. Details about the component Virtual Agent, which acts as a chatbot through which users can provide their requests and get work done. This includes users' HR requests, self-service requests, and providing automation by which manual tasks are reduced. The Knowledge Management module provides a repository in which knowledge base articles can be stored and referenced. Service Catalog provides a list of products that employees order internally in the organization.

Chapter 5: Database Management- This chapter details database concepts that are applied in ServiceNow. ServiceNow stores all the data in internal tables. Data schema refers to the organization and structure of the database tables, how they relate to each other, and how the data is stored and accessed. This chapter details the importing of data into ServiceNow tables from external sources. A unique feature of ServiceNow is that all data is stored and ready to pull in the needed format, which is useful from a business, functional, and technical point of view for an organization. This chapter talks about the **configuration management database** (**CMDB**), which is available for organizations to use as a single source of truth. Complete IT infrastructure is stored as **configuration items** (**CIs**). This concept enable to pull the data from all sources into ServiceNow by a concept called ServiceNow Discovery.

This concept also provides faster resolution of incidents and problems by pinpointing which CI is having an issue.

Chapter 6: Data Migration and Integration- This chapter details components of ServiceNow, such as UI policies, business rules, update sets, and scripting options. Update sets capture all configurations made, and those are moved to the higher environment.

These are the components for the ServiceNow release. This chapter details data that is not captured by the update set as well. The data that was not captured can be stored as XML and exported into a higher environment. Details about the UI policy by which the behavior of fields is configured. Describes business rules that can be triggered under specific conditions for the database operations. Apart from this, ServiceNow facilitates scripts for functionalities, including integration. Glide API is the main API available, and details are provided in this chapter.

Chapter 7: Case Studies CSA- This chapter details a few practical scenarios, tasks that ServiceNow admins perform in managing the ServiceNow instances. To start with, when a new, fresh ServiceNow instance is created, plugins are the first thing that needs to be loaded according to the license obtained by the organization. Plugins are the way in which ServiceNow pulls out-of-the-box functionality into that ServiceNow instance. Admins add users, roles, and groups as per organizational needs. Jobs are configured and maintained by admins.

Chapter 8: ServiceNow CSA Practice Exams- This chapter provided two sample CSA practice exams. Once this is understood, it will provide a good approach towards the certification exam. Concepts are already explained in the previous chapter. Vision is such that to provide the reader with the best with all inputs to pass the certification. Also, practical concepts are explained in chapters that they can apply as ServiceNow system admins, explaining why they do the work for organizations.

Chapter 9: Summing Up and Future Trends- This chapter sums up the concepts understood towards the ServiceNow CSA certification exam. Details about future trends. AI is becoming a big part, and explained how it started being applied in ServiceNow. There is a Now Assist functionality which will help to summarize the Incidents and can perform other functions that will help to avoid manual work and repeated tasks. Other expansions of AI concepts, such as generative AI and agentic AI, are explained to the reader to provide an idea of future trends.

Coloured Images

Please follow the link to download the
Coloured Images of the book:

https://rebrand.ly/5a4d8e

We have code bundles from our rich catalogue of books and videos available at **https://github.com/bpbpublications**. Check them out!

Errata

We take immense pride in our work at BPB Publications and follow best practices to ensure the accuracy of our content to provide an indulging reading experience to our subscribers. Our readers are our mirrors, and we use their inputs to reflect and improve upon human errors, if any, that may have occurred during the publishing processes involved. To let us maintain the quality and help us reach out to any readers who might be having difficulties due to any unforeseen errors, please write to us at:

errata@bpbonline.com

Your support, suggestions and feedback are highly appreciated by the BPB Publications' Family.

Piracy

If you come across any illegal copies of our works in any form on the internet, we would be grateful if you would provide us with the location address or website name. Please contact us at **business@bpbonline.com** with a link to the material.

If you are interested in becoming an author

If there is a topic that you have expertise in, and you are interested in either writing or contributing to a book, please visit **www.bpbonline.com**. We have worked with thousands of developers and tech professionals, just like you, to help them share their insights with the global tech community. You can make a general application, apply for a specific hot topic that we are recruiting an author for, or submit your own idea.

Reviews

Please leave a review. Once you have read and used this book, why not leave a review on the site that you purchased it from? Potential readers can then see and use your unbiased opinion to make purchase decisions. We at BPB can understand what you think about our products, and our authors can see your feedback on their book. Thank you!

For more information about BPB, please visit **www.bpbonline.com**.

Join our Discord space

Join our Discord workspace for latest updates, offers, tech happenings around the world, new releases, and sessions with the authors:

https://discord.bpbonline.com

Table of Contents

Chapter 1
CSA Platform Overview and Navigation

Introduction

ServiceNow **Certified System Administrator** (**CSA**) certification provides an entry point to understanding the ServiceNow platform. This certification demonstrates a candidate's ability to configure, implement, and maintain the ServiceNow platform. The platform overview and navigation concepts cover 7% of the 60 questions for the ServiceNow's CSA exam.

Structure

This chapter covers the following topics:

- ServiceNow platform overview
- The ServiceNow instance
- Next Experience Unified Navigation
- Certification sample questions

Objectives

This chapter provides insights about ServiceNow platform overview, platform capabilities and services, ServiceNow instance, Next Experience Unified Navigation pertaining to CSA certification. This includes sample questions at the end, providing a good understanding of these topics.

ServiceNow platform overview

ServiceNow is a cloud-based platform that helps organizations automate processes and improve productivity. The overview is as follows:

- **Digital transformation**: ServiceNow helps businesses digitize and automate workflows and create digital experiences. ServiceNow uses workflows to automate processes, primarily categorized into IT, employee, customer, and creator workflows.

IT workflows streamline IT operations for faster service, resource management, and issue resolution. Employee workflows create connected employee experiences for HR, IT, and services like new hire onboarding. Customer workflows focus on customer service functionalities. Creator workflows enable developers to build applications.

- **Real-time analytics**: ServiceNow analytics and AI capabilities help businesses predict issues, anticipate trends, and prioritize resources. Turns operational data into actionable insights. Key components are Reporting, Performance Analytics, and Platform Analytics.
- **Unified architecture**: ServiceNow's unified architecture and data model help ensure that all products work together.

The following figure shows the ServiceNow platform overview:

Figure 1.1: ServiceNow platform overview

- **Security**: ServiceNow includes automated security controls, certified integrations, and multilayer encryption. ServiceNow system security settings are platform configurations controlling access, data protection, and behavior, encompassing **role-based access control** (**RBAC**), encryption, authentication (MFA, IP Access), instance hardening (password policies, default deny), and comprehensive auditing/monitoring (Activity Logs, Security Center) to secure the platform and its sensitive data. Key features include the High Security Plugin, which enables stricter defaults like denying access until explicitly granted, ensuring only authorized users and actions are permitted. provides **access control lists** (**ACL**), which define who can access specific records and fields as part of RBAC.
- **Compatibility**: ServiceNow is compatible with third-party software, including legacy on-premises solutions.

- **Environment**: ServiceNow provides sub-production environments for building, testing, and implementing applications. These lower environments are termed as development, testing, and **user acceptance testing** (**UAT**).

Platform capabilities and services

The ServiceNow platform addresses three common business challenges, which are:

- **Case management**: Processing of case outcomes involving human tasks and complex processes.
- **Enterprise service**: End user portal for requesting services.
- **Operations management**: Inventory, equipment, systems, facilities, and people.

Case management involves ticket-based business processes that require workflows and knowledge workers to move a case to its outcome. It usually involves unpredictable events such as customer complaints, litigation, insurance claims, service requests, and many other scenarios. Managing and resolving these kinds of events requires a combination of human intelligence and electronic workflows. Comprehensive case management solutions include workflow management, content management, collaboration, decision-making, and digital filing.

Operations management is all about business process automation and record keeping that involves things such as managing inventory, equipment, systems, facilities, and people. For business operations analysts, this means keeping track of configurations and item relationships, quickly addressing problems and changes, and ensuring regular events like planned maintenance and training happen consistently and on time. It is a job with responsibility that requires orchestrating numerous, interrelated tasks.

Enterprise service management is the delivery of services throughout the enterprise and often involves the need to aggregate disparate IT systems. Major enterprise service providers include IT, HR, and finance, although any team can deliver services. Service management solutions are designed to improve service efficiency and access to critical services. Most of these solutions offer a service portal for service requests, self-service, and collaboration options, as well as status lookups and notifications.

ServiceNow offers a wide variety of packaged applications, including **IT service management** (**ITSM**), security operations, customer service, and human resources.

The following figure shows ServiceNow **Products**:

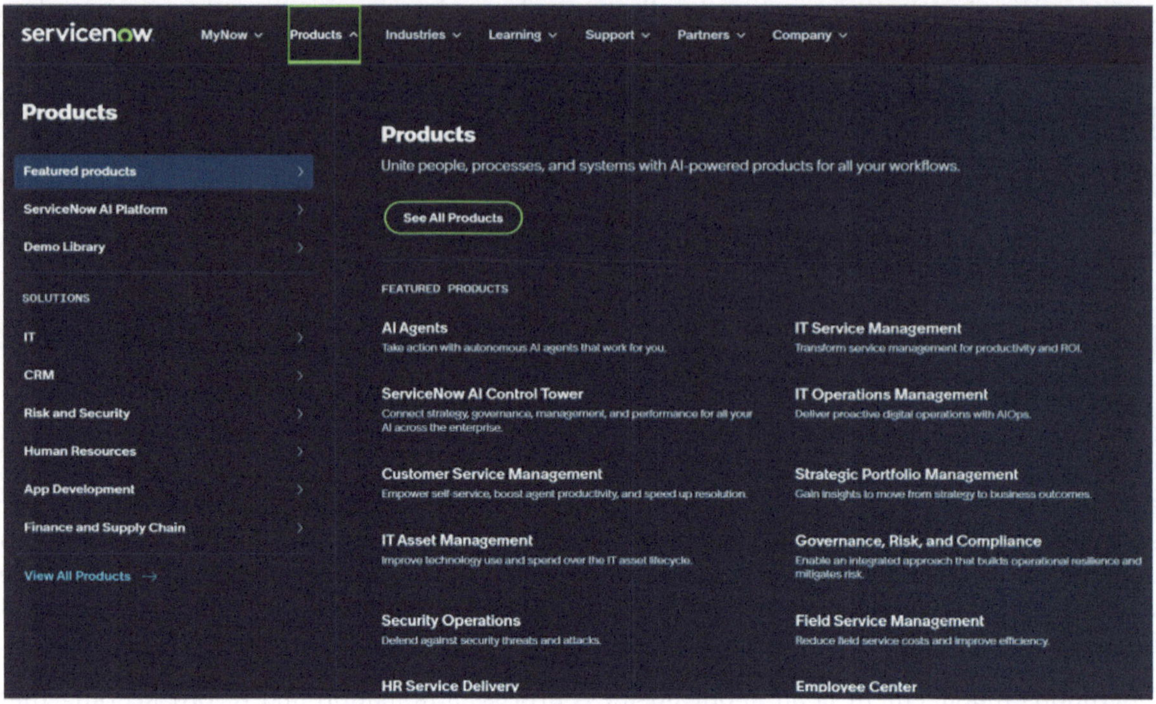

Figure 1.2: ServiceNow Products

Customers can extend the functionality of these apps or create custom business apps with the Now Platform. The Now Platform's environment, which is used for development, is the foundation underlying all our packaged application subscriptions. (It can also be purchased separately per app or with platform licenses.).

ServiceNow platform capabilities include comprehensive workflow automation, customizable dashboards, mobile app access and specialized features for managing IT services, customer service, and HR functions, with key service examples like **IT asset management** (**ITAM**), incident management, knowledge base creation, **field service management** (**FSM**), and customer service case management, all built on a low-code development environment allowing for customization based on specific business needs.

The key service examples are as follows:

- **ITSM**: Managing IT incidents, requests, problems, and changes efficiently through automated workflows and ticket tracking.
- **ITAM**: Tracking and managing IT hardware and software licenses, including alerts for expiring licenses.
- **Knowledge Management**: Creating a centralized knowledge base for employees and customers to access solutions to common issues.

- **FSM**: Scheduling and dispatching field technicians to customer locations, managing work orders, and tracking progress in real-time.
- **Customer service management (CSM)**: Managing customer inquiries, complaints, and support cases through a unified platform.
- **HR Service Delivery**: Automating HR processes like leave requests, employee onboarding, and expense reporting.

Platform capabilities and overview include ITSM, Service Operations Workspace, and Employee Center portal.

Service Operations Workspace, previously called **Agent Workspace**, provides a unified workspace to view, edit, and create cases by agents, help desk, and incident managers.

Employee Center portal, also known as **Employee Service Center** (**ESC**), provides employees with a unified portal with functionalities of HR, IT, and workplace services.

IT service management incident management

To navigate to an **Incident** from the **All** menu, go to **All**, select **Incident**, and choose **Create New**:

- **Incident lifecycle**: States are New, In Progress, On Hold, Resolved, Closed, and Canceled.
- **incident assignment/groups**: In ServiceNow, assignment groups are essential for efficiently routing tickets or tasks to a designated team or department based on specific criteria. This provides an organized work distribution.

The steps for creating an assignment group are as follows:

1. Go to **All** in the navigation menu.
2. Select **User Administration**.
3. Click on **Groups**.
4. Click **New** to create a new assignment group.
5. Enter the necessary details like group name, manager, and group type.
6. Click **Submit** to save the assignment group.

Work notes and additional comments

In ServiceNow, there are two types of notes that can be used to provide additional information about an incident task or an incident. They are work notes and additional comments. While both serve the same purpose of providing additional context to a record, they differ in their accessibility and intended use. Work notes are viewable only within the task for the fulfiller groups to review.

Additional comments are viewable by the requester, so whenever you need to reach out to the customer, always use additional comments.

Incident prioritization and handling based on **Impact** and **Urgency** fields.

The ServiceNow incident priority matrix automatically determines the priority of an incident based on its impact and urgency levels. Impact measures business loss, and urgency measures the speed of resolution needed. The matrix uses combinations of these two fields to automatically set a priority, such as Critical, High, Moderate, or Low. This priority is a read-only field, and its value changes automatically if the impact or urgency fields are modified.

This is setup as priority lookup rules in system policy.

The following figure shows the incident priority matrix:

Priority Matrix		Impact		
		1 - High	2 - Medium	3 - Low
Urgency	1 - High	1 - Critical	2 - High	3 - Moderate
	2 - Medium	2 - High	3 - Moderate	4 - Low
	3 - Low	3 - Moderate	4 - Low	5 - Planning

***Figure 1.3**: Incident priority matrix*

A **service level agreement** (**SLA**) is a contract between a service provider and a customer, defining the types and standards of services to be offered. As an example, an SLA can state expected timing for ticket resolution based on priority.

Service Operations Workspace (Agent Workspace)

Workspaces are collections of curated, task-based workflows that enable users to complete their work easily and effectively. Individual widgets are available on dashboards to navigate in the workspace. In this workspace view, the classic view (list view) is available in the left side menu bar.

The following figure shows the unified navigation of the Service Operations Workspace:

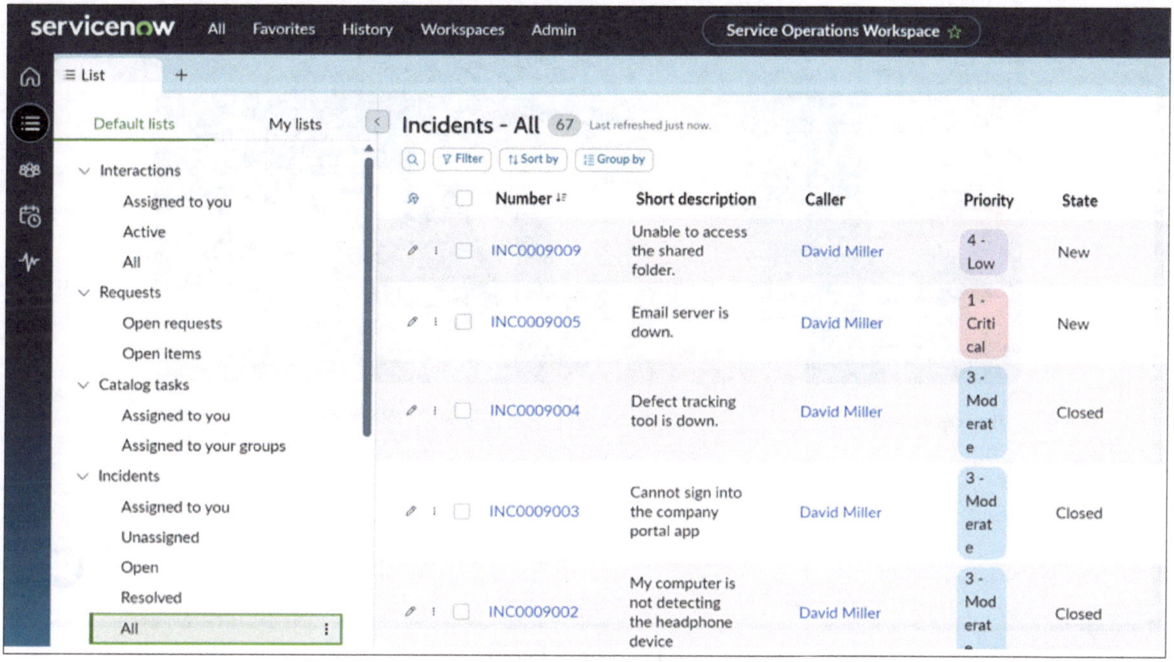

***Figure 1.4**: Service Operations Workspace*

Employee Center portal

The Employee Center portal provides employees with a unified portal to access services, communications, apps, and tasks. It also boosts productivity, enhances self-service, and reduces costs. This is termed the Employee Center. An enhanced version of the Employee Center is also introduced by ServiceNow, and it is called Employee Center Pro.

Navigating to the Employee Center

The following link brings up the ESC portal: **https://devxxxxxx.service-now.com/esc**.

To access the Employee Center in ServiceNow from the **All** menu:

1. Navigate to **All**.
2. Go to the **Employee Center**. This will open the dedicated **Employee Center** portal within your ServiceNow instance.

The following figure shows the dynamic portal of **Employee Center**:

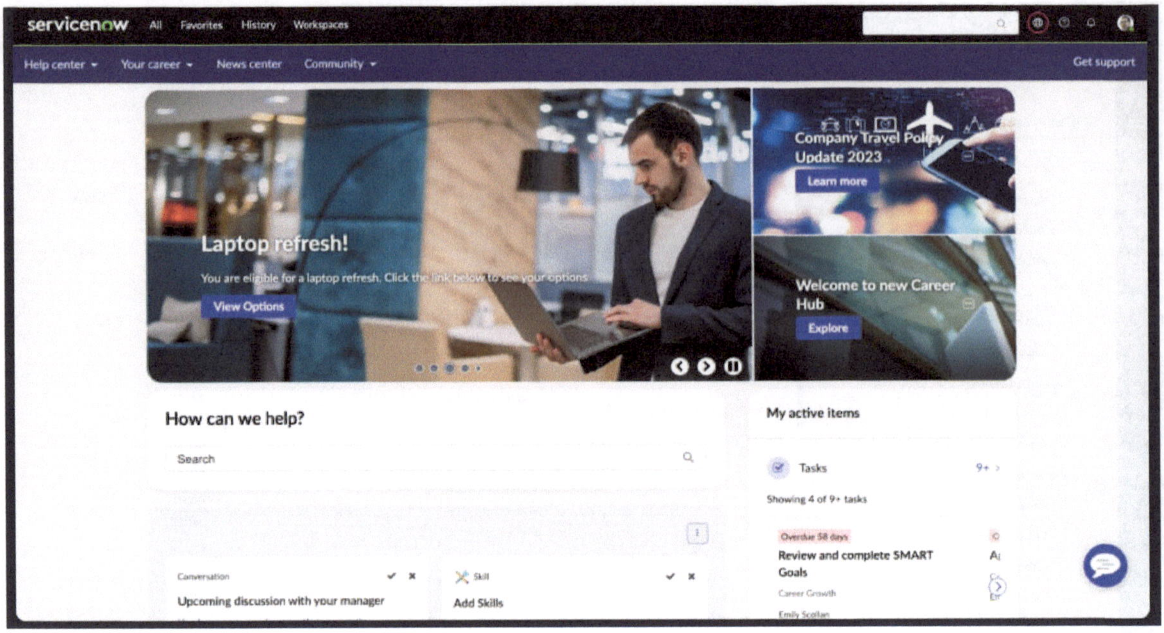

Figure 1.5: ESC

Workflow

A workflow comprises the interdependent processes and people required to reach a result that no single participant can achieve alone.

Manual workflows can become digital workflows when companies use software, automation tools, and other technologies to digitize and/or automate manual tasks, processes, and workflows.

ServiceNow, for example, uses digital workflows to automate a company's quarterly financial close, as opposed to forcing accountants to enter massive amounts of financial data manually into a system. Digitizing this workflow eliminates needless busy work. The time saved in doing so allows finance employees to concentrate on higher level tasks like analyzing key metrics that drive our business.

New efficiencies reduce frustrating delays that might have been caused by manual paperwork.

The four types of workflows in ServiceNow are:

- IT workflows
- Employee workflows
- Customer workflows

- Creator workflows

ServiceNow offers a range of solutions to support the organization's IT workflows, including ITSM and **IT operations management (ITOM)**. ServiceNow also offers solutions to support other types of workflows, including customer, employee, and creator workflows:

- **IT workflows**: Automate and manage IT services, improving operations and agility.
    - o **Examples**: Incident management (routing tickets), request fulfilment (new laptop/ software), change management, problem management.
- **Employee workflows**: Connect employees to HR, facilities, and other departments for seamless service delivery.
    - o **Examples**: New hire onboarding, employee self-service (payslips, benefits), Support requests, HR cases.
- **Customer workflows**: Deliver great customer experiences across all service touchpoints, extending beyond traditional CRM.
    - o **Examples**: CSM for resolving issues, FSM for on-site support.
- **Creator workflows**: Empower developers (pro-code and low-code) to build custom applications and automate complex processes.
    - o **Examples**: Building custom apps with App Engine, integrating systems via Integration Hub, creating approval flows for purchase orders, and automating document approvals.

The four primary interfaces of the ServiceNow platform are:

- Next Experience UI.
- Workspace UI includes the Service Operation Workspace.
- Service portal is the latest version, termed as Employee Center and Employee Center Pro.
- Classic environment, which is also called **Core UI**.

A transform map matches the columns from the staging table to the columns in the target table. Every import operation requires at least one transform.

Two ServiceNow applications that comprise customer experience (modernized work experience) are as follows:

- CSM
- FSM

The following figure shows FSM:

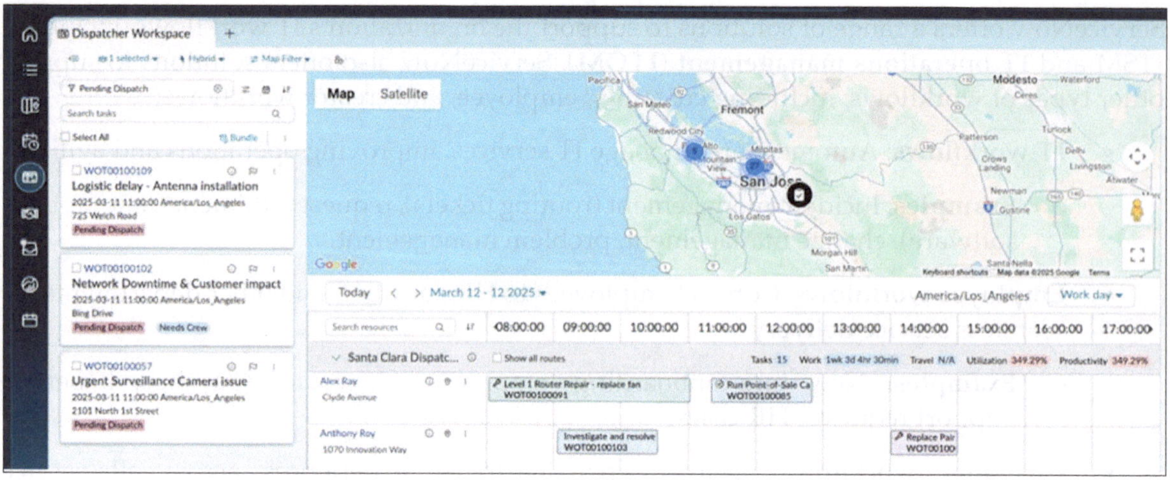

Figure 1.6: FSM

Four ServiceNow applications that comprise employee experience are as follows:

- **HR Service Delivery (HRSD)**: It workflows automate HR processes (like onboarding, offboarding, and benefits).
- **Workplace Service Delivery (WSD)**: Its workflows are automated processes that manage various workplace tasks, such as desk bookings, facility requests, and location management.
- **Safe Workplace Suite**: Key workflows involve automated case creation, task assignment for cleaning/sanitization, health screenings, temperature checks, tracking occupancy, and leveraging the platform's case and Knowledge Management for efficient resolution and communication.
- **Employee Center portal**: ServiceNow Employee Center workflows automate and unify employee requests (like HR, IT, facilities) through a central portal.

The following figure shows the HRSD Employee Center sample page:

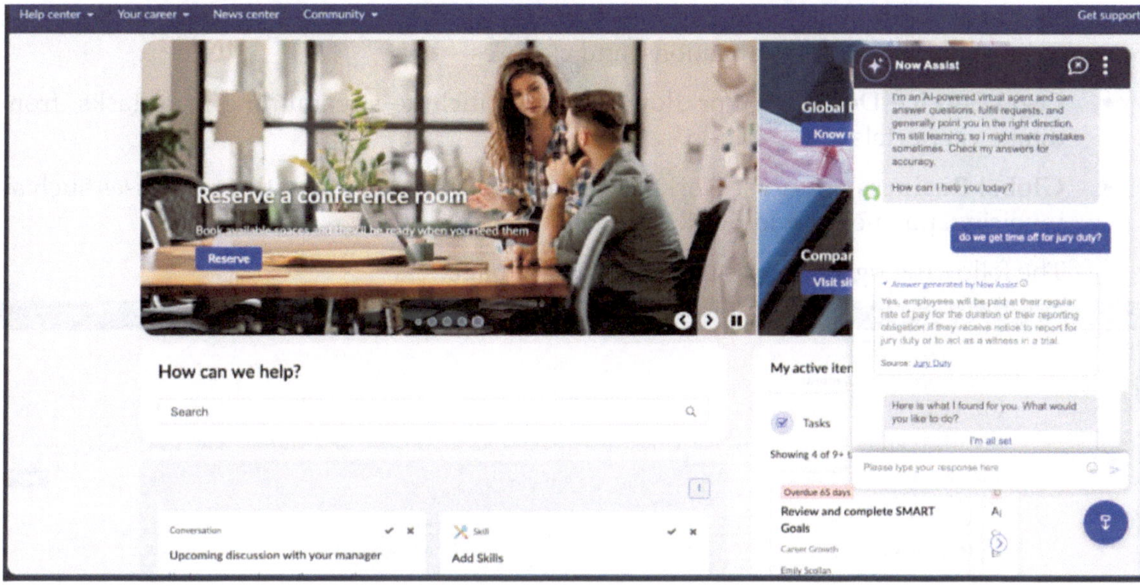

Figure 1.7: HRSD Employee Center

The following figure shows the WSD sample page:

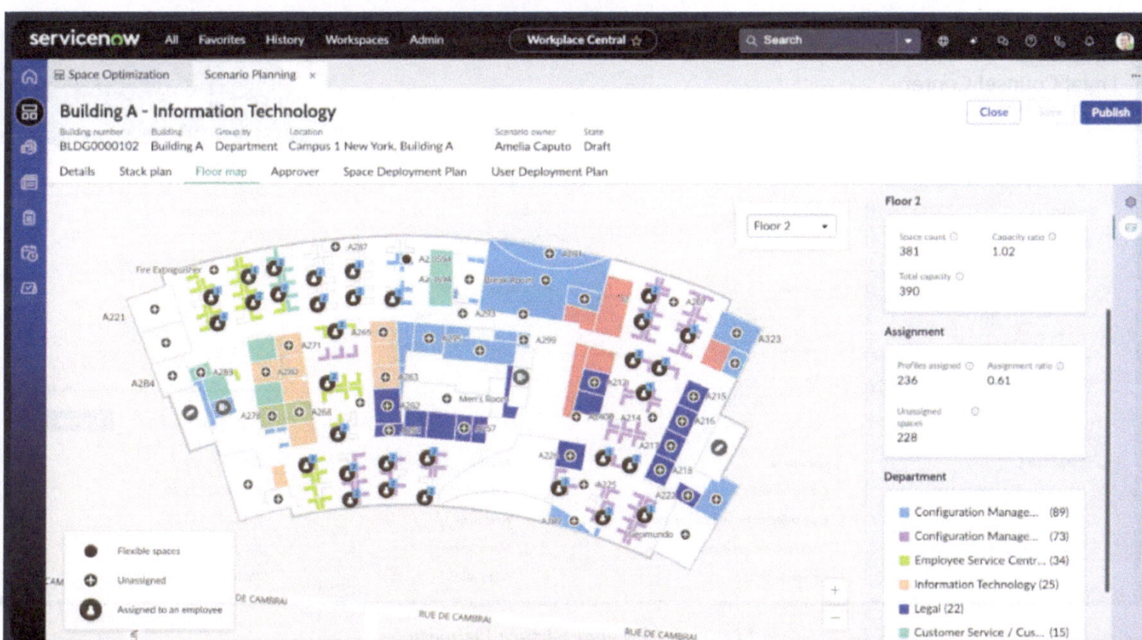

Figure 1.8: WSD

Three ServiceNow applications that comprise operating excellence are as follows:

- **Strategic Portfolio Management (SPM):** Workflow examples include auto-approvals of low-risk demands, notifications, and closures.
- **Legal Service Delivery**: Workflow examples include streamlining legal tasks, from intake via portals to resolution.
- **Global Business Services**: Workflow examples include automating processes such as invoicing, payments, and SPM.

  The following figure shows the SPM sample page:

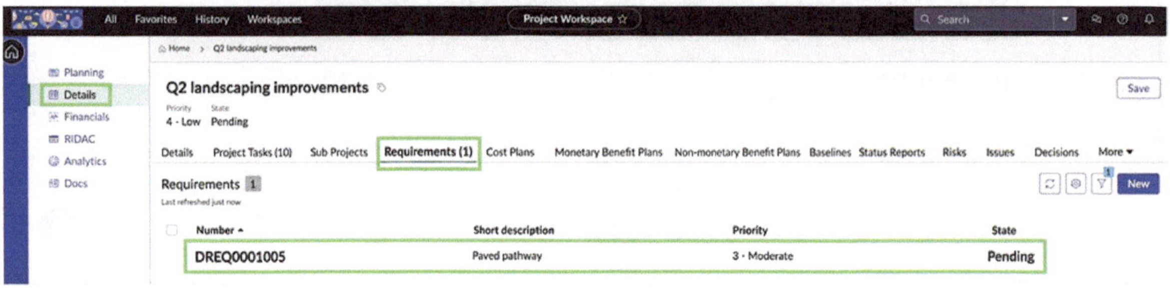

***Figure 1.9**: SPM*

The following figure shows an example of the Legal Service Delivery sample page:

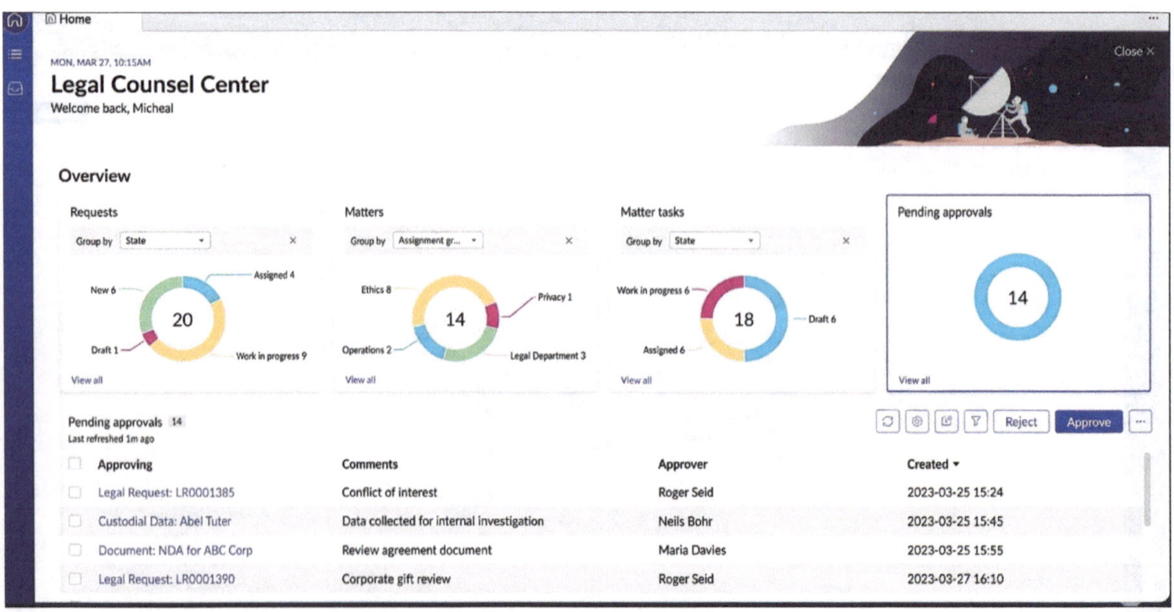

***Figure 1.10**: Legal Service Delivery*

Four ServiceNow modules that provide technology excellence are as follows:

- **ITSM**: It workflows automate core IT processes like Incident, Problem, Change, and Request Management.
- **ITOM**: Workflow examples include automating and optimizing the monitoring, management, and health of an organization's IT infrastructure.
- **Security**: Workflow examples include automating responses to threats.
- **ITAM**: IT workflows automate the entire IT asset lifecycle, from procurement to disposal

Service Now provides a modernized work experience and makes use of the latest technologies to enable seamless communication and collaboration among team members, regardless of their physical location. The modern workplace emphasizes the well-being of employees by promoting a healthy work-life balance and providing options for remote or hybrid working arrangements.

Employee Service Portal (**ESP**) provides a modern employee experience in a single portal, offering a personalized experience for the respective companies. ServiceNow applications provide operating excellence and technology excellence. Service Portal, the previous UI solution provided by ServiceNow, requires customization, whereas Employee Center and Employee Center Pro have modern UI with pre-built widgets, smart search, and personalized content.

When impersonating a user with an application-specific admin role, the following cannot be accessed:

- Security incidents.
- Profile information, including password changes.
- Filter navigator access is restricted.

ServiceNow is fundamentally a **platform as a service** (**PaaS**) and a **software as a service** (**SaaS**) solution.

PaaS is a cloud computing model where a third-party provider delivers hardware and software tools to users over the internet. A couple of examples are AWS and Microsoft Azure.

The ServiceNow platform is a PaaS, considering that the ServiceNow platform allows users to create custom applications to specific needs using the tools and platform.

SaaS is a service that provides ready-made suites and applications. ServiceNow provides various services such as ITSM, HRSD, and CSM without extensive customizations. In this way, ServiceNow is termed as a SaaS solution.

Admins can choose to elevate a role. Roles that can be elevated are as follows:

- **security_admin**: Allows users to modify ACL.
- **workplace_admin**: May be an option as well.

Flow Designer

The core concepts are as follows:

- Flow Designer automates processes.
- Flows trigger is based on:
  - o A record creation or update.
  - o A schedule.
- A flow is a sequence of actions and flow logic to define a process.
- Data pills are variables from triggers and actions.
- Flow logic allows flows to branch:
  - o Based on a condition.
  - o For each record in a set.
- Actions and flow logic for a branch are in a block.
- Flows should be tested in the following manner:
  - o In a non-production environment.
  - o Before activation.
- A flow execution is a flow's runtime environment.
- Activation causes a flow to execute when the trigger condition is met.

  The following figure shows the Flow Designer:

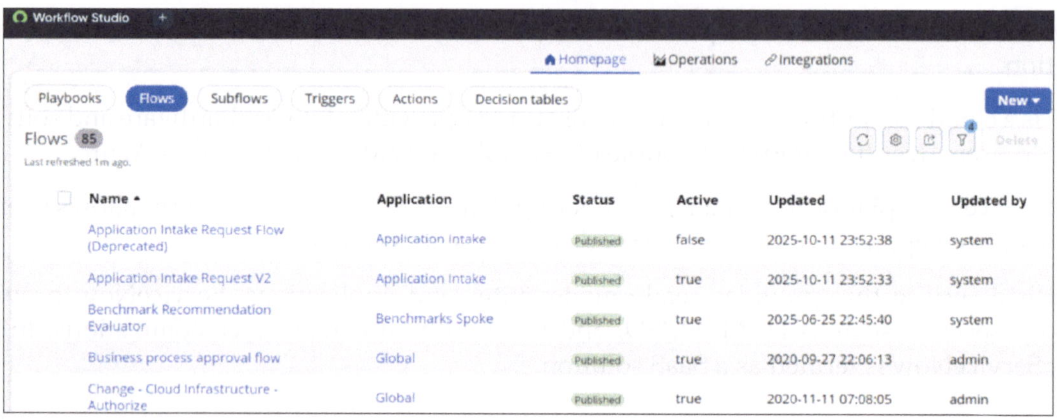

Figure 1.11: Flow Designer

Knowledge Management

In ServiceNow, the Knowledge Management application is used for managing and accessing a knowledge base. This facilitates users to create, edit, and view knowledge articles. A knowledge article provides information about a product or service to help users solve common issues or understand how to use a product. Knowledge articles contain information and can pull the articles with respect to incidents and so forth.

The following figure shows the **Knowledge Home**, which displays knowledge articles:

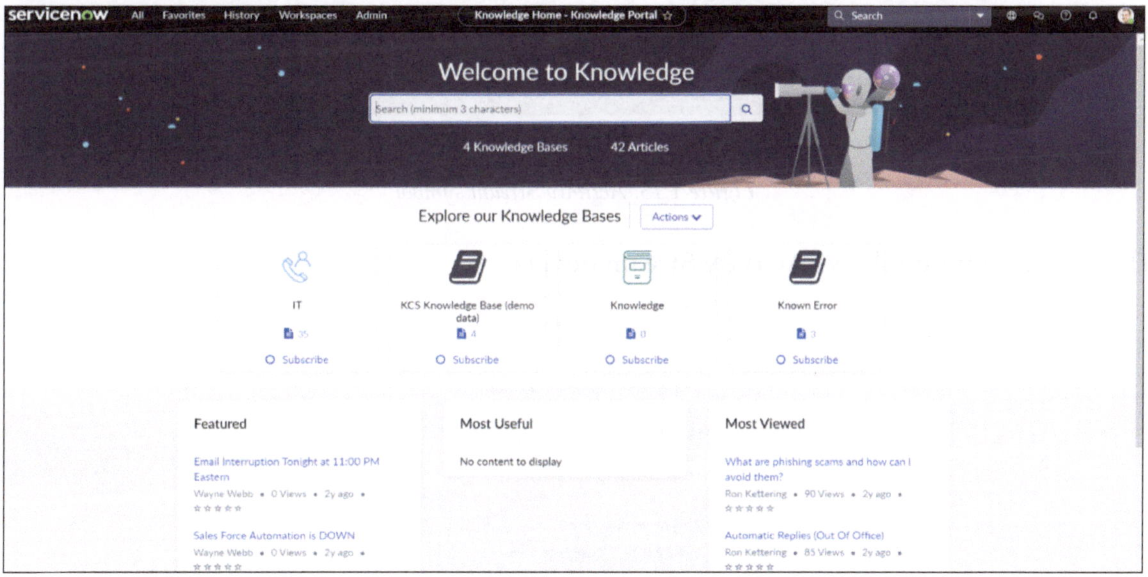

***Figure 1.12**: Knowledge Home*

Dashboards and reports

Dashboards and reports are visualizations of data. These help to make business decisions, as follows:

- **Dashboard**: A ServiceNow dashboard is a visual display of data that provides an overview of the needed details for the company or department. Dashboards comprise widgets, reports, and other visualizations that can be dragged and dropped into place.
- **Widgets**: Widgets are reusable components that make up the functionality. In ServiceNow, widgets are added in the Service Operations Workspace, Employee Center, and dashboards.
- **Reports**: In ServiceNow, the reports application enables us to create, view, and analyze data within the platform by generating reports with customizable filters, visualizations, and data breakdowns.

Activity Stream

Activity Stream enables agents to communicate with requesters and make internal notes about the work done on record. Configure the Activity Stream and Activity Stream Compose components in UI Builder to setup the Activity Stream in the Configurable Workspace.

To access the Activity Stream in ServiceNow, navigate to the record you want to view the activity for, then click on the icon that looks like an EKG symbol in the title bar. The Activity Stream flyout window opens, where all related events, notes, and tasks associated with that record are displayed.

The following figure shows the Activity Stream:

***Figure 1.13**: Activity Stream symbol*

The following figure shows **Activity Stream** details:

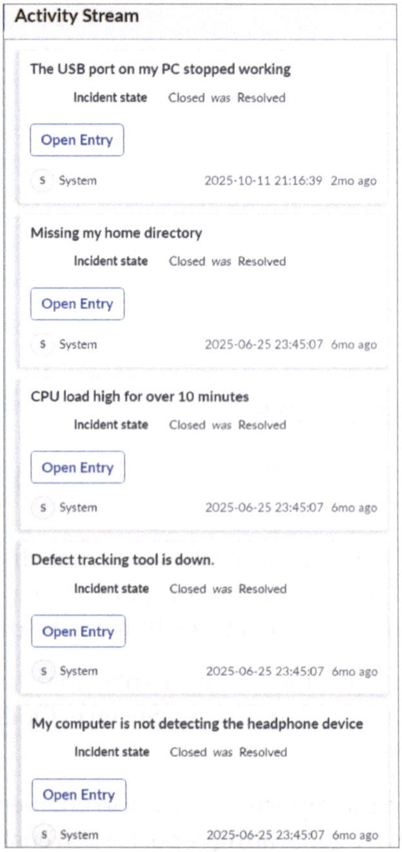

***Figure 1.14**: Activity Stream*

Tags

Tags are text labels that can be associated with items like records and pages. Tags enable grouping and organizing the items.

To add a tag to an incident in ServiceNow, you can open the incident form and select **Add Tag**. You can also create a new tag and then apply it to an incident.

The following figure shows tags:

Figure 1.15: Tags

The ServiceNow instance

ServiceNow offers free **personal developer instances** (**PDIs**) to registered users who want to develop applications on the ServiceNow platform or improve their skills with ServiceNow. New developer program members automatically receive a PDI running the latest release. Members of the ServiceNow developer program can use their PDI if there is activity on the instance.

ServiceNow releases two new versions per year. The *Xanadu* release was delivered in Q3 2024. Prior to Xanadu were the *Washington* releases in Q1 2024 and the *Vancouver* and *Utah* releases of 2023.

The Next Experience Unified Navigation runs across the top of every page and includes controls that help you navigate your instance. Easily access your workspace and classic environment, search your instance, and receive notifications.

To turn Next Experience on or off in ServiceNow, users can go to their **Profile Icon** | **Preferences** | **Display,** select **Turn on Next Experience** to switch from **User Interface 16** (**UI16**) back to **Next Experience**:

The steps to getting assigned a ServiceNow PDI are as follows:

1. The URL is **https://developer.servicenow.com/.**
2. **Home** | **ServiceNow developers**.
3. Click on sign up and start building.
4. Complete sign up and get a username and password.
5. Free PDI will be assigned.
6. Then sign in. Signing in will provide you with a ServiceNow PDI.

ServiceNow Administration Fundamentals course

The **ServiceNow Administration Fundamentals** (**SNAF**) course is mandatory to understand ServiceNow fundamentals with respect to the CSA exam. You can practice the lessons provided.

All on-demand courses are free in now learning: **https://nowlearning.servicenow.com/lxp?id=learning_course_prev&course_id=fbb6cc4847f5dd505cbdaf44846d436a.**

Free training plan and practice are provided by ServiceNow. The training path is provided as follows:

ServiceNow administrator | ServiceNow developers

The ServiceNow concepts are as follows:

- In ServiceNow, an application represents a larger functional area within the platform, like incident management or change management. A module is a specific section or feature within that application, which essentially acts as a sub-menu that provides access to related functions and data within the application. Applications contain multiple modules that provide a more granular level of access to features within the application.
- In ServiceNow, workflow refers to a traditional, often more technical tool for automating processes with a linear, step-by-step logic. Flow represents a more modern, user-friendly approach using the Flow Designer, which provides a drag-and-drop interface for creating complex workflows with greater flexibility and accessibility, even for non-technical users.
- ServiceNow uses a single tenant architecture, which means that each ServiceNow customer gets their own instance of the Now platform to run apps instead of sharing resources as occurs in a multi-tenant environment. Single tenant tends to cost more to operate, but grants the customer additional flexibility to customize their instance to meet their needs.

- In ServiceNow, baseline implementation refers to the standard out-of-the-box configuration. This includes the core modules, tables, workflows, and flows acting as a starting point for further customization and development.
- Cloning allows you to copy everything in a database from one instance to another. All records from one instance are copied to another instance. Practically, a production instance will be cloned to lower instances, keeping the lower instances' data in sync with the production instance. The steps for cloning are as follows:
    1. Create a clone target.
    2. Log in to your instance, which needs to be cloned.
    3. Navigate to **System Clone**.
    4. **Clone Targets**.
    5. Click **New**.
    6. Navigate to **System Clone**.
    7. **Request Clone**.
- A customization is a feature, extension, or modification of a ServiceNow feature that requires custom coding and some form of implementation outside the out-of-the-box context.
- A configuration is where we use native ServiceNow capabilities and tools in the system to change its behavior or features to address business needs. Any change to the configurable data that changes the functionality of the application is considered a configuration change. Adding a **Department** field to the incident form is configuration, and building a new custom app for asset tracking is customization.
- Zurich is the latest ServiceNow release as of December 2025. ServiceNow releases every six months and keeps the name of the release in a continuing alphabetic sequence. The names of the releases are named after city names.
- ServiceNow Security Center is an application added recently. This is provided in the Now Platform at no additional cost, which helps customer admins to uphold their security responsibilities and manage and monitor the security of their ServiceNow instance. Access to ServiceNow Security Center (for hardening, scanning, metrics) is primarily for system administrators and designated security roles who manage instance security, but granular access (like viewing specific security incidents) can be granted to specific users via roles. The steps to access it are as follows:
    1. **Use the filter navigator**: In the search box (`Filter Navigator`) at the top left, type `Security Center`.
    2. **Select from results**: Click on **Security Center** when it appears in the dropdown.

The following figure shows **Security Center**:

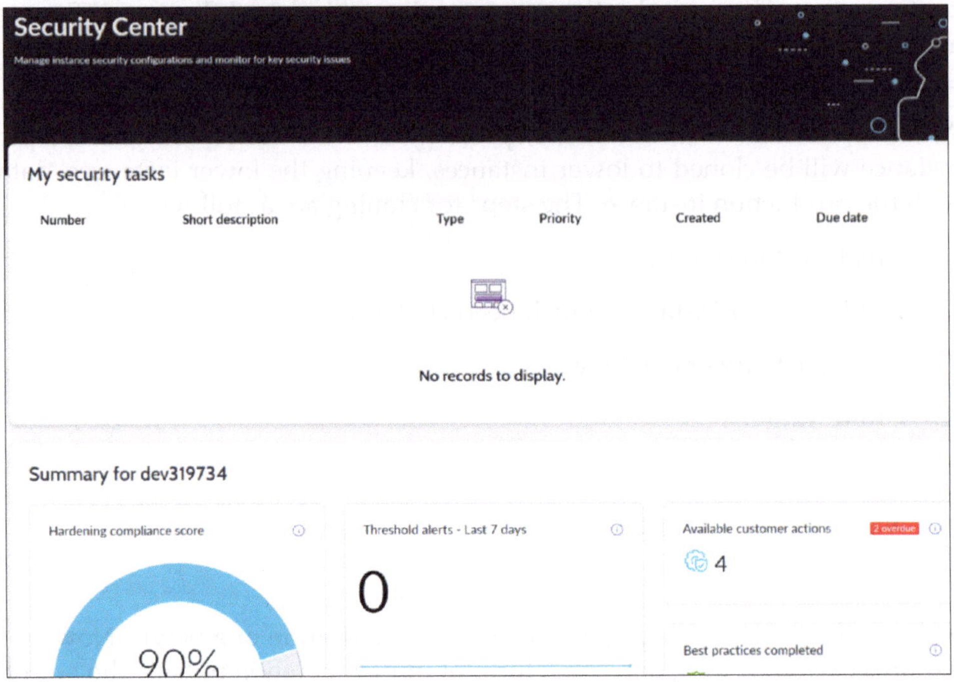

Figure 1.16: Security Center

The following figure shows **Security consoles** and **Tools**:

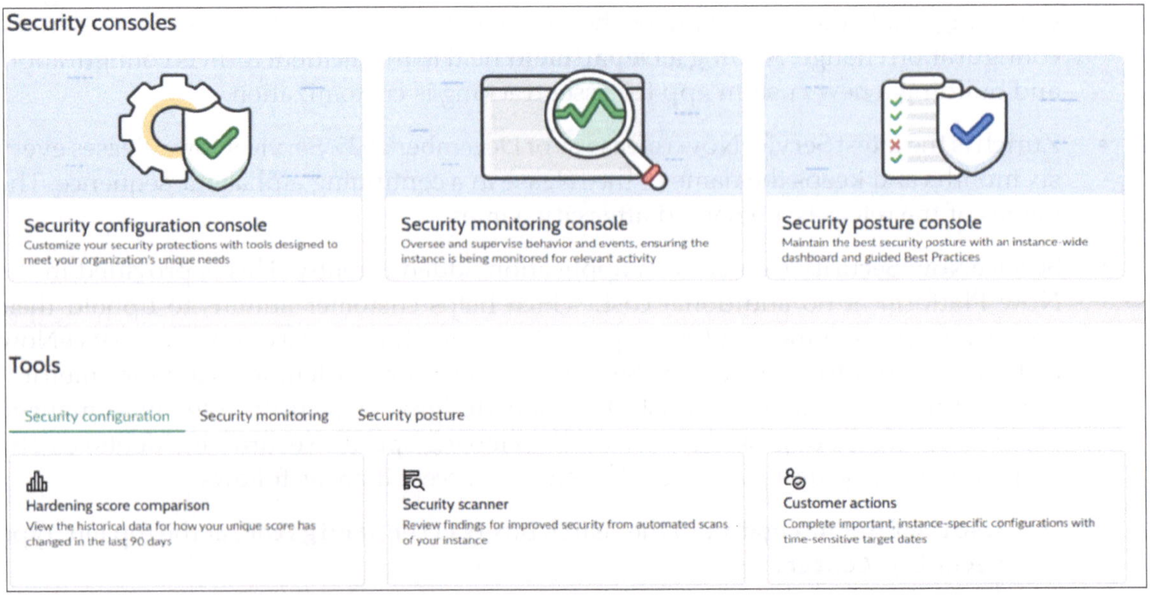

Figure 1.17: Security consoles and Tools

- An update set is a group of configuration changes that can be moved from one instance to another. It allows administrators to group a series of changes into a named set and then move them as a unit to other systems for testing or deployment. Development is done and grouped as Update Sets, and it is moved across instances.

  The following figure shows **Update Set** creation:

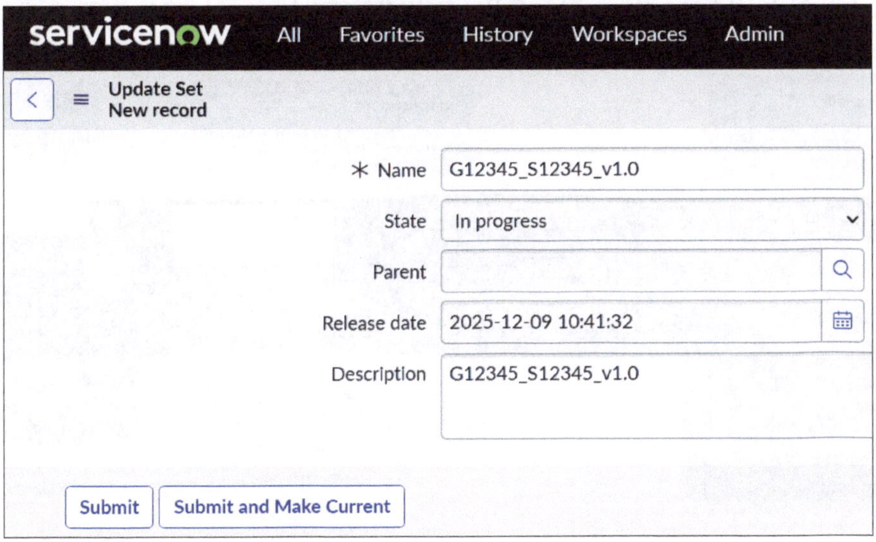

Figure 1.18: Update Set creation

The following figure shows the **Update Set** creation details:

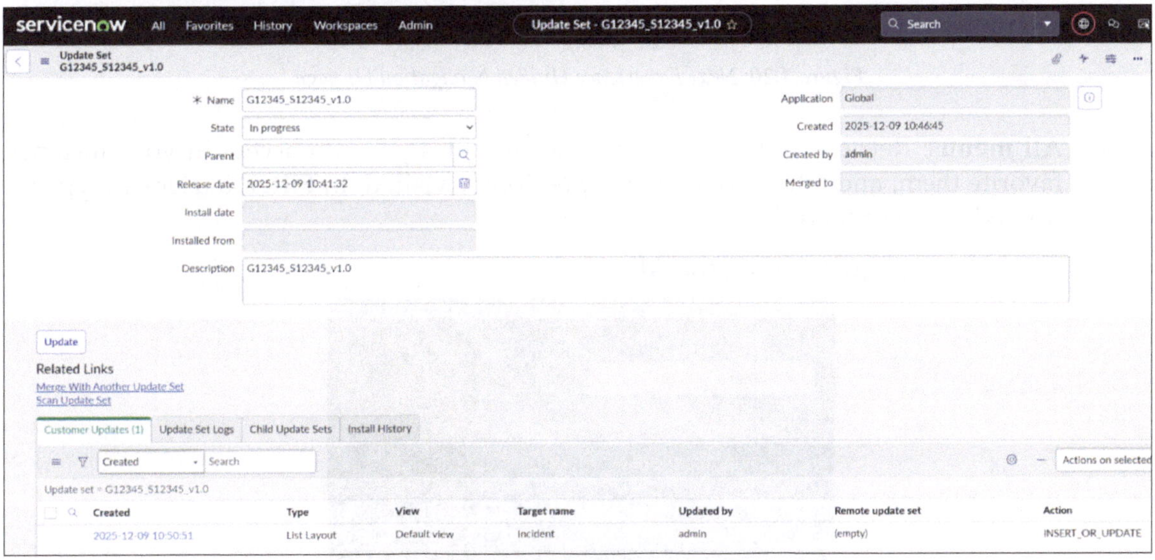

Figure 1.19: Update Set details

Next Experience Unified Navigation

Next Experience UI Navigation includes logo, filter, All menu, Favorites menu, History menu, Workspaces menu, Admin menu, Global Search field, globe setting application scope and update set (selected), Now Assist, side bar discussions, help, Notifications menu, User menu.

These are detailed in this section. The following figure shows the Next Experience Unified Navigation UI page:

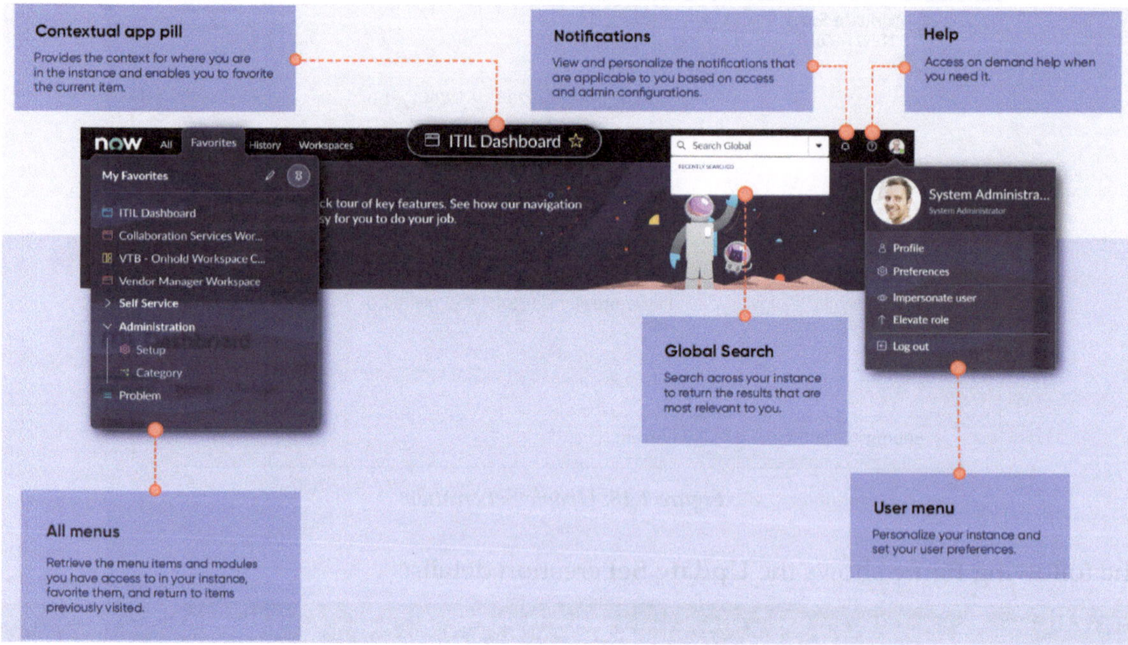

Figure 1.20: Next Experience Unified Navigation UI page

- **All menus**: Retrieve the menu items and modules you can access in your instance, favorite them, and return to the items previously visited. In **Filter**, a user can type the needed menu or module.

  The following figure shows the **All** menu:

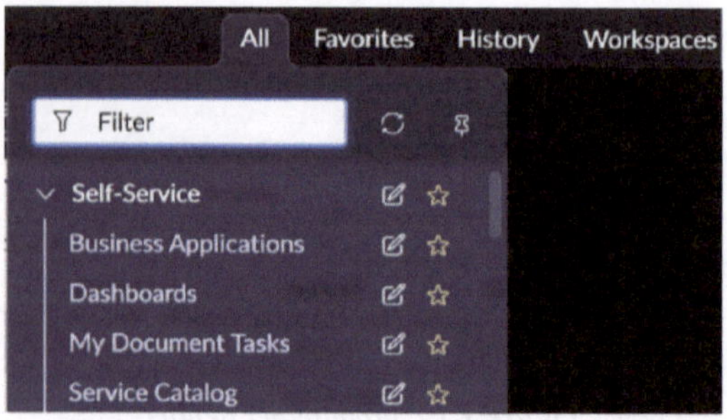

Figure 1.21: All menu

- The main navigation bar is the **application navigator**, a collapsible left-side panel featuring the **All** menu, **Favorites**, and **History**, providing access to all platform applications and modules like Incident, Problem, Change, and Service Catalog. This is the central hub for finding and launching different functionalities within the platform.

  The following figure shows the application navigator:

Figure 1.22: Application navigator 1

The following figure shows the application navigator:

Figure 1.23: Application navigator 2

- **Contextual app pill**: See where you are in the instance and favorite the current item if desired.
- **Global search**: Search across your instance to return the results that are most relevant to you.
- **Notifications**: View and personalize notifications applicable to you based on access and admin configurations.
- **Help**: Access on-demand help when you need it.

  The following shows the Show help in the application navigator:

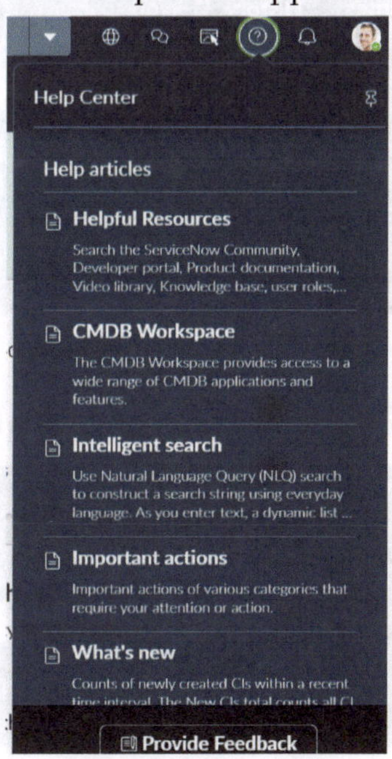

Figure 1.24: Show help

- **User menu**: Personalize your instance and set your user preferences.
- **Favorites menu**: The following figure shows the **Favorites** menu:

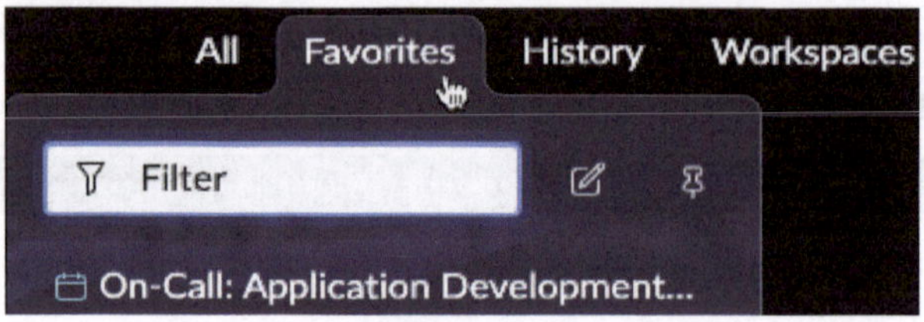

Figure 1.25: Favorites menu

- **History menu**: The following figure shows the **History** menu:

Figure 1.26: History menu

- **Workspaces menu**: The following figure shows the **Workspaces** menu:

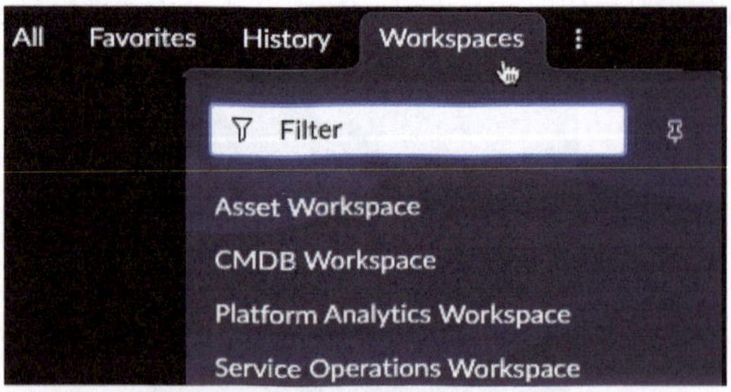

Figure 1.27: Workspaces menu

- **Admin menu**: The following figure shows the **Admin** menu:

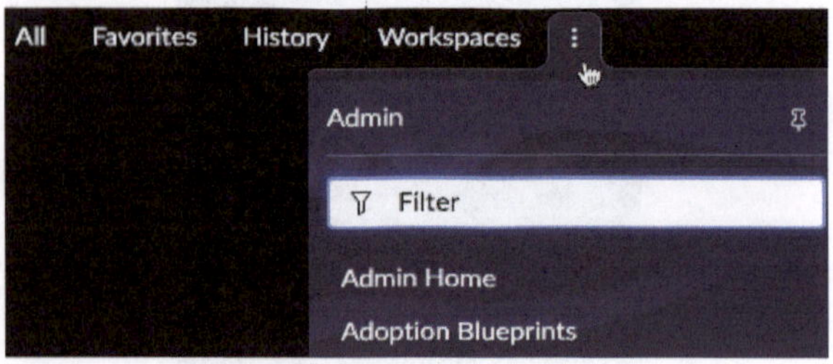

Figure 1.28: Admin menu

- **Application scope**: The following figure shows the **Application scope** icon:

Figure 1.29: Application scope icon

- **User menu**: The following figure shows the user menu:

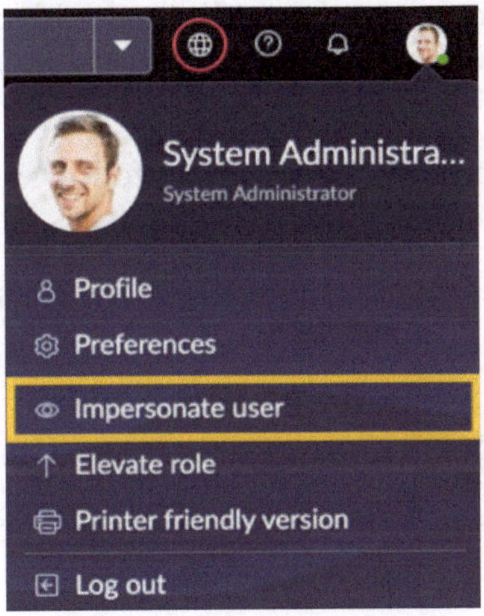

Figure 1.30: User menu

- **Profile**: Your instance profile, which includes your personal information displayed in the instance.
- **Preferences**: Display, accessibility, notifications, and workspace preferences.
- **Impersonate user**: Administrators can impersonate other authenticated users for testing purposes and viewing impersonation logs.
- **Elevate role**: Designate any role as an elevated privilege role and then assign that role to one or more users. Do this when you want to restrict users from having access to the rights that the role provides immediately after logging in.
- **Printer-friendly version**: A printer-friendly version of the current content frame.
- **Now Assist (if enabled)**: The following figure shows the Now Assist icon:

Figure 1.31: Now Assist icon

- **Chat**: The following figure shows the Chat icon:

Figure 1.32: Chat icon

Engages in real-time collaboration with others based on a Workspace task-based or interaction-based record. Sidebar discussions facilitate the exchange of information and knowledge to help resolve issues faster and with higher-quality outcomes. Select the pin icon to pin a menu to the page.

In ServiceNow, a classic view refers to the traditional, older user interface for viewing and interacting with data on lists and forms as opposed to the newer, more customizable *Next Experience* interface.

Some common types of fields found in **Forms** are as follows:

- Choice
- True/False
- Reference
- Date/Time
- String
- List

Roles, users, and groups

In ServiceNow, roles, users, and groups are used to control access to features and capabilities in applications and modules.

Roles

Roles do not protect data until they are assigned to specific users or groups. Creators typically work with a system administrator to assign and manage roles.

A few common platform roles are `admin`, `security_admin`, `user_admin`, `snc_internal`, and `snc_external`.

The core platform roles are as follows:

- **Admin**: Full system access, configuration, security.
- **security_admin**: Manages ACLs and security settings, often elevated.
- **user_admin**: Manages users, groups, and roles.
- **impersonator**: Allows impersonating other users for testing or support.
- **snc_internal**: Identifies internal employees and users.
- **snc_external**: Identifies external users.

The primary roles table is named `sys_user_role` in ServiceNow.

Users

Every user who logs in to ServiceNow has a user record that includes information such as:

- Username
- First name
- Last name
- Password
- Email address

The user record also includes a list of roles that are assigned to the user. To see a user record, in the main ServiceNow browser tab, use the **All** menu to open **User Administration** and then select **Users**. The primary user table is named **sys_user**, which stores detailed records for all individuals who access the platform, containing info like user ID, name, roles, and contact details, as shown in the following figure:

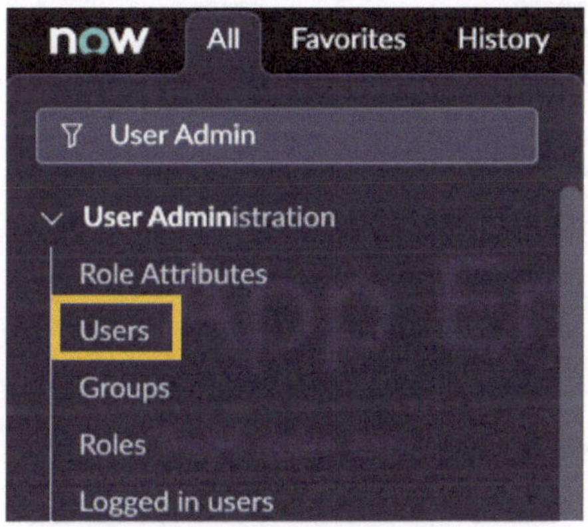

***Figure 1.33**: Users menu*

Groups

Groups are collections of users who need the same permissions and are a shortcut way of assigning roles to users. System administrators assign roles to groups rather than adding a role individually to each user. Group members have all the roles assigned to a group. The following figure shows the same:

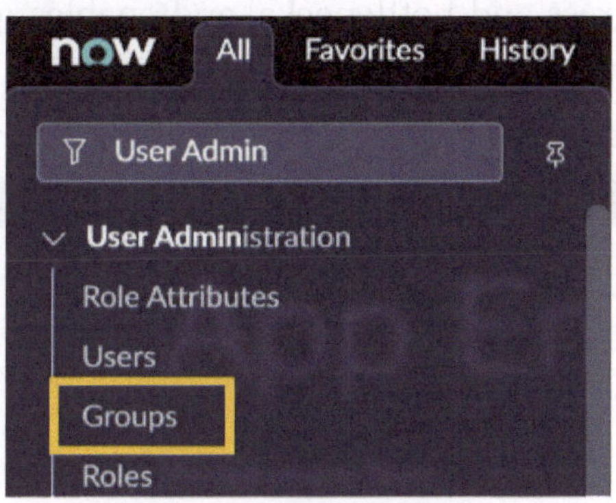

***Figure 1.34**: Groups menu*

Slushbuckets

Slushbuckets allow users to select multiple items from a list of available items. They are used in many operations, such as personalizing lists, adding items to related lists, and personalizing lists.

Pressing the gear icon in the list brings the slushbucket. The following figure shows the slushbuckets:

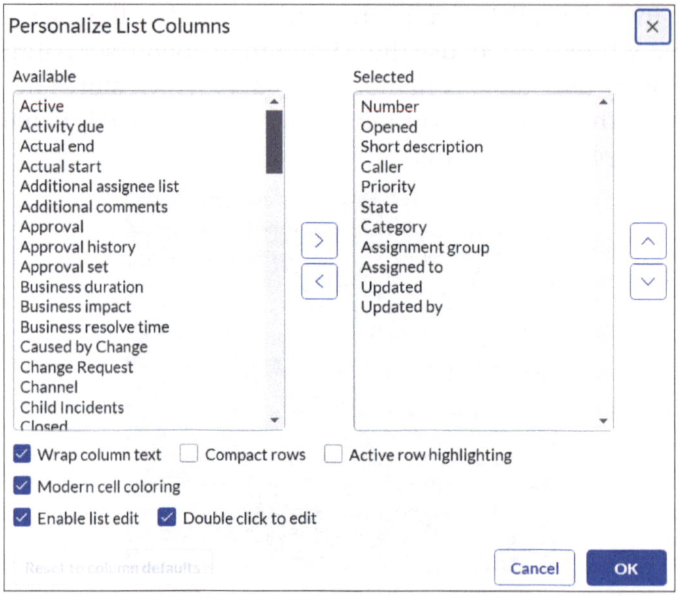

Figure 1.35: Slushbuckets

Visual Task Board

Visual Task Board in ServiceNow allows users to visually track and manage tasks across different stages of a process by displaying them on a Kanban-style board. This provides a clear overview of work progress and bottlenecks, and enables quick updates through drag-and-drop functionality.

The following figure displays an example of the Visual Task Board:

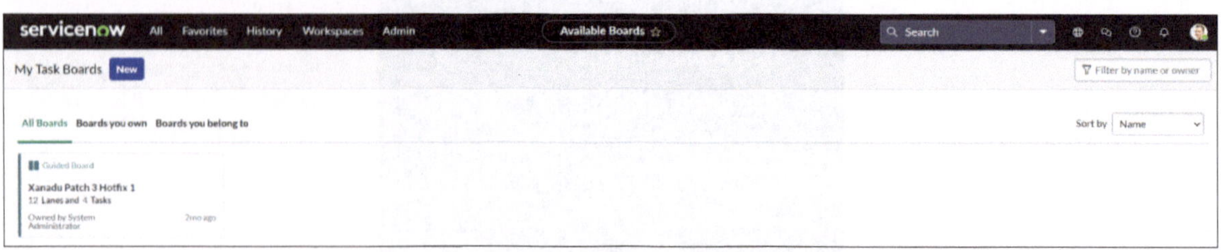

Figure 1.36: Visual Task Board

Three main types of task visualization in the Visual Task Board are as follows:

- **Freeform**: Fully customizable for personal tasks/ideas.
- **Flexible**: Data-driven from a table with custom lanes for specific data sets.
- **Guided**: Data-driven with lanes tied to field values, updating underlying data when moved.

Service Catalog

A **Service Catalog** provides access to request services for the users and teams of the company. Customers' requests are sent to the correct team, providing solutions quickly and efficiently.

The following figure shows the service catalog for various service requests:

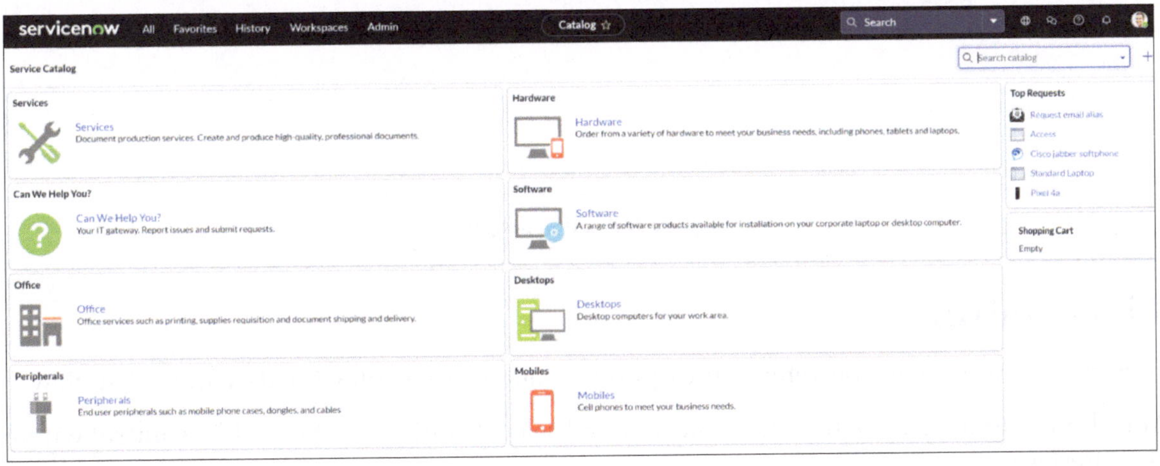

Figure 1.37: Service Catalog

Form designer

Form designer is a drag-and-drop interface used to:

- Create form layouts.
- Create form views.
- Create and delete form sections.
- Add fields to tables.

To access the form designer in ServiceNow, navigate to the record, then click on **Configure** in the header and select **Form Design**.

In ServiceNow, a header refers to the top section of a page or form that usually displays key information about a record. The following figure shows a quick change view for form views.

The following figure shows form designer:

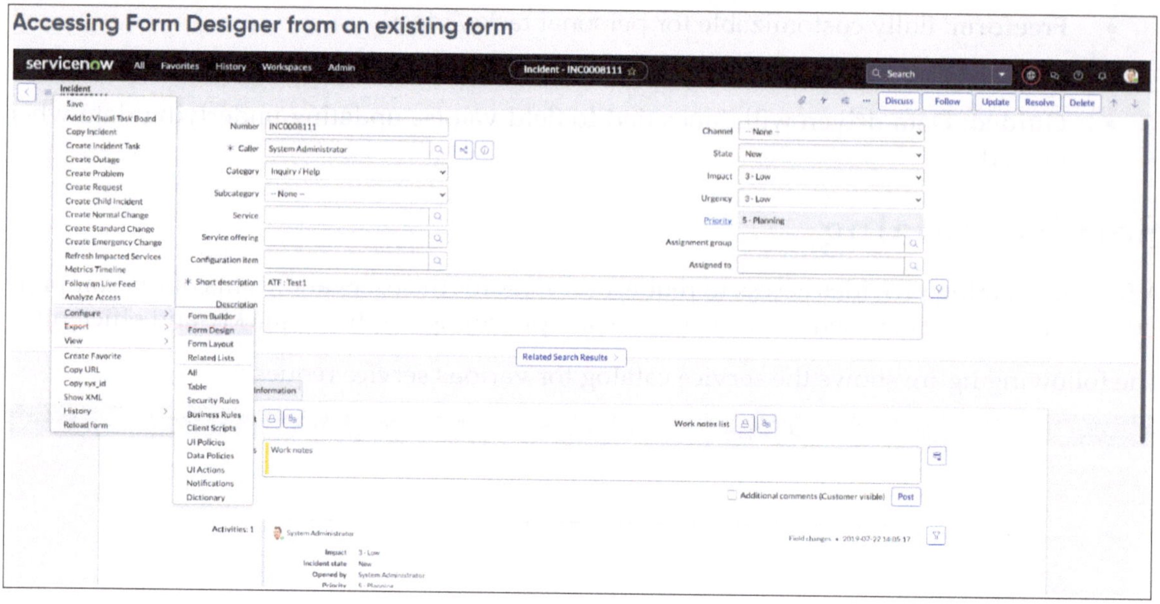

Figure 1.38: Form designer

List Control

In ServiceNow, list controls refer to the options available to display the data in the list view.

You should right-click on the column header and select **Configure**. Choose **List Control** within the interface.

Main aspects of list controls in ServiceNow are as follows:

- **Field selection**: Fields form a table to display in list view.
- **Display formatting**: Data presented in date format, currency symbol.
- **Sorting options**: Sorting the list by needed fields.
- **Filtering capabilities**: Filters to narrow down the displayed records.

The following figure shows **List Control**:

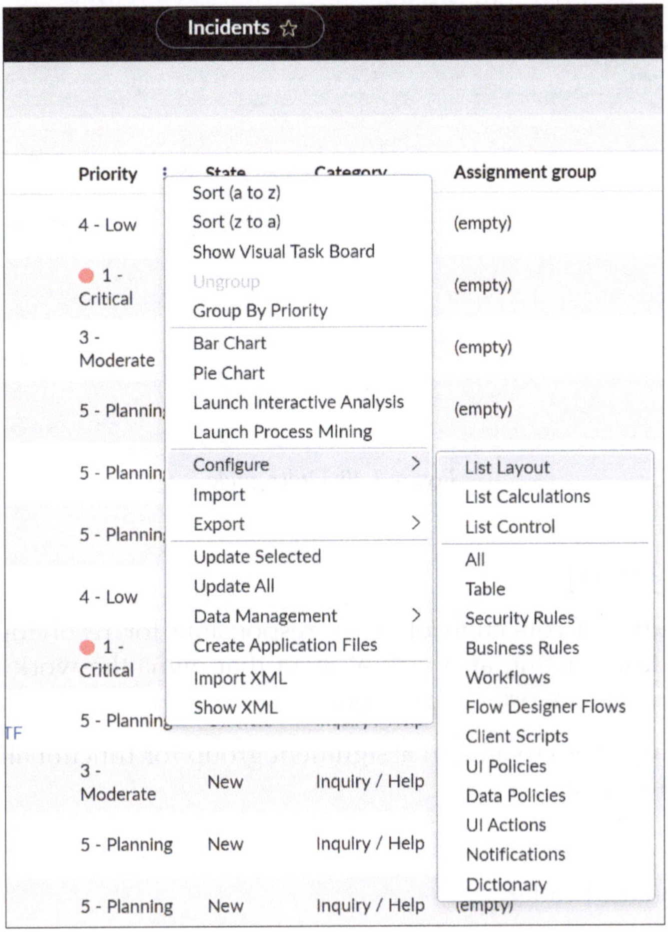

Figure 1.39: *List Control*

Order guide

An order guide is a bundle of catalog items in the Service Catalog grouped together, which ultimately generates a single request and several requested items.

Order guide is developed by creating a central form that collects common details once, then using **Rule base** to dynamically bundle and populate multiple catalog items, passing variables across them (cascading) for a single, simplified request, often for scenarios like new employee onboarding.

The following figure shows the order guide:

***Figure 1.40**: Order guide*

Assignment group

An assignment group is a collection of users responsible for resolving specific tasks, like incidents or project tasks, acting as a virtual team that owns the work rather than just one person. This allows efficient work distribution.

The following steps will help to add an assignment group for functionalities for a group that is allowed to access incidents:

Open an incident.

1. Right-click on the header.
2. Configure form layout.
3. Select the assignment group from the left slushbucket and move it to the right.
4. Adjust to where you want it in the list.
5. Click **Save**.

The following figure shows assignment groups:

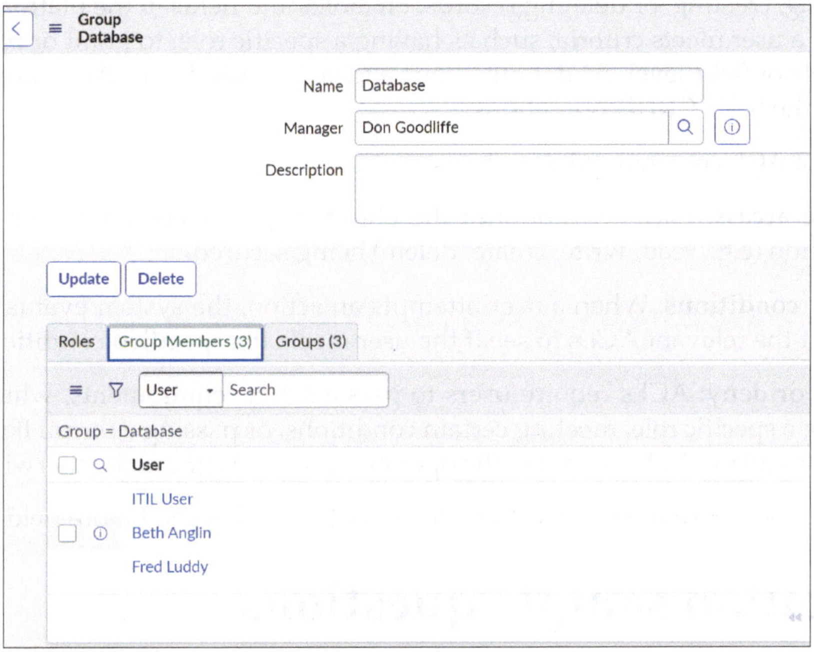

***Figure 1.41**: Assignment groups*

Security groups

Security groups focus on what users can do rather than who gets assigned. To add ACLs to a security group in ServiceNow, typically assign roles to the group, then create ACLs that require those roles, or use the group directly via scripts or conditions.

ACL is applied to security groups.

The easiest way to remember this is to keep the following terms:

- **Who**: Roles of people.
- **What**: System security.
- **Which**: Creating a type (record).

To create ACL, go to the **All** menu, type **`System Security`**, and type **`ACL`**.

Create a type and write a record. This accesses a particular table record as per the **Create, Read, Update, and Delete** (**CRUD**) level, write, which can be controlled.

Roles can contain multiple child roles. Once a role is assigned to a user, the user inherits all child roles.

A ServiceNow ACL is a security rule that determines who can perform specific operations, like reading, writing, creating, or deleting records, on tables and fields in the platform. ACLs work by checking if a user meets criteria, such as having a specific role, to grant or restrict access to data at the table or field-level. By default, when a table is created, four ACLs are automatically generated for the basic CRUD operations.

The working of ACLs is provided as follows:

- **Define access**: Each ACL defines the object (e.g., a specific table or field) and the operation (e.g., read, write, create, delete) being secured.
- **Check conditions**: When a user attempts an action, the system evaluates the request against the relevant ACLs to see if the user meets the specified conditions.
- **Grant or deny**: ACLs require users to pass a set of requirements, which can include having a specific role, meeting certain conditions, or passing a script. If the user passes all the required ACLs for a specific operation, access is granted; otherwise, it is denied.

ACLs follow a specific sequence. The table-level ACLs are checked before field-level ACLs.

Certification sample questions

1. **From the user menu, which actions can a user select? (Choose three.)**
   a. Send notifications
   b. Logout ServiceNow
   c. Elevate
   d. Impersonate users
   e. Order from the Service Catalog
   f. Approve records
2. **Which term refers to application menus and modules that you may want to access quickly and often?**
   a. Breadcrumb
   b. Favorite
   c. Tag
   d. Bookmark
3. **What are the roles required to impersonate other users?**
   a. Impersonator, admin
   b. Application specific role
4. **Which icon in the banner do you use to turn on the application picker and the update set picker?**
   a. Magnifier
   b. Checkbox
   c. Question mark
   d. Gear
   e. Globe icon on the top right corner

5. **Where is the global search banner located?**
   a. Banner frame
   b. Favorites menu
6. **What is the language used for scripting in ServiceNow?**
   a. Java
   b. AngularJS
   c. JavaScript
   d. Jelly
7. **Which one of these applications is available to all users?**
   a. Change
   b. Incident
   c. Facilities
   d. Self-service
8. **Which one of the following is a definition for transform maps in ServiceNow?**
   a. A map that is used to store the history of the incident records
   b. A map used to add data to encrypted fields
   c. A map used to trigger business rules before the data is queued in the outbound web service
   d. A map to determine relationships between fields, displaying in an import set to fields in an existing table
9. **What section on a task record is used to see the most recent updates made to a record?**
   a. Related list
   b. Activity stream
   c. Audit log
   d. Timeline
10. **While showing a customer their incident form, they ask to change the priority field title to display their internal terminology value. How would you do that? Choose two answers.**
   a. Right-click on priority and select configure dictionary
   b. Right-click on priority and select configure label
   c. Right-click on priority and select configure display settings
   d. Right-click on priority and select configure column
11. **What type of rules specify which user groups are responsible for working on different types of tasks?**
   a. On call
   b. Assignment
   c. Routing
   d. Calendar
   e. Escalation

12. **What are examples of UI actions relating to lists? Choose four answers.**
    a. List buttons
    b. List context menu
    c. List choices
    d. List links
    e. List control
    f. Lists overwrite
13. **From the form designer, how would you define a section so that it displays as a tab?**
    a. Click the gear and check the tab option
    b. Click context menu | configure tabs
    c. Add .tab to the end of the section name
    d. Add _tap to the end of the section name
    e. Name the section
14. **Only production instances can be cloned.**
    a. True
    b. False
15. **What do you click when you have made modifications to your report, and you want to see the results without saving?**
    a. Run
    b. Execute
    c. Test
    d. Preview
    e. Try it
16. **What types of elements are Single Line Text and Select Box in ServiceNow?**
    a. Order guides
    b. Request types
    c. Variable types
    d. Related lists
17. **How is access to the application or modules in the navigator restricted?**
    a. ACL
    b. Roles
    c. Application scope
18. **What is ServiceNow's default service engine?**
    a. AnswerNow
    b. Search
    c. GoogleNow
    d. Zing
19. **Changing the list layout by clicking on 'gear' icon will impact all users.**
    a. True
    b. False

20. **What are the operations done by user menu? Select three that apply.**
    a. Impersonate
    b. Elevate privileges
    c. Send notifications
    d. Logout

21. **The _________ protects applications, application files and data from being edited?**
    a. ACL
    b. Application scope

22. **Knowledge articles can be visible to end users in which state?**
    a. Draft
    b. Review
    c. Published
    d. Retired

23. **You are looking at the list of active incidents that you want to exclude incidents with the state of resolved. What might you do?**
    a. On the list of records, locate and right-click on the resolved value, select Filter Out.
    b. Use the search bar

Answers

1. b, c, d	2. b	3. a
4. e	5. a	6. c
7. d	8. d	9. b
10. a, b	11. b	12. a, b, c, d
13. e	14. b	15. a
16. c	17. b	18. d
19. b	20. a, b, d	21. b
22. c	23. a	

Conclusion

This chapter covered the concepts of the ServiceNow platform overview and navigation, and sample questions towards CSA for this section. This provided a good understanding of the ServiceNow platform and concepts.

The next chapter will cover the ServiceNow instance configuration, which will cover 11% of the questions towards the CSA certification.

Chapter 2
CSA Instance Configuration

Introduction

ServiceNow CSA instance configuration refers to the process of setting up a ServiceNow instance, including installing applications, adjusting user interfaces, and personalizing features.

This includes the implementation of unique needs of the organization, such as flows, basic settings, service catalog requests, users, access, and applications.

Structure

This chapter will cover the following topics:

- Installing applications and plugins
- Personalizing and customizing the instance
- Common user interfaces of the platform
- Certification sample questions

Objectives

This chapter provides insights about installing applications in ServiceNow, personalizing/customizing the instance, and common user interfaces of the platform pertaining to CSA certification. This chapter will provide users with the skills to configure ServiceNow for the unique needs of the organization.

Installing applications and plugins

ServiceNow offers enhanced application functionality via plugins and stores applications with each release. Plugins are software components that add functionality to installed applications on ServiceNow instances.

In ServiceNow, an application installation refers to the process of adding a new application (a set of features or functionalities) to your ServiceNow instance. This can be done by accessing the ServiceNow Store, selecting the desired application, and initiating the installation process to make it available for users within your platform. The steps are as follows:

1. Your licensed applications and plugins can be found under **All | System Definition | Plugins**.

   The following figure shows an example of licensed applications and plugins:

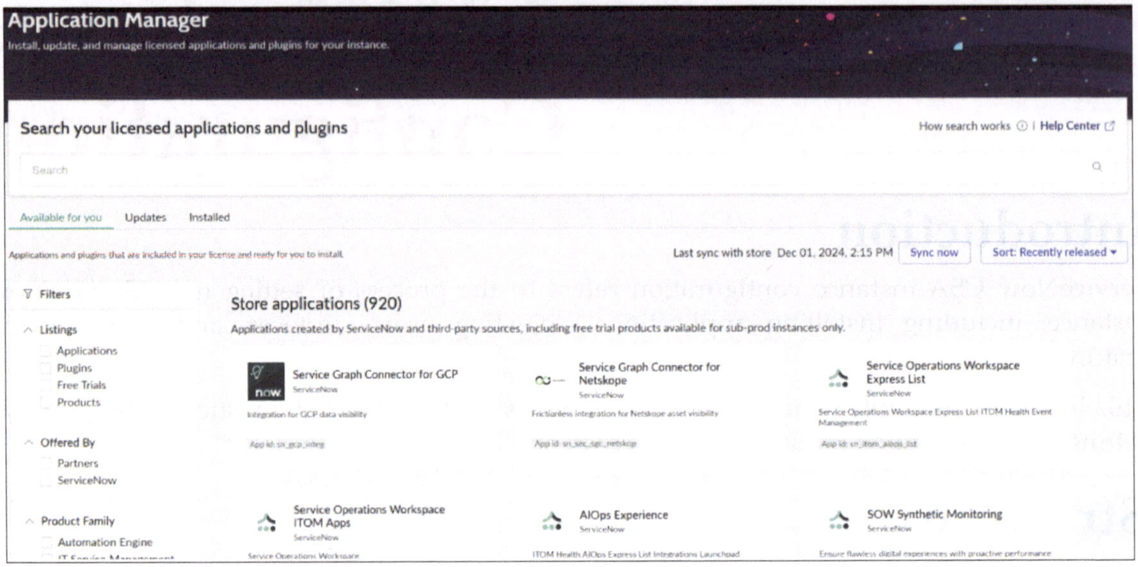

Figure 2.1: Application Manager

   a. The following path in the **All** menu brings up the **Plugins** module:

      All | System Definition | Plugins

2. Once the needed plugin is found, click on it. An **Install** button is shown. Click on the button for installation.

   An example is shown in the following figure:

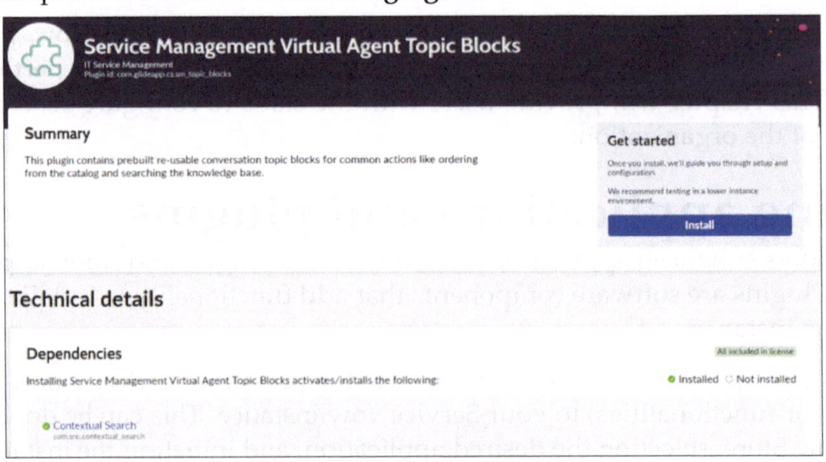

Figure 2.2: Plugin installation

a. The two checks you perform before installing a new plugin are:

   i. The role required to activate the plugin.

   ii. The related plugins that will be activated/installed (dependencies).

b. If you cannot find a plugin, the other options available are:

   i. Check the ServiceNow Store.

   ii. Submit a request on ServiceNow.

To check the ServiceNow Store steps, look at the details via the link: https://store.servicenow.com/sn_appstore_store.do#!/store/home

The following figure shows an example of applications other than licensed ones:

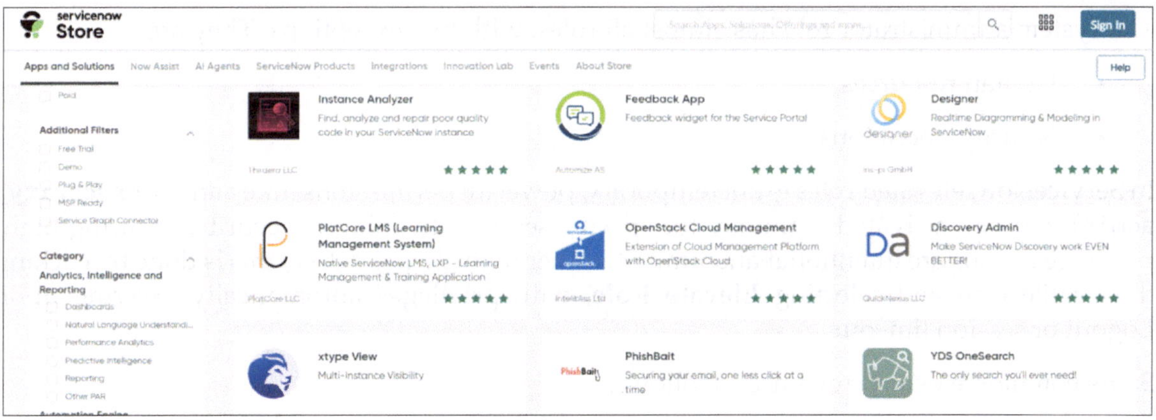

Figure 2.3: ServiceNow Store

To submit a request on ServiceNow, the steps are provided as follows:

1. To submit a request on ServiceNow, in the ServiceNow instance, navigate to the **Self-service** module.

2. Access the **Service Catalog**, where you can choose the relevant service.

3. Fill out the request form with the necessary details.

4. Click **Order Now** to submit your request.

Roles and groups

The path in the **All** menu that brings up **Users**, **Groups**, or **Roles** administration modules is as follows:

- **All | User Administration | Users**
- **All | User Administration | Groups**

- **All | User Administration | Roles**
- **All | System Security | Users and Groups | Users (or) Groups (or) Roles**

A role is a collection of permissions that defines what a user can access and do within the platform.

Best practice: Rather than adding roles to individual users, the best practice is to create a group for the required role, assign the role to the group, and add the users to the group.

In ServiceNow, a role is a collection of permissions that defines what a user can access and modify within the platform, essentially determining their level of authority based on their job function. A role is created by specifying which tables, fields, and operations it can perform on, effectively setting up access control for different user types within the system.

The system administrator role has almost all roles, with two exceptions. They are:

- Human resources
- Security operations

In ServiceNow, elevated roles grant temporary, powerful permissions (like `admin` or `security_admin`) to users, activated manually for specific sessions to enhance security, ensuring high-privilege actions are intentional and limited, rather than always active; this is done by clicking the profile icon and selecting **Elevate Role**, with privileges automatically expiring upon Logout or session timeout.

Some common elevated roles are as follows:

- **security_admin**: Required to modify **access control lists** (**ACLs**) and other security settings, even for users with the admin role.
- **admin**: Full system access.
- **user_admin**: Manages users, groups, and roles.
- **itil_admin, itil**: For managing **IT service management** (**ITSM**) processes.
- **catalog_admin, catalog_editor**: For Service Catalog management.

Personalizing and customizing the instance

Each customer gets their own copy or multiple copies of ServiceNow in the cloud. These copies are known as ServiceNow instances.

The three typical environments are:

- Production
- Non-production (called **test**)
- Development

Service Now applications and functionalities, as they are available as per acquired licenses, are termed to be **out-of-the-box** (**OOTB**). Changes made to the OOTB are considered to be customization. This is to modify the platform to meet the particular needs and requirements of an organization. Changes made to the ServiceNow system for only user changes are considered personalization.

Personalization will not impact both configuration and customization. Personalized settings within ServiceNow are similar to the user preferences. Personalization allows users to change the following:

- Their list view.
- Change the form to make reports.
- Adjust notification preferences.
- Add themes.
- Change how fields look, and all kinds of other features.

User-level personalization

This method allows individual users to customize their own view of a list without affecting others. These changes can be saved as personal lists for future use.

- **Add, remove, or rearrange columns**:
  - Navigate to a list (e.g., **All Open Incidents**).
  - Click the gear icon (personalize list mechanic) to open the slushbucket interface.
  - In the slushbucket, move available fields from the left column to the **Selected** (right) column to add them, and vice versa to remove them.
  - Drag-and-drop fields within the right column to reorder them.
  - Click **OK** or **Save** to apply the changes instantly.
- **Create and save personal lists**:
  - After applying filters to a list, you can save that specific list configuration (filters and personalized columns) for future access under the **My Lists** section in the navigation menu.

The following figure shows **Personalize List Columns**:

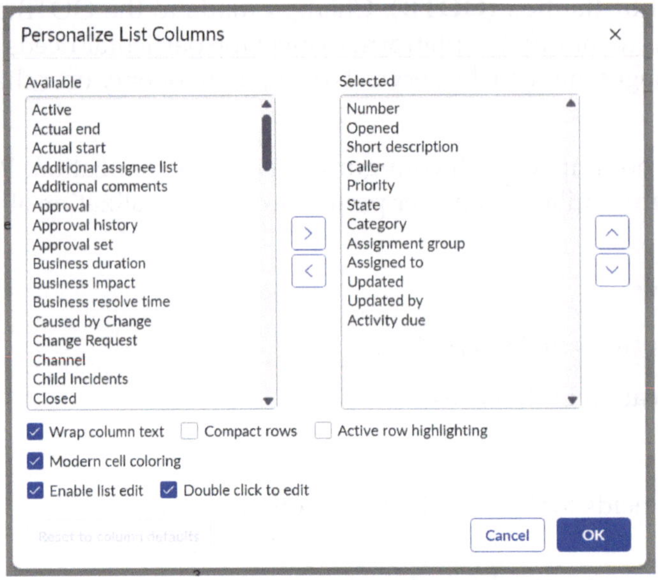

Figure 2.4: Personalize List Columns

Administrator-level configuration

Users with appropriate roles (like admin) can configure the list layout to apply changes to the default view for all users.

- **Modify the default view**:
    - o Right-click on any column header in the list view.
    - o Select **Configure** | **List Layout**.
    - o Use the slushbucket to add, remove, and reorder fields.
    - o Ensure the **View name** is set to the **Default view** (or a specific custom view you wish to modify for all users).
    - o Click **Save**. The changes will appear for all users who have not set their own personal list preferences.
- **Create new global views**:
    - o Follow the same steps as above (right-click | **Configure** | **List Layout**).
    - o Instead of modifying the default view, select **New** at the bottom of the **View name** dropdown.
    - o Give the new view a clear, descriptive name (e.g., `High Priority Incidents View`, `HR Agent Workspace View`).

- Configure the columns and click **Save**.
- Users can then switch to this view via the view selector in the list view context menu.

The following figure shows an example of the personalization list view:

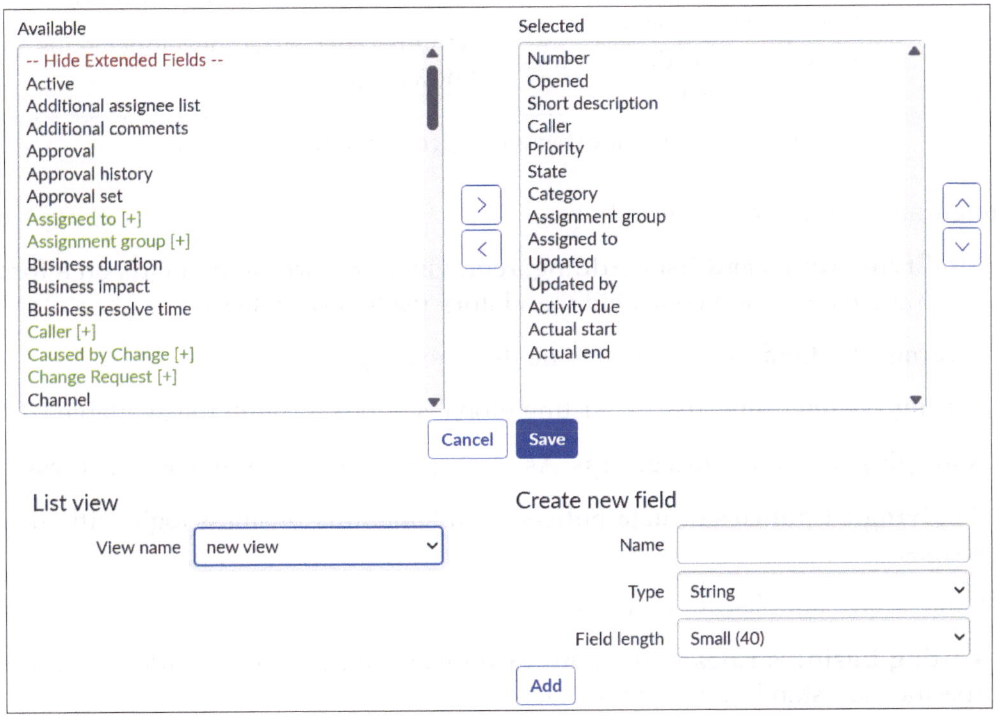

Figure 2.5: Personalization list view

The key difference between configuration and customization is that configuration uses built-in, no-code tools to meet requirements without changing the baseline code, while customization involves writing new code or modifying the OOTB functionality.

The following table shows key differences between configuration and customization:

Feature	Configuration	Customization
Code requirement	No new code is written; uses built-in tools.	Involves writing new code (JavaScript, Jelly, etc.).
Baseline code	Does not alter the baseline (OOTB) installation code.	Modifies or extends the baseline code/ functionality.
Upgrades	Generally, upgrade-safe and easy to maintain during platform upgrades.	Can complicate and potentially break future upgrades, requiring dedicated testing and resources.

Feature	Configuration	Customization
Flexibility	Limited to the options provided by the platform's standard features.	Offers greater flexibility to meet unique and specific business needs.
Resources	Can often be done by a system administrator or less specialized user.	Requires specialized developer skills and knowledge.

***Table 2.1**: Key differences between configuration and customization*

The configuration examples are as follows:

- **Modifying forms and lists**: Adding, removing, or rearranging fields on a form (e.g., making the resolution code field mandatory using a UI policy).
- **Adding new fields**: Creating new fields on existing tables.
- **Setting system properties**: Adjusting global settings through the available UI.
- **Managing user roles and groups**: Assigning roles to groups to control access.
- **Applying UI policies or data policies**: Implementing business logic without writing scripts.

The customization examples are as follows:

- **Writing business rules with complex logic**: Creating a server-side script to enforce specific, non-standard business logic.
- **Developing custom applications**: Building a completely new application from scratch (e.g., an application to track company assets or a new leave management system).
- **Creating custom widgets**: Building new interactive elements for portals using HTML, CSS, and JavaScript.
- **Modifying OOTB workflows**: Altering the default change request approval workflow to function differently from the baseline.
- **Changing UI macros**: Modifying Core UI components that require using Jelly coding.

In general, ServiceNow best practices recommend pursuing configuration options wherever possible to ensure easier maintenance and seamless upgrades. Customization should be a last resort when unique business requirements cannot be met through configuration alone.

This user enablement, along with self-service, Service Catalog, and Knowledge Management, has instilled a **do it yourself** (**DIY**) approach to issue resolution at many companies.

A configuration is where ServiceNow native capabilities and tools in the system are changed with their behavior or features to address business needs. Change to the configurable data, which will end in a change of the functionality of the application, is considered a configuration.

Configuration is to set the following:

- **Assignment groups**: Assignment groups are a set of users who are authorized to perform a set of functionalities.
- **Security groups**: Security groups are in addition to the responsibilities in assignment groups. An ACL is applied to have granular access control.
- Assignment rules.
- Preferences within ServiceNow.
- Email configurations and notifications.

Baseline implementation is a set of installed applications on an instance prior to configuration or customization. System properties store configuration information that rarely or never changes.

The path in the **All** menu allows you to customize system properties like this:

All | System Properties | System

The following figure shows the menu for **System Properties**:

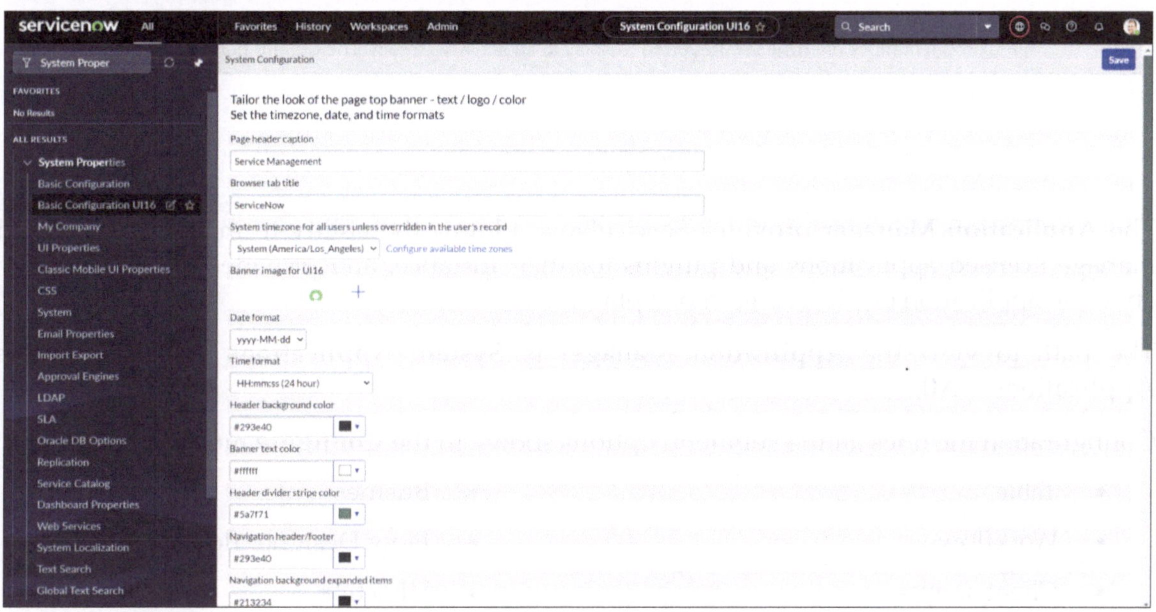

Figure 2.6: ServiceNow System Properties

The following figure shows a sample page of **System Properties**:

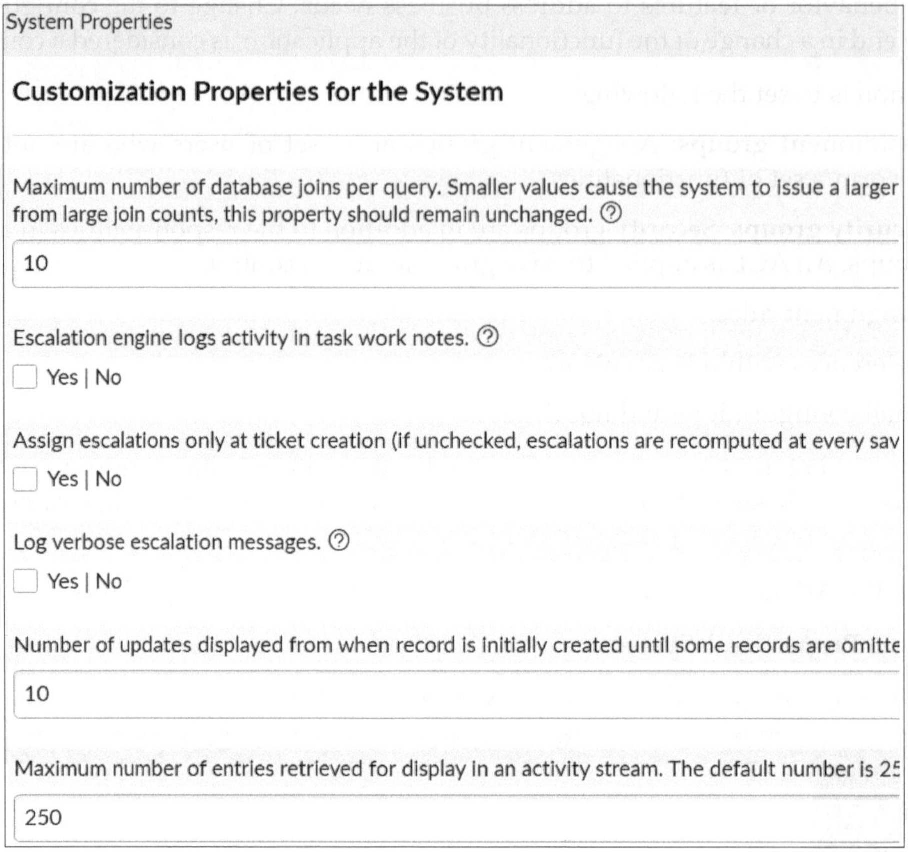

***Figure 2.7**: System Properties*

The **Application Manager** provides ServiceNow admins the ability to install, update, and manage licensed applications and plugins for their instance, and provides key information about an application or plugin, all in one place.

The path to view the **Application Manager** is **System Applications | All Available Applications | All**.

Configuration includes all the submenu options shown in the **Configure** menu:

- Table
- Workflows
- Client scripts
- UI policies
- ACLs
- Business rules
- Flow Designer flows
- UI action
- Data policies
- Notifications

Workflow distinctions examples between configuration and customization

The distinction also applies to building and modifying workflows.

Configuration examples

Configuration leverages the Flow Designer and workflow properties to adapt processes to specific needs without hard-coding the logic.

- **Modifying a form layout**: Adding, hiding, or restyling fields on an existing form using UI policies or form design tools.
- **Defining approval rules**: Setting conditions in a workflow to automatically route approvals based on a user's role, department, or request cost, using standard workflow activities.
- **Setting system properties**: Adjusting system-wide settings like the company name, logo, or email configurations using available menus.
- **Adding new fields**: Creating a new custom field on an existing table (e.g., incident table) using the system dictionary.

Customization examples

Customization involves significant changes to baseline code or creating entirely new applications, often using server-side or client-side scripting.

- **Modifying an OOTB business rule**: Changing the existing script logic of a default business rule (e.g., changing how an incident's priority is calculated in the baseline script).
- **Creating a new application from scratch**: Building a new application to manage a unique business process, such as tracking loaner equipment or managing marketing events, which requires creating new tables, modules, and scripts using ServiceNow Studio.
- **Altering OOTB UI actions**: Modifying the existing JavaScript code behind a standard button (e.g., the **Resolve** button on an incident form) to make it function differently than its original design.
- **Integrating with a unique external system via custom code**: Writing bespoke script includes or an integration spoke from scratch when the OOTB Integration Hub functionality does not meet the specific requirements.

As a best practice, organizations are strongly encouraged to use configuration as the first option to meet business requirements and avoid unnecessary customizations to ensure smooth upgrades and support.

The following figure shows the **Configuration** submenus:

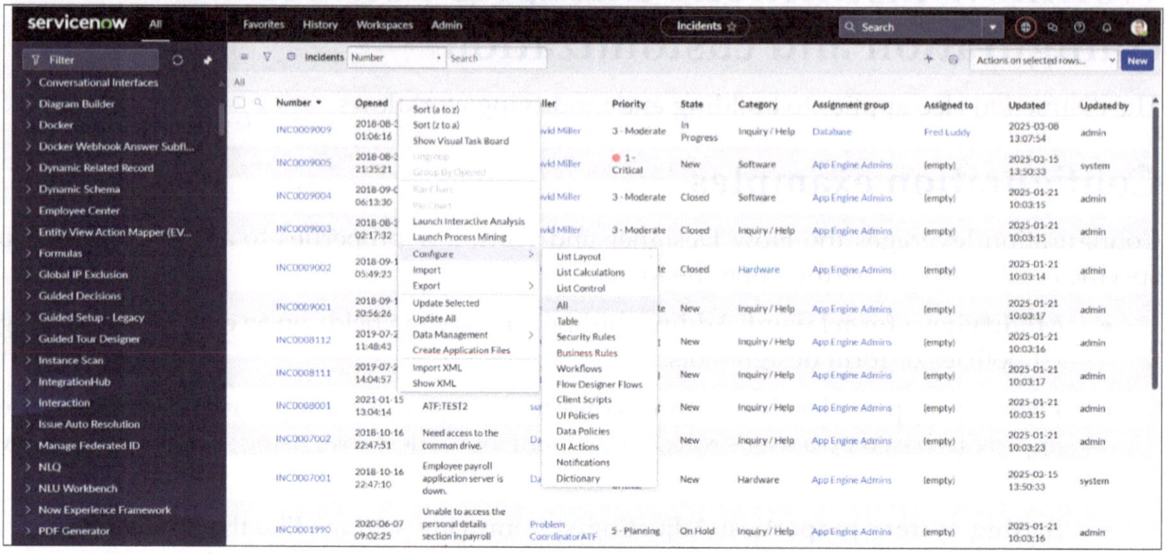

Figure 2.8: Configuration

A context menu in ServiceNow is a pop-up menu that appears when you right-click. It provides options for navigation and functionality. The menu items vary depending on the context, such as what is selected or hovered over.

The following figure shows a sample of **Context** menu:

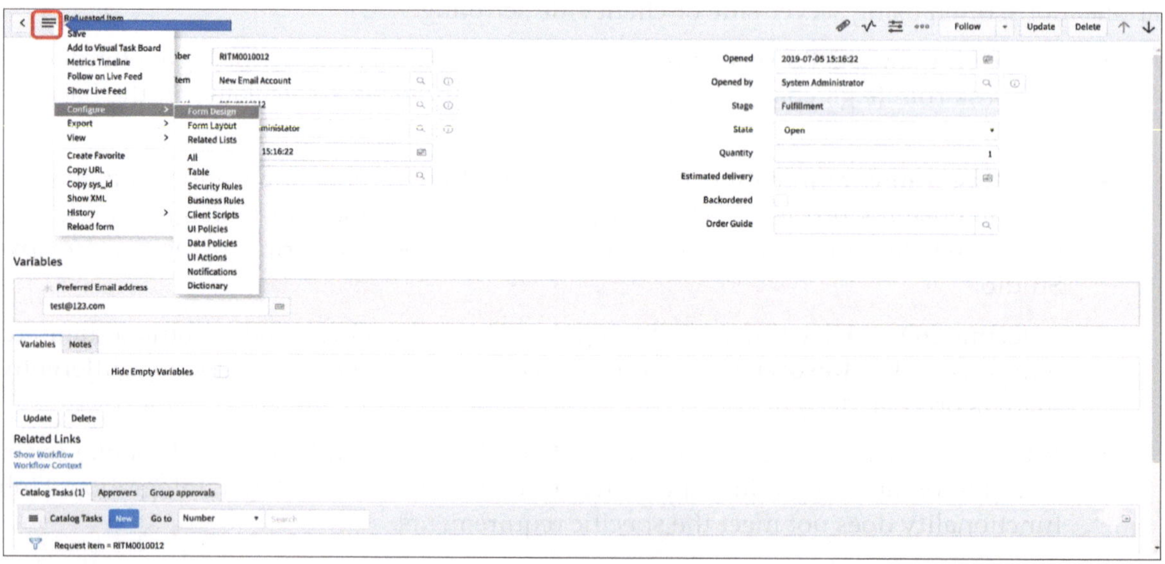

Figure 2.9: Context menu

ServiceNow UI action is a configurable element that allows you to add buttons, links, or context menu options to forms and lists within the ServiceNow platform.

The business rule in ServiceNow is a server-side script that runs when a record is created, updated, deleted, or queried. Business rules are written in JavaScript and are used to automate actions that happen to records.

The following figure shows an example of a **Business Rules**:

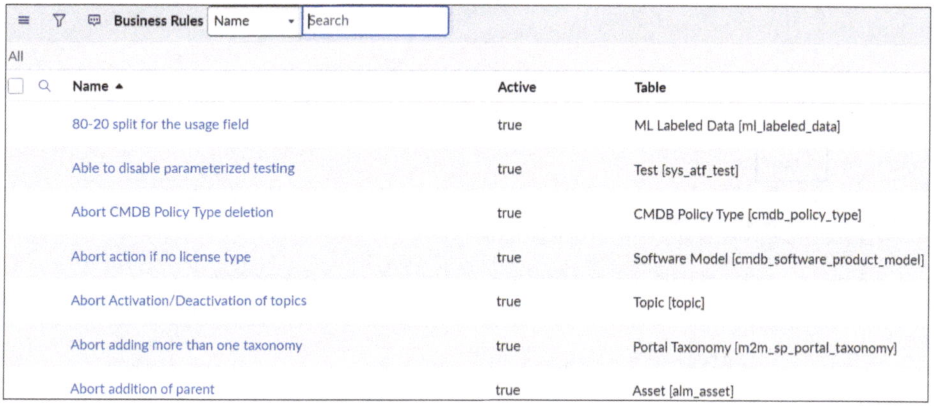

***Figure 2.10**: Example–Business Rules*

A business rule in ServiceNow is a server-side script that executes when a record is displayed, inserted, updated, deleted, or queried. It automates tasks, enforces logic, and performs actions based on specific conditions, allowing administrators to customize platform behavior. For example, a business rule can automatically update a field when a record is saved or prevent a user from saving a record unless a required condition is met.

The following figure shows the creation of **Business Rule**:

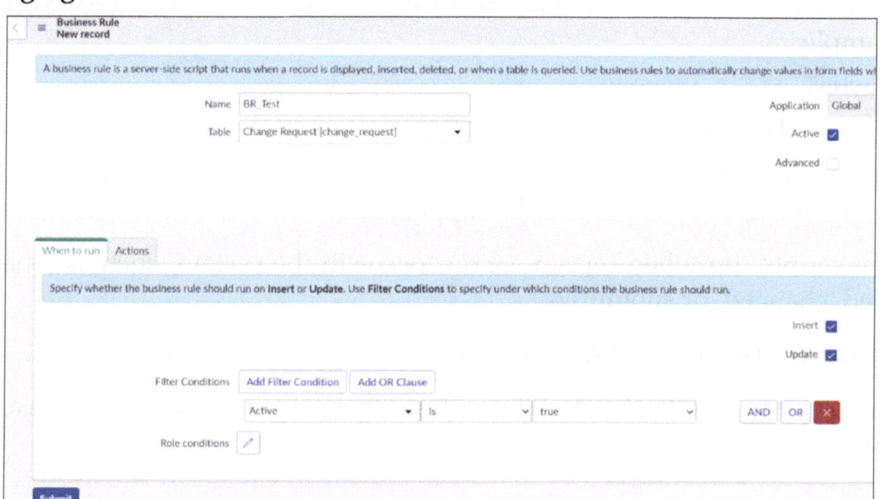

***Figure 2.11**: Creation of Business Rules*

The following figure shows the creation of **Business Rules** with the **Actions** field:

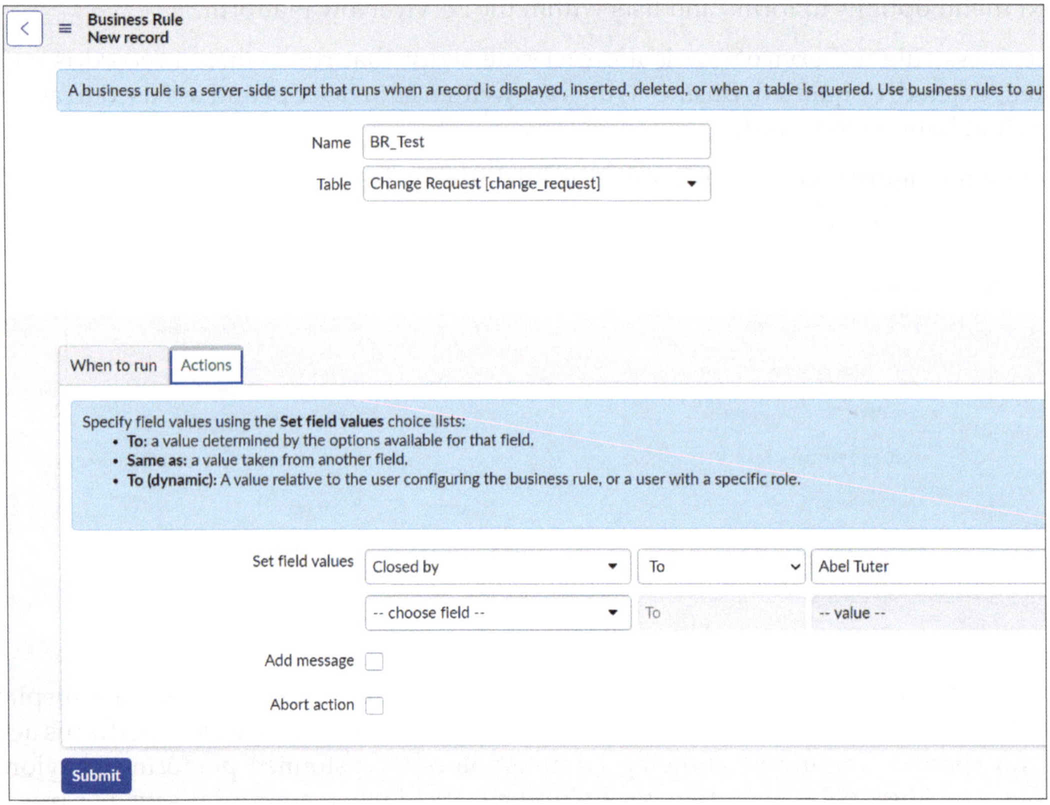

***Figure 2.12**: Creation of Business Rules–Actions field*

UI Scripts are blocks of code that are available to any client-side script on a page on which they load. For example:

```
function sayHello()
 {     alert('Hello!'); }
```

Client scripts in ServiceNow are JavaScript scripts that run in a user's web browser. They are used to control how fields on forms and lists appear and behave. Further details are as follows:

- Client scripts run when certain actions occur in the system, such as when a form is loaded, changed, or submitted.
- They can be used to validate forms, set field values, and more.
- They can be used to update the client state through events, such as when a user selects a radio button.

The following figure shows an example of **Client Script**:

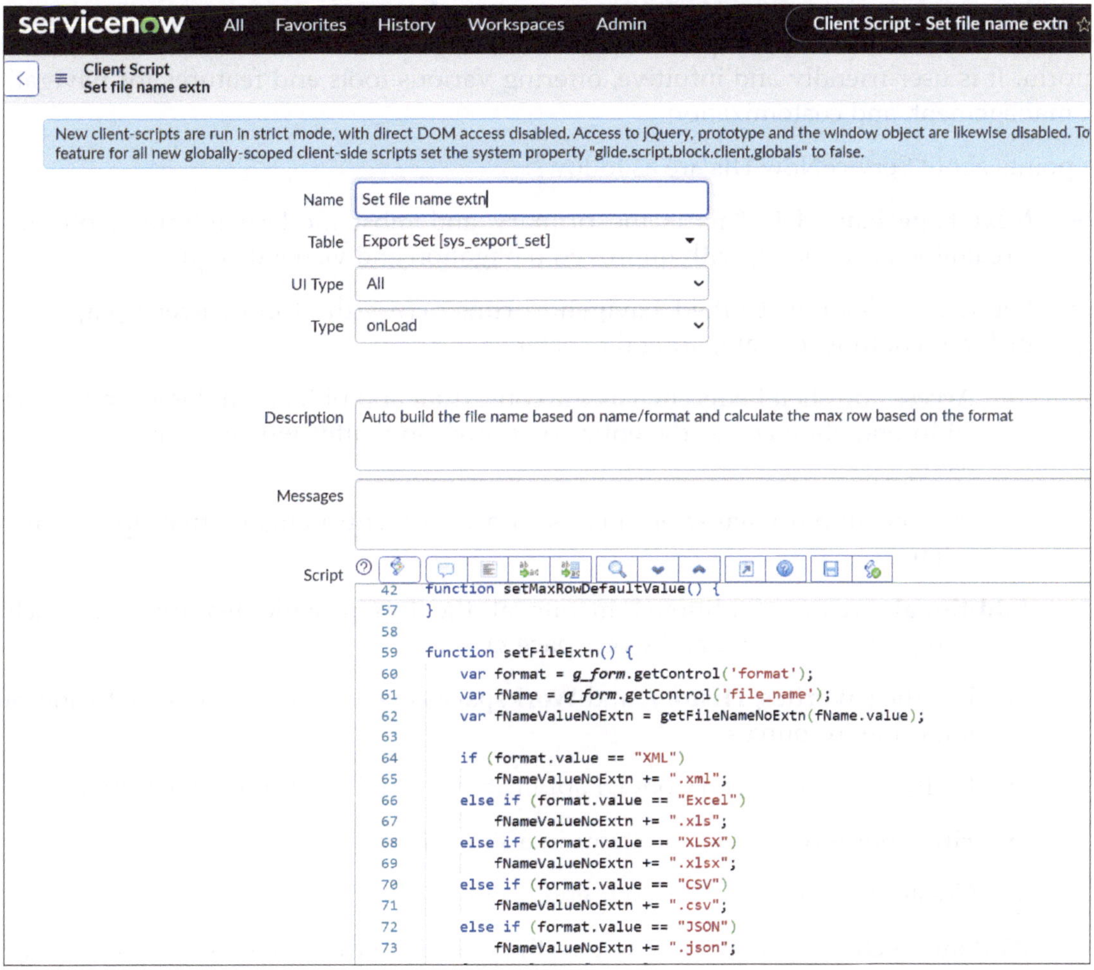

Figure 2.13: Client Script

Client script types

There are mainly four types. They are **onLoad**, **onChange**, **onSubmit**, and **onCellEdit**. Each type runs under different conditions and often has a different use than the others. Examples of tasks you can perform using client-side script in ServiceNow are provided as follows:

- Make the field mandatory.
- Make the field read-only.
- Make the field hidden.
- Make the field visible.
- Validate the form on submission.
- Display messages.
- Add more fields dynamically.

Common user interfaces of the platform

ServiceNow's UI is a web-based platform that allows users to interact with the ServiceNow platform. It is user-friendly and intuitive, offering various tools and features for navigation, task management, and customization.

Key points about ServiceNow UIs are as follows:

- **Next Experience UI**: This is the primary and most modern interface, offering a streamlined experience with improved navigation and visual design.
- **Unified navigation**: Unified navigation runs across the top of every page, which includes controls for navigating the instance.
    - Access app shell items such as the contextual app pill, menu items, and search—all in one place across the entire platform, no matter which application you are using.
    - Pin and unpin navigation menus to access menu items or free up screen real estate.
- **Additional menus**: Additional menus at the top provide features that include switching between classic and workspace views.
    - Use the **Favorites**, **History**, and **Workspaces** menu items to navigate to and pin important resources.
    - Easily switch between Core UI applications and Configurable Workspaces.
    - Find your recently viewed items in a single menu.
    - Create custom menus for your end users.
- **Workspace UI**: A specific view within the Next Experience UI focused on managing individual tasks and work items, often with customizable lists and views:
    - Improved agent efficiency.
    - Work on multiple issues concurrently in an optimized, intuitive layout.
    - Speedy resolution.
    - Resolve issues faster with automated suggestions powered by machine learning.
    - Proactive identification of major incidents.
    - Get notified of potential major incidents based on issue frequency and impact.
    - Greater visibility for agents.
    - Keep informed of updates and surface important insights with a live activity feed and analytics.

- **Core UI**: While considered older, the Core UI is still accessible and provides a more traditional interface for users familiar with earlier ServiceNow versions. The Core UI interface provides an updated look and usability improvements.

  Notable features include real-time form updates, user presence, a redesigned application navigator with **Favorites** and **History** tabs, and improved Activity Streams. Core UI is the default user interface for new instances. For upgraded instances, an administrator must activate Core UI.

Common UI elements within ServiceNow are as follows:

- **Unified navigation**: A consistent top bar allowing users to access different applications, favorites, and recent activity.
- **Application navigator**: A menu for selecting specific applications within ServiceNow.
- **Favorites**: Ability to pin frequently used applications or views for quick access.
- **History**: A list of recently accessed records and pages.
- **Workspaces**: Customizable dashboards or views to manage specific work items.
- **Lists**: Table-like views to display data in a structured format.
- **Forms**: Detailed views for creating, editing, and viewing individual records.

Working in the classic environment provides the following features:

- Work in lists and forms.
- Work in the classic Now Platform environment, creating lists from records.
- Powerful app creation and development.
- Create applications and develop with the full power of the Now Platform.
- Application scoping protects applications by identifying and restricting access to application files and data.

The **Workflow Studio** is used to create the flows. The following figure shows the **Workflow Studio** panel:

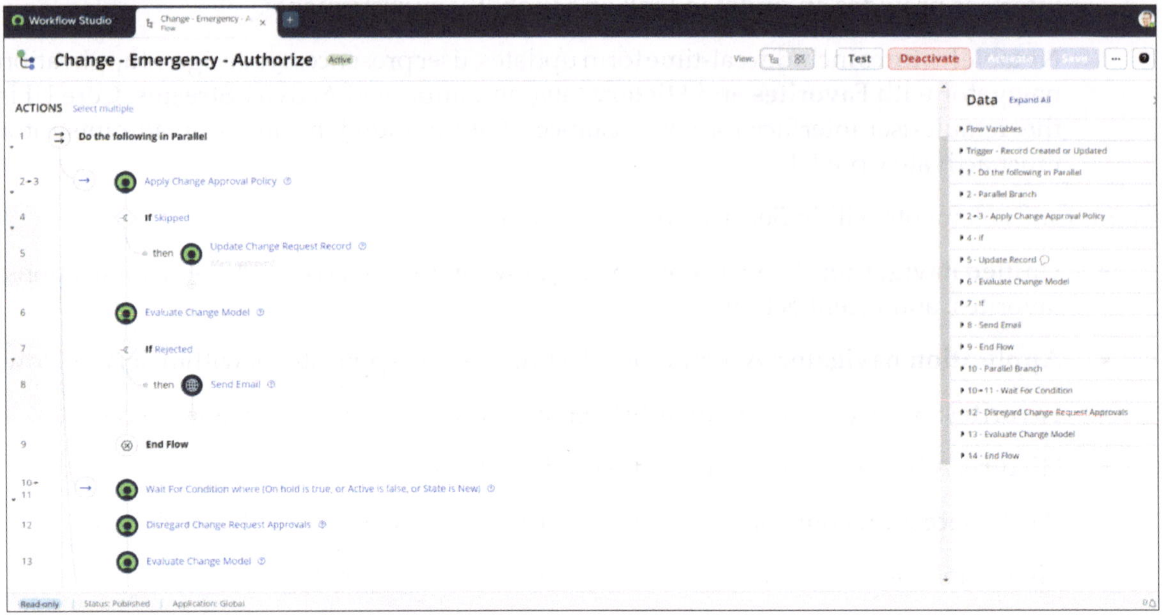

***Figure 2.14:** Workflow Studio*

Update sets do not capture data like users, roles, or groups, and reports, scheduled jobs, homepages, etc.

The steps to capture customization work are as follows:

1. Go to **All**.
2. Select **Local Update Sets**.
3. Create **New Update Set**.
4. Use the **Update Set** picker to set the newly created update set. That will be the current **Update Set**, and all customizations will be captured. Update status should be in the progress state.
5. Customizations or changes completed are captured.
6. Once completed and verified, change the status of the update set to closed.
7. Now, the **Update Set** is ready to be retrieved in a higher environment.

A template is a pre-defined record structure that automatically populates certain fields when creating a new record.

Assignment rules are configurations that automatically assign a task or record to a specific user or group based on predefined conditions within the record.

System identifier (**sys id**). Refers to a unique 32-character code that identifies every single record within the platform, acting as a **globally unique identifier** (**GUID**) for each data entry across all tables and modules.

A merge update set in ServiceNow is a feature that allows you to combine multiple individual Update Sets into a single update set, effectively merging all the configuration changes from each source set into one unified set. This is with the latest changes taking precedence in case of conflicts between different Update Sets.

Merging is recommended when:

- **Consolidating small changes**: When several small update sets (e.g., tiny tweaks for a single feature) are done, merging them into one larger set before final promotion makes migration simpler.
- **Cleaning up development**: To tidy up your development environment by combining work from multiple In Progress sets into a single, cleaner set for testing.

Merging is not recommended for the following conditions:

- **For release management**: Merging permanently combines updates, making it impossible to back out just one change.
- **With complex changes**: If sets have different development timelines or are for different features, merging mixes them, losing logical separation.

The system property required to be activated and set to true to implement the dark theme is:

```
glide.ui.polaris.dark_themes_enabled
```

In ServiceNow, ACL execution happens from specific to generic, meaning the system evaluates the most specific ACL rules first, and then moves to more general rules if needed, to determine if a user has access to a record or field.

Key points about ACL execution:

- **Evaluation order**: Table-level ACLs are checked first, then record-level ACLs, and finally field-level ACLs.
- **Both field and row-levels must be true**: For a user to access a field, both the row-level ACL (access to the record) and the field-level ACL (access to that specific field within the record) must evaluate to true.

Example scenario

Reading an incident: Imagine a user trying to read the `short_description` field on an incident record:

- **ACL 1 (specific field)**: `incident.short_description` (Requires service desk role, `Condition: Active=true`, `Script: false`).

  - **Result:** User does not have service desk, so this ACL returns `false` (denied).
- **ACL 2 (table wildcard)**: `incident.*` (Requires itil role, `Condition: true, Script: true`).
  - **Result**: User has itil role, condition met, script true, so this ACL returns `true` (granted).
- **Final**: Processing stops, access is granted because the second rule (more general, but still specific enough) passed.

The key takeaways are as follows:

- **Specificity wins**: More specific rules (field-level, parent tables) are checked before broad rules (table-level, wildcards).
- **Default deny**: Access is denied by default; one must create rules to allow it.
- **Stop processing**: Once any rule returns true, access is granted, and evaluation stops.

Knowledge articles are pieces of information, like release notes or policies, that are stored in a knowledge base. Knowledge managers manage the knowledge base.

In ServiceNow, knowledge articles can be in the following states:

- **Draft**: The content is available for editing and has not been published.
- **Review**: The article is waiting for approval before publishing.
- **Published**: The article is visible to users with read access.
- **Pending retirement**: The article is waiting for approval before being retired.
- **Retired**: The article is only visible to the knowledge base owner and managers.

The key stages of the lifecycle are as follows:

- **Draft (creation)**:
  - A need for information arises (e.g., from an incident, user request, or proactive capture).
  - An article is created in a specific knowledge base with required fields and detailed content (instructions, FAQs, etc.).
  - The article starts in a draft state, awaiting review.
- **Review (approval)**:
  - Content is checked for accuracy, clarity, and adherence to style guides.
  - Approvals are obtained from designated owners or managers.

- **Published (distribution and use):**
    - o Approved articles are made available in relevant knowledge bases (Service Portal, Agent Workspace).
    - o Users find solutions via search, preventing new incidents.
- **Retire (maintenance/archival):**
    - o Articles become outdated or redundant and are moved out of active search.
    - o This prevents users from relying on old information.

The following figure shows the **My Knowledge Articles** panel:

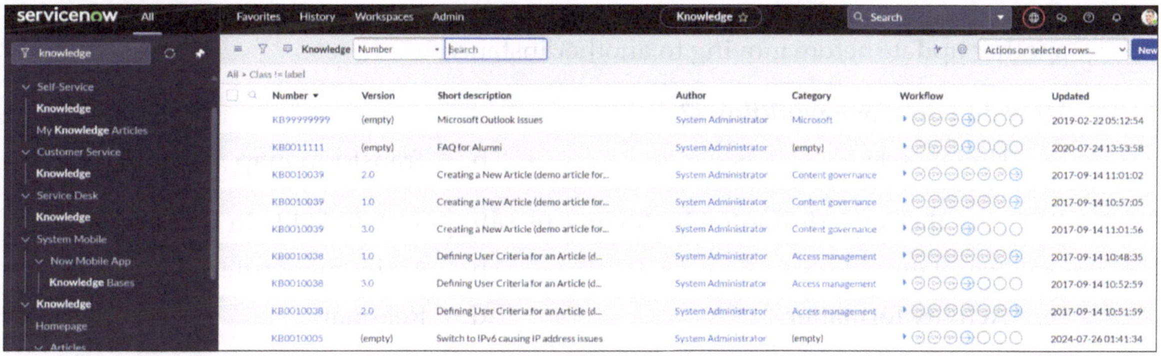

Figure 2.15: *My Knowledge Articles*

The **Knowledge Articles** are visible to end users in the published state.

Certification sample questions

1. **Which storefront is a single location for accessing prebuilt spokes to quickly integrate with third-party services to build and share content?**
    a. Integration portal
    b. Integration store
    c. ServiceNow spoke store
    d. Integration one stop
    e. ServiceNow Store
    f. Integration spoke hub
2. **User records are stored in the user [sys_user] table?**
    a. True
    b. False
3. **What are the steps to retrieve and commit an update set?**
    a. Check, retrieve, and apply
    b. Retrieve, preview, and commit

4. **Which of the following options are captured in the update set?**
   a. Scheduled jobs
   b. Groups users
   c. Workflow
   d. CI data
   e. Workflow
5. **Which of the following options is a group table?**
   a. sys_user_group
   b. sys_group
   c. sys_groups
   d. Groups
6. **State whether the following statement is true or false:**

   It is a good practice to open a complete update set to In Progress in order to recapture another update before moving to another instance.
7. **How do you move workflows?**
   a. Update sets
   b. Transform map
8. **What are the ways through which you can auto-populate fields in ServiceNow?**
   a. Template
   b. Assignment rule
   c. Activity formatter
   d. Ref qual
9. **What is a sys_id?**
   a. 32-digit GUID
   b. 64-digit GUID
10. **What is the base module to load data?**
    a. Incident
    b. Change
    c. Import set
11. **Where can the applications, modules, or tables be saved that are used frequently?**
    a. Favorites
    b. Bookmarks
    c. Header bar
    d. Applications
12. **Anyone should click on validate before moving the update set to another instance to avoid conflicts.**
    a. False
    b. True
13. **Where can the ServiceNow version of the instance be seen?**
    a. System Diagnostics | Stats
    b. Memory Stats
    c. System logs
    d. System upgraded

14. **What role is required to create ACLs?___________**
15. **What is impersonation used for?**
16. **What is a metric?**
17. **Personalized filter will be available for which option?**
    a. For me
    b. For group
    c. For company
18. **If there are multiple update sets and those update sets are merged, which of the following happens?**
    a. Only the latest update will be present in the merged update set.
    b. Only the old updates will be present in the merged update set.
    c. We cannot merge update sets.
    d. All the updates will be merged into one update set.
19. **Which option states the correct difference between form configuration and form personalization?**
    a. Configure is for all users, and personalization is for one user only
    b. Configure is for one user, and personalization is for one user
    c. Configure and personalization is for all users
    d. Configure is for one user, and personalization is for all users
20. **True/False**: Applying a role to a user will apply that role's permissions as well as the permissions of any role contained within.

Answers

1. e	2. a	3. b	4. c	5. a
6. False	7. a	8. a, b	9. a	10. c
11. a	12. a	13. a	14. Security_admin role	

15. Testing and visibility

16. A metric is a measure that can evaluate the effectiveness of ITSM processes

17. a	18. d	19. a	20. True

Fill in the blanks

1. **Users are represented by a record on the ______ table.**

   Ans: sys_user table.

2. **Groups are represented by a record on the ______ table.**

   Ans: sys_user_group

3. **Roles are represented by a record that exists on the______ table.**
   Ans: sys_user_role

Conclusion

This chapter covered the concepts of ServiceNow instance configuration and sample questions towards CSA. Personalization, customizations, and UI concepts explained.

The next chapter covers ServiceNow, configuring applications for collaboration. This includes details about lists, filters, tags, list configuration, form configurations, Form Templates, Task management, Visual Task Boards, Reporting, Dashboards, and Notifications.

Chapter 3
Configuring Applications for Collaboration

Introduction

Configuring applications for collaboration refers to the process of configuring lists, forms, dashboards, reports, **Visual Task Boards (VTBs)**, notifications, and customizing a ServiceNow instance. Configuring of tags, filters is detailed in this chapter. Setting of favorites is discussed in this chapter. Configuration of VTB, Reporting, Performance Analytics, Notifications, HealthScan, Instance Scan, Upgrade Center is detailed in this chapter. This chapter includes the customization of the unique needs of the organization using service operation workspace views. This section covers the related concepts, covering 20% of CSA questions.

Structure

This chapter covers the following topics:

- Lists, filters, and tags
- Dot walking
- Form configuration
- Notifications
- HealthScan
- Instance Scan
- Upgrade Center

Objectives

This chapter provides insights into ServiceNow about configurations of lists, forms, dashboards, reports, VTB, notifications, and customizing the instance for the needs of the organization. This chapter will provide users with the skills to configure ServiceNow for these aspects for the unique needs of the organization.

Lists, filters, and tags

Lists display data. Basically, a set of records from a table. Filters show the needed data based on conditions. Tags are labels or keywords that can be attached to records (like incidents, tasks, etc.) to help organize and filter them. Say, for example, menu **Incident–All**, fetches the **Incident** list.

The following figure shows the list view (**Incidents**):

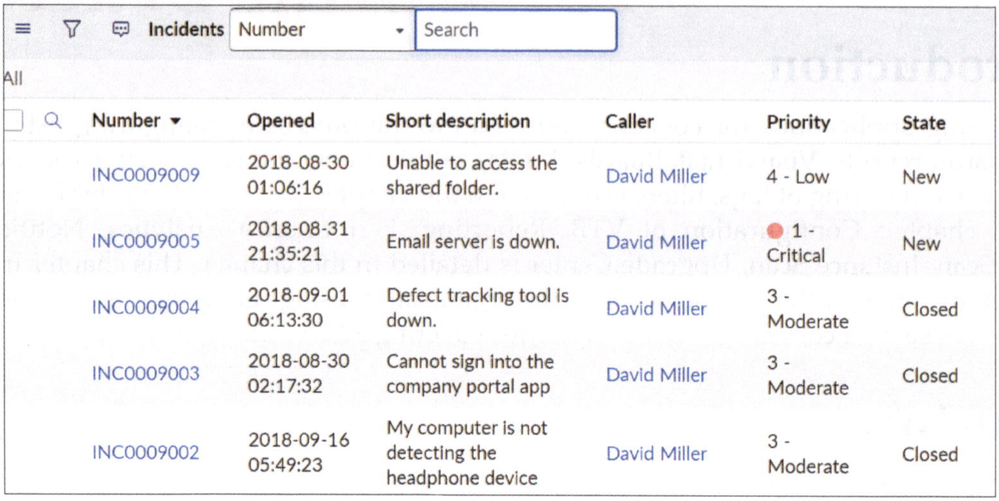

***Figure 3.1**: List view*

Classic list view refers to the traditional way of displaying records from a table, offering a tabular format with rows and columns, allowing users to view, search, and filter data.

In ServiceNow classic list view, you have three types of context menus: list header (Title bar), column header, and list item (row). These menus provide options for sorting, filtering, grouping, exporting, and manipulating the list view and data.

The following figure shows details of classic list view elements:

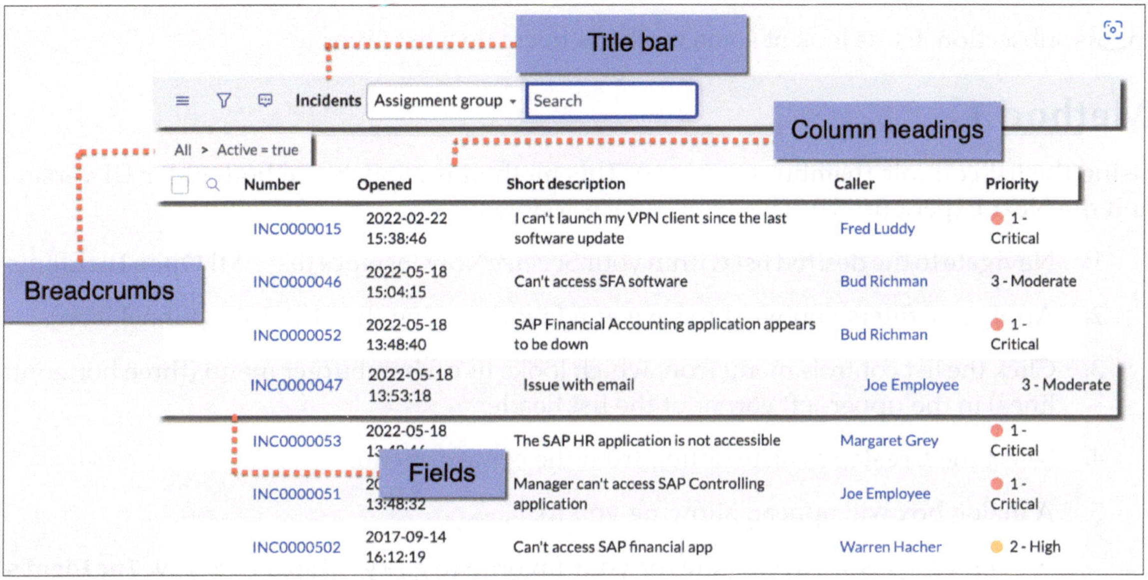

Figure 3.2: Classic list view context menus

The following figure shows details of the list features and actions:

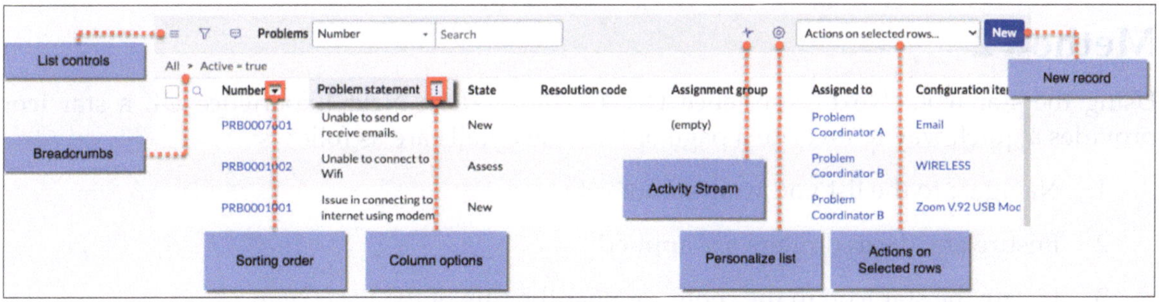

Figure 3.3: List features and actions

In ServiceNow, breadcrumbs are navigation aids that show your path through a hierarchy (like **Home | Catalog | Item**) and act as dynamic filters on lists, letting you see and quickly modify complex search conditions (e.g., **Active=True AND Priority=High**) to refine data views without rebuilding filters from scratch. They provide context, consistency, quick navigation back up the structure, and allow easy removal or modification of filters by clicking on parts of the breadcrumb.

Methods to create a list favorite

In this subsection, let us look at some methods to create a list favorite.

Method 1

Using the list controls (hamburger menu). This method is available in both older UI versions and the Next Experience UI. The details are as follows:

1. Navigate to the desired list within your ServiceNow instance (e.g., **All Open Incidents**).
2. Apply any filters you want to save as a favorite using the filter icon (funnel icon).
3. Click the list controls menu icon, which looks like a hamburger menu (three horizontal lines) in the upper-left corner of the list header.
4. Select the **Create Favorite** option from the context menu.
5. A dialog box will appear, allowing you to:
    - Enter a descriptive **Name** for your favorite (e.g., `My High Priority Incidents`).
    - Choose a specific **Color** and an **Icon** for easy identification in your favorites list.
6. Click **Save** to add the list view as a favorite.

Method 2

Using the star icon (Next Experience UI). In the modern Next Experience UI, a star icon provides a quick way to favorite a page or list. The details are as follows:

1. Navigate to the list you want to favorite.
2. Ensure any desired filters are applied.
3. Locate the star icon in the center or near the title of the list/page.
4. Click the star icon.
5. A confirmation and options menu will appear, letting you name the favorite and select an **Icon** and **Color**.
6. Click **Save** or **Add** to finish.

Accessing your favorites

Once created, all your favorites are accessible from the **Favorites** tab (the tab with the star icon) in the left-hand navigation pane. You can manage, reorder, and group your favorites from this tab.

The following figure shows the **Create Favorite** menu:

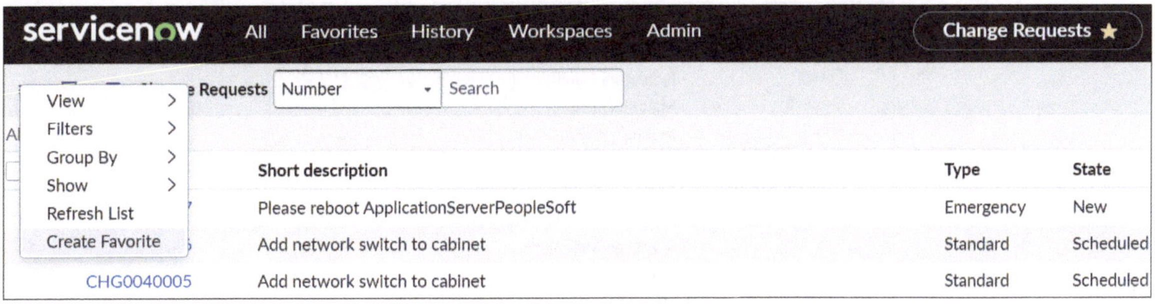

Figure 3.4: Create Favorite

The pin filters in the list work using the following steps:

1. Open your list (e.g., **Incidents | Open**).
2. Click the filter icon (looks like a funnel or three horizontal lines) to open the condition builder.
3. Click the pin icon (a small pin) within the filter builder to keep it expanded by default for that list view.

The following figure shows the menu to pin filters:

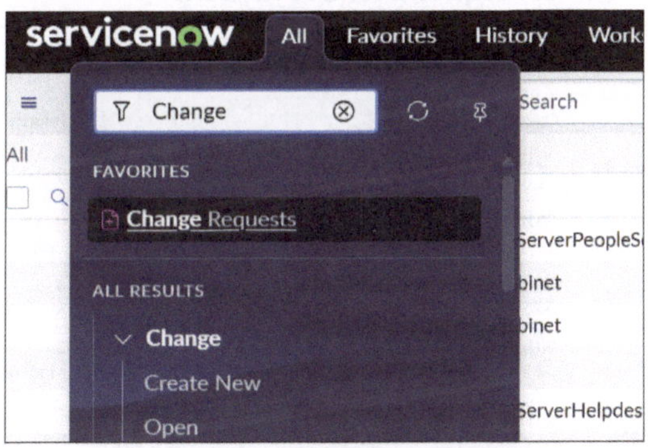

Figure 3.5: Pin filters

In ServiceNow's classic list view, the know the field right-quick functionality, or quick-edit, allows for editing of field values directly from the list without navigating to a form. This is achieved by double-clicking on a field to open the list editor, enabling inline editing.

The procedure is as follows:

1. Navigate to the list you want to configure.
2. Open the **List controls** menu and select **View | (view name)** to select the view you want to configure.

The following figure shows the configuration list controls with different views:

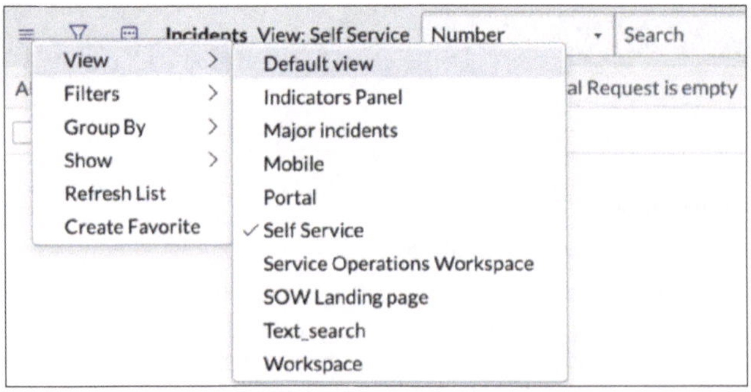

***Figure 3.6**: Configure list controls-view*

3. Right-click any column heading and select **Configure | List Layout**.
4. Add, remove, or reorder fields to configure the columns displayed and their order of appearance.

   The first non-reference field automatically links to the form view of the record. For this reason, consider using the record number as the first column in the list layout.
5. Select **Save**.

The following figure shows the configuration list layout:

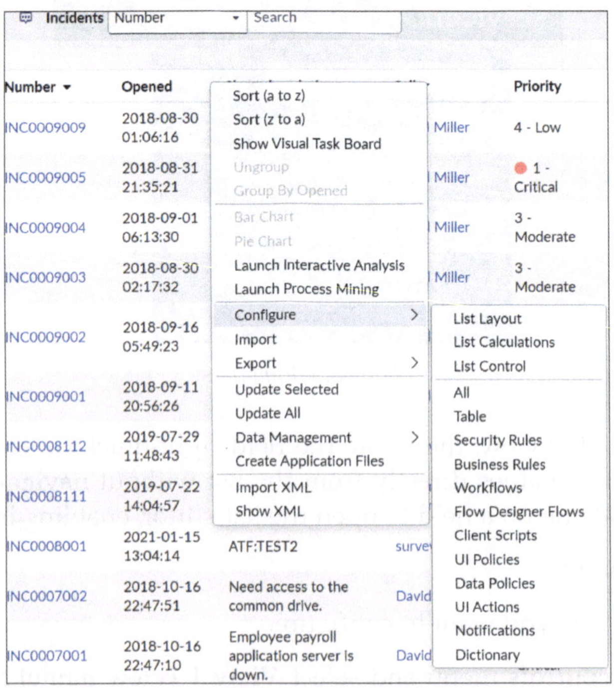

***Figure 3.7**: Configure list layout*

In ServiceNow, users can create and modify filters to limit the list of records that appear. Filters can be saved and shared.

The following figure shows filters in the classic list:

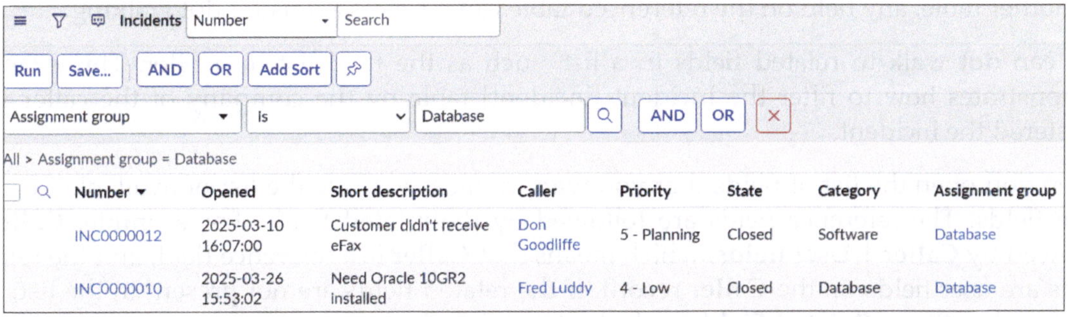

***Figure 3.8:** Classic list filters*

List view enables you to see high-level information for all records in a list filter. Normally, clicking a field in a record in a list opens that record.

The list in the **Service Operations Workspace** is detailed here. The procedure is as follows:

1. Click the list icon.
2. Find a list category that contains the records you want to work on.

The following figure shows filters in the **Service Operations Workspace** list view:

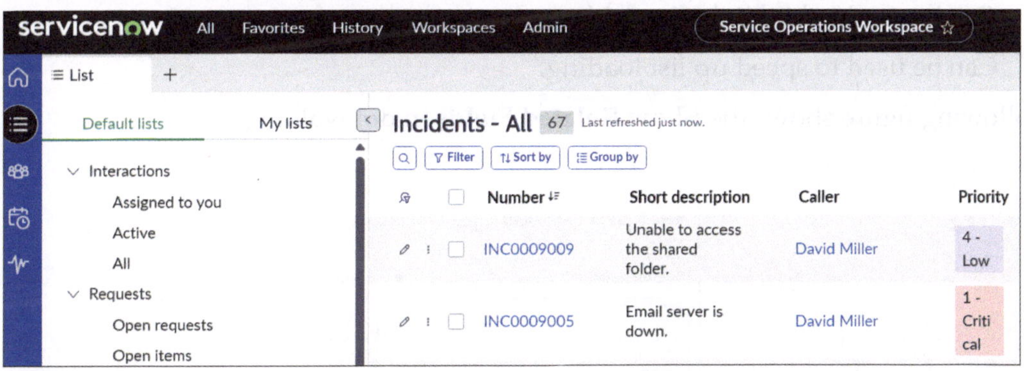

***Figure 3.9:** Service Operations Workspace, list*

Dot walking

The steps to dot walk in ServiceNow are as follows:

1. Use the **Show Related Fields** option on any filter list to display dot walking options.

2. Visit the ServiceNow wiki for a video tutorial and step-by-step guide on how to dot walk.

Dot walking provides access to fields on related tables. If the current table contains a reference to another table, any field on the referenced table can be accessed using dot walking.

You can dot walk to related fields in a list, such as the field list in a filter. This example demonstrates how to filter the Incident [incident] table by the company of the caller who registered the incident.

When you open the list of fields that you want to filter, you see the list of available incident table fields. The reference fields are followed by the related fields. For example, **Caller** is followed by **Caller | User fields**, which means that **Caller** is a reference field, and the related fields are user fields on the **Caller** record. If the related fields are not present in the list, you would select **Show Related Fields** at the bottom of the list.

In ServiceNow, dot walking allows users to access fields from related tables, while list collectors provide a container of items for selection.

Dot walking performs the following functions:

- Allows users to access fields on related tables.
- Can be used on forms, lists, and scripts.
- Can be used to customize reports.
- Can be used to setup list categories, filtered lists, and custom list operations.
- Can be used to highlight list fields.
- Can be used to speed up list loading.

The following figure shows the **Show Related Fields** in dot walking:

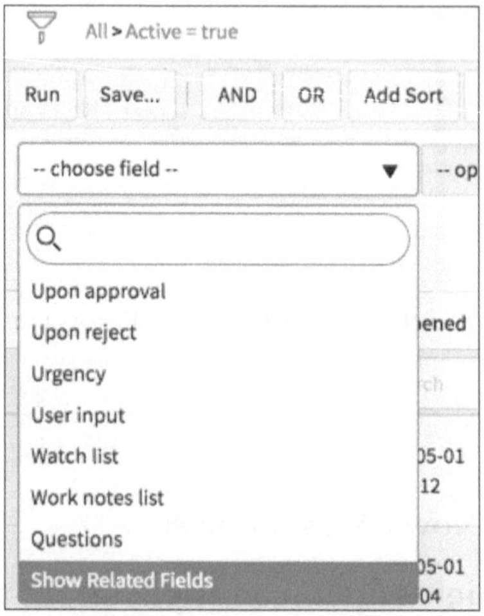

***Figure 3.10**: Dot walking 1*

When you select **Show Related Fields**, the menu reloads to display related fields.

The following figure shows creating a menu with reloading the related fields in dot walking:

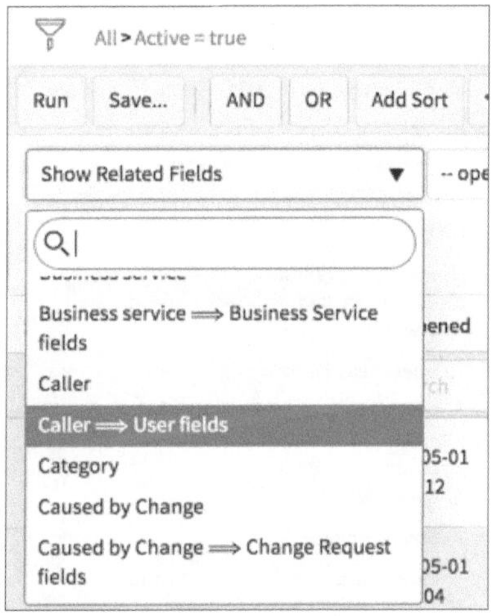

***Figure 3.11**: Dot walking 2*

When you select a related field, the menu reloads with the fields of the related table.

The following figure shows creating a menu with reloading the related table in dot walking:

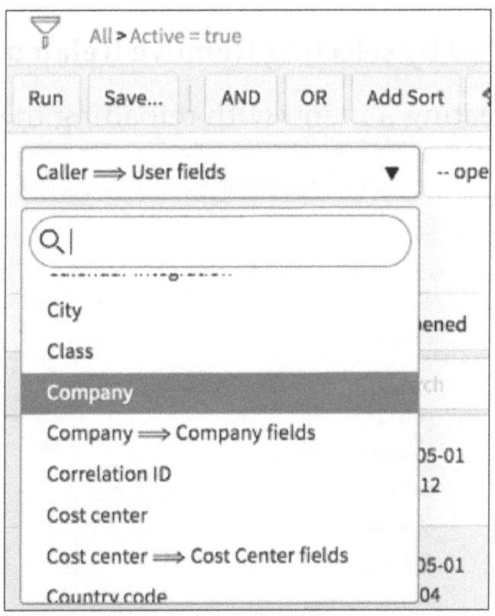

***Figure 3.12**: Dot walking 3*

When you select **Company** under the **Caller | User fields**, the field then becomes **Caller**. The following example shows where you are in the dot walk. Each selected reference is stored at the top of the fields menu, and the number of dots preceding the field label indicates how many dots from the initial record the user has reached.

The following figure shows creating a menu with reloading the 'second related table (**Incident fields**)' in dot walking:

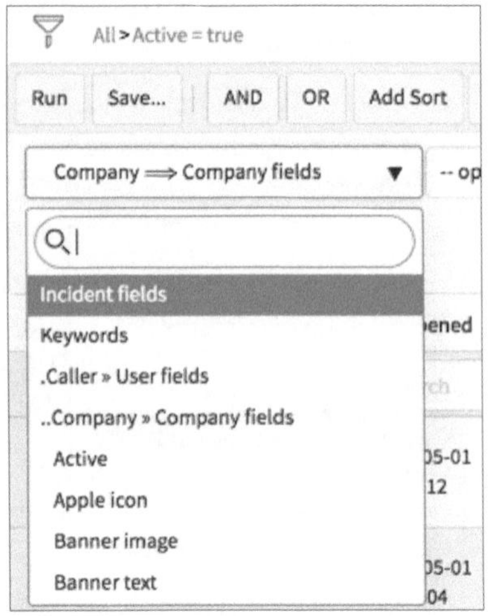

***Figure 3.13**: Dot walking 4*

The example shows that the user is at **Incident.Caller.Company**. You can return to higher levels in the hierarchy by selecting fields located at the top of the menu. For instance, selecting Incident fields returns to the list of incident fields.

The related fields can be removed by selecting **Remove Related Fields** at the bottom of the list.

The following figure shows creating a menu with reloading the related table in dot walking:

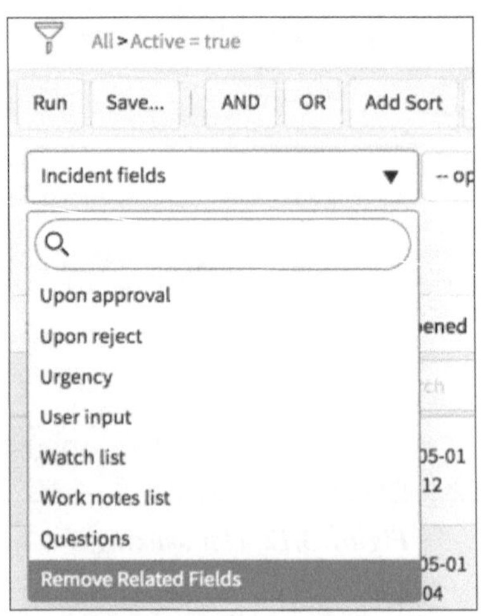

***Figure 3.14**: Dot walking 5*

To configure a list (add, remove, reorder) for all users in ServiceNow, the required role is admin.

List collectors

List collectors (slushbuckets) perform the following functions:

- Provide a container of items for selection.
- Contain nodes that users can click to dot walk to referenced items.
- Contain a search field for searching for specific entries.
- Contain a configurable label that shows the count of items available for selection.
- Contain a return icon that moves focus to base items in the first container.
- Contain a dot walk path that shows the reference path for the items selected.

A ServiceNow list collector is a variable type that allows users to select multiple items from a list. It is useful when you want users to be able to select more than one option without creating a lot of extra variables.

Tags

Tags are text labels. These are associated with items like records and pages. Tags enable grouping and organizing the items. Tags are visible to the user (global), visible only to specific groups or users (shared), or visible to a single user (private).

Tags are stored in the tag table. Viewing tags in a list, go to **System Definition | Tags** or **Self-Service | My Tags**.

If you tag an incident with Low Priority, the **label_entry** table will contain a record referencing the incident's **sys_id** and the "Low Priority" tag in the **label** table. Creating a tag from the list view is shown below. Right-click on a field and choose **New Tag** and click.

The following figure shows creating tags from the list view:

Figure 3.15: Create tag from list view

Form configuration involves changing the form layout and the related list layout. The form layout changes what appears on the form, and the related list layout changes which related lists appear at the bottom of the form.

Tags are visible in the list view by adding the **Tags** column in the personalized list slushbucket.

The following figure shows an example of a **Tags** in a list view:

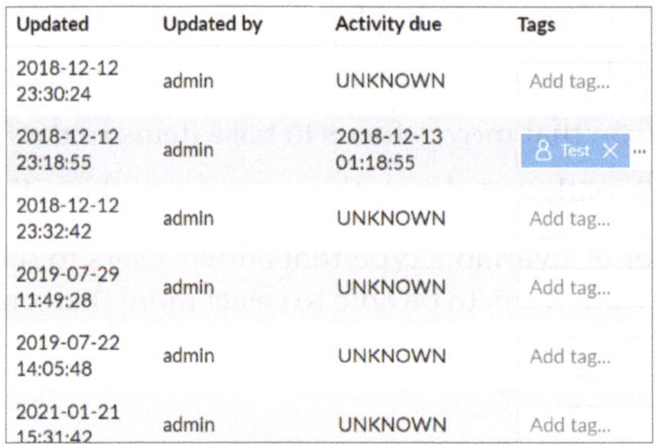

Figure 3.16: Tag

The following figure shows the menu to **Add Tag**:

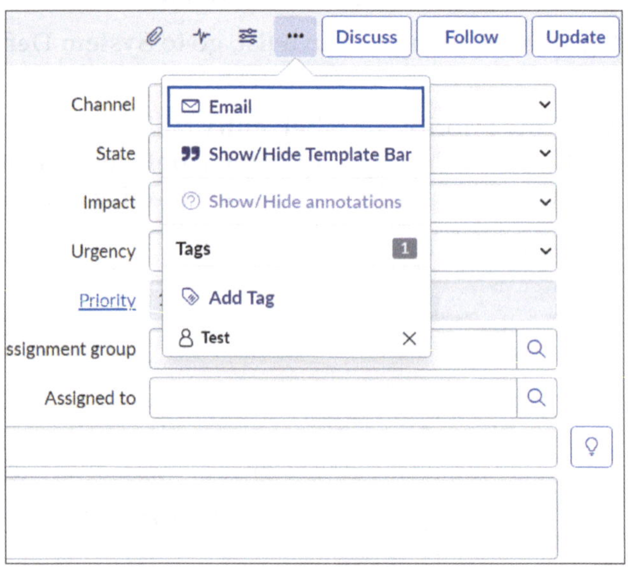

Figure 3.17: Add a tag

Form configuration

The following figure shows the configuration **of Form Builder**:

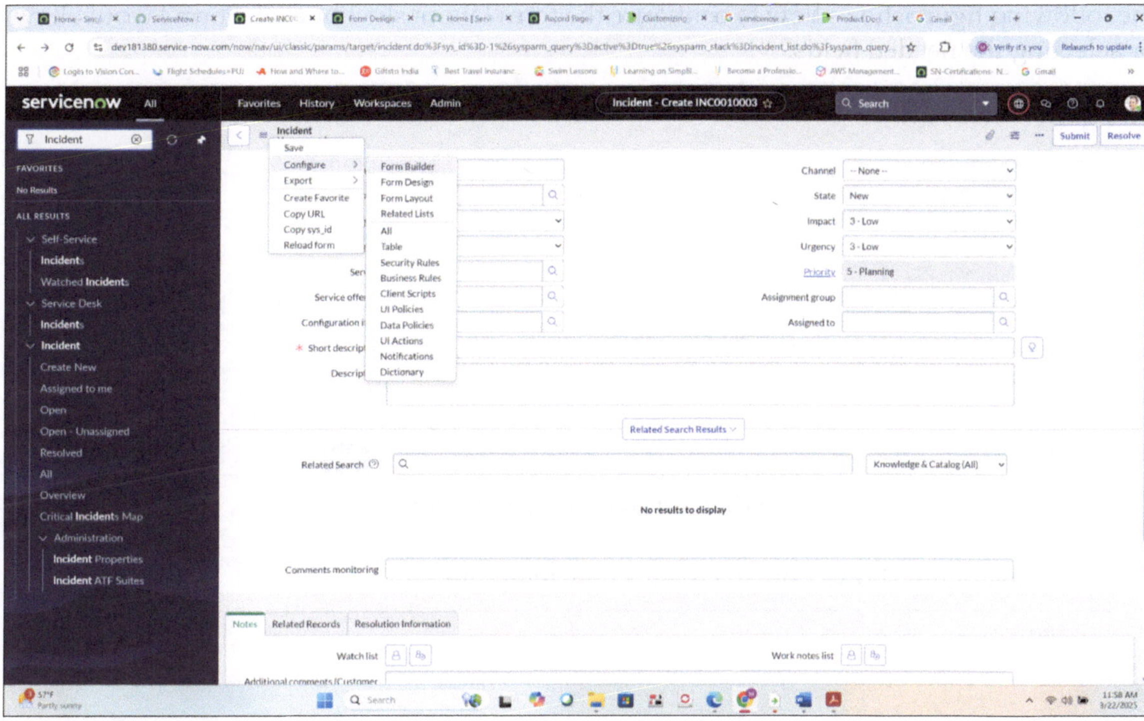

***Figure 3.18**: Configure Form Builder*

The following figure shows the configuration of **Form Builder** fields:

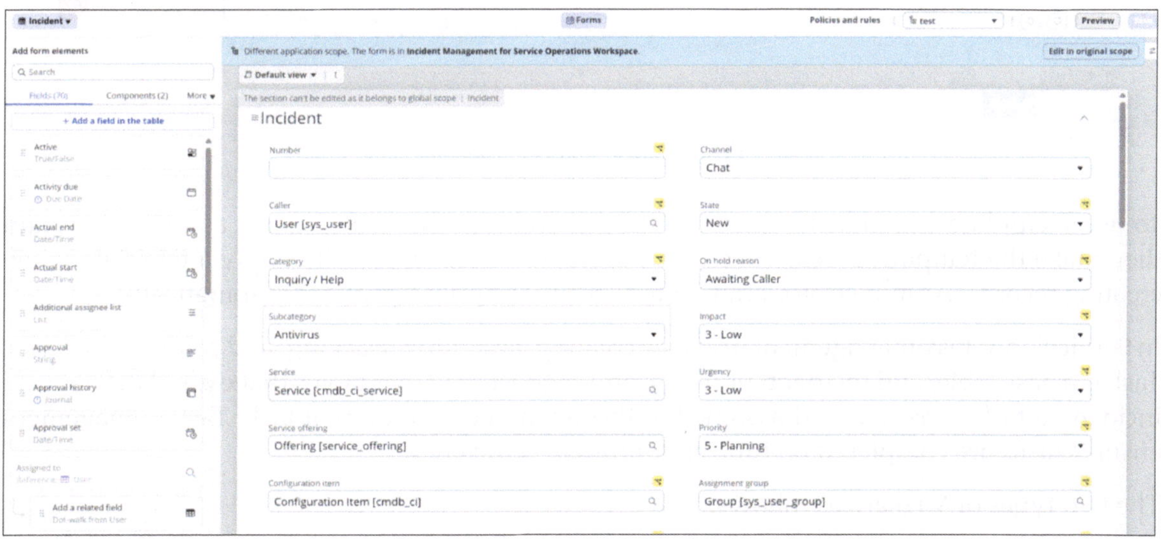

***Figure 3.19**: Configure Form Builder fields*

The following figure shows how to configure the form layout slushbucket. Form layout allows for selecting the needed fields:

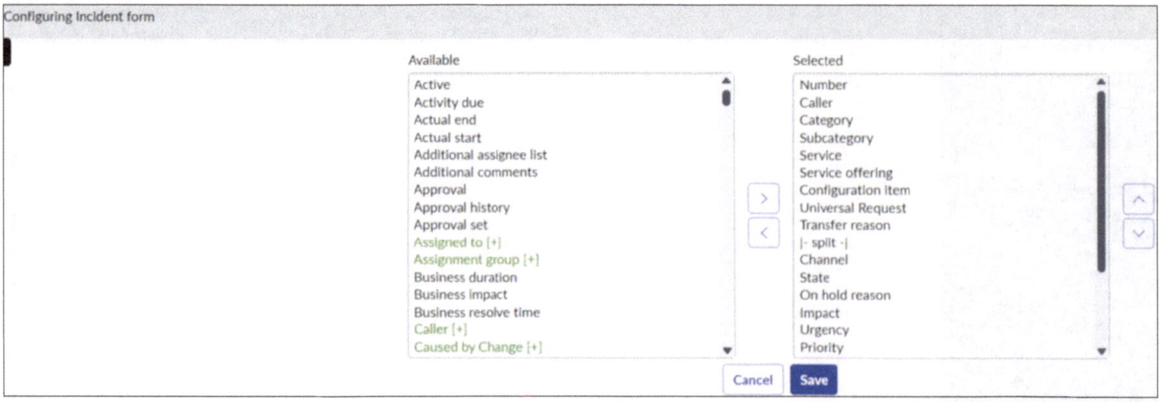

***Figure 3.20**: Form layout slushbucket*

The following figure shows how to create a new template:

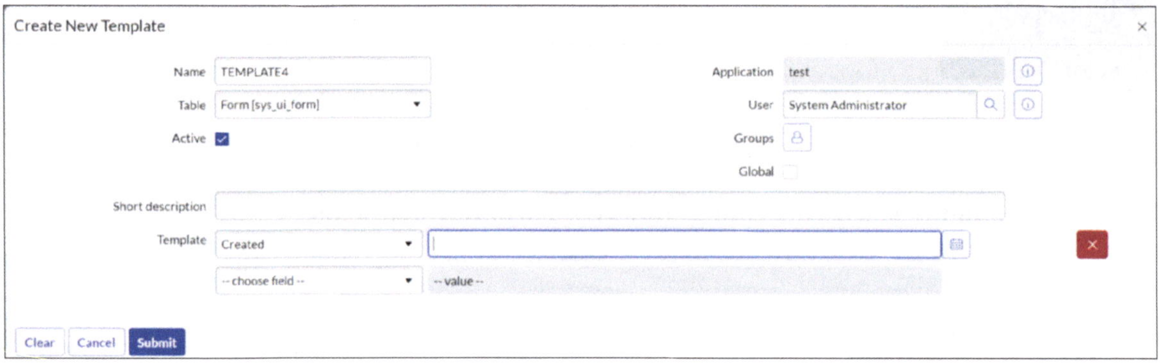

***Figure 3.21**: Creating a template*

To use a template, populate the most-used fields for a specific table, save it as a template, and then make the template accessible to your users. Users can manually apply a template when creating records. Administrators can define scripts to apply templates automatically.

In ServiceNow, task management involves creating, assigning, tracking, and prioritizing tasks. Task is a base table, and incident, problem, and request are other tables that extend it. Say in an incident, a task is created and assigned to those who need to do that task. Task management ensures tasks are completed on time and improves efficiency.

The two types of VTB are as follows:

- **Freeform**: This is customizable.
- **Data-driven**: Linked with data. Lane titles cannot be changed.

The following figure shows VTB:

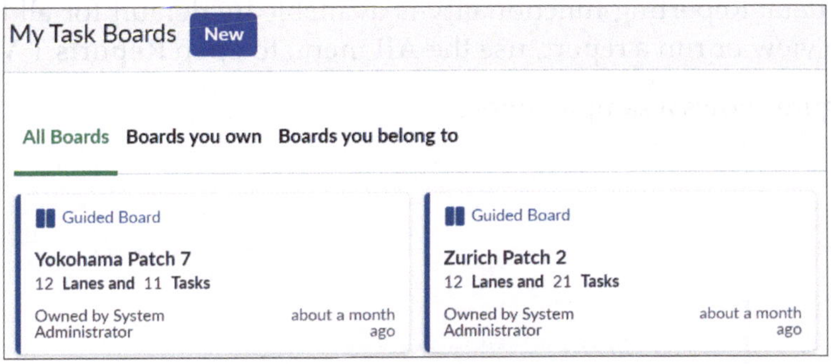

***Figure 3.22:** VTB*

In the **All** menu type, the VTB and available VTBs are displayed. Click on **Create New** to create a new VTB. Arrangement of cards can be horizontal or vertical; they are called Lanes. The categories are called Lanes. Cards are records. The Quick Panel on top shows assignees. Taskboard tools are shown at the top, showing **Activity Stream**, **Configuration**, and **Users**.

Dashboards are a visual display of multiple reports and widgets in one place, providing a real-time overview of critical data.

To create a new dashboard, follow these steps:

1. Go to **All**.
2. Go to **Dashboard**.
3. Create a new dashboard.

The following figure shows a **Sample_Dashboard**:

***Figure 3.23:** Dashboard (sample)*

ServiceNow Reporting enables the creation and distribution of reports that show the current state of instance data. Reporting functionality is available by default for all tables, except for system tables. To view or run a report, use the **All** menu to open **Reports | View/Run**.

The following figure shows a sample report:

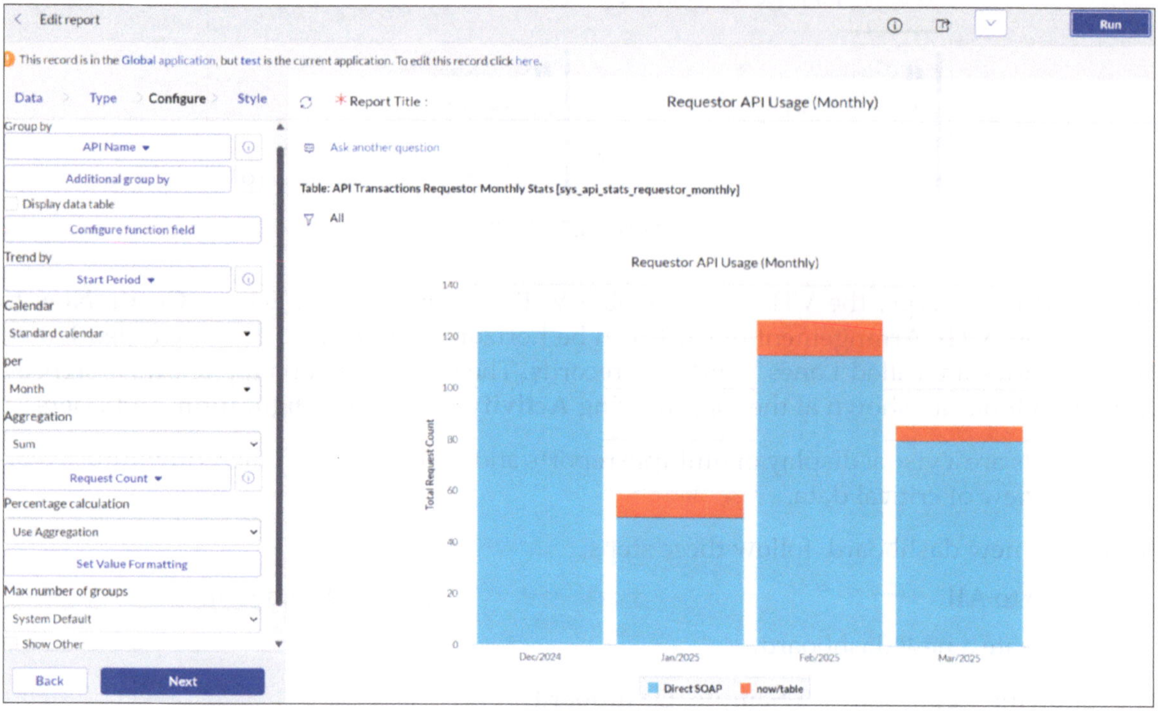

Figure 3.24: Report

ServiceNow Performance Analytics is an in-platform process optimization solution to create management dashboards, report on KPIs and metrics, and answer key business questions to help increase quality and reduce the costs of service delivery.

The steps to configure a report are as follows:

1. **Navigate and initiate**: Go to the **Reports** app and click **Create New**, or start from a list view.
2. **Define data source**:
   - Name the report.
   - Choose a **Source Type** (**Table** or **Data Source**).
   - Select the specific **Table** (e.g., **Incident**, **Change Request**).
3. **Select report type (visualization)**: Choose a visual to best display data.

4. **Configure data**:
   - **Filter**: Add conditions (e.g., state is 'In Progress', created within the last 30 days).
   - **Group and aggregate**: Group data by fields like **Priority** or **Assignment Group** and choose aggregation (**Count**, **Sum**, **Average**).
   - **Sort**: Order the data.
5. **Style and customize**: Use the **Presentation** tab to change colors, labels, titles, and axes for clarity.
6. **Set interactions**: Configure drill-downs to see underlying records or add links.
7. **Save and share**: Save the report with a clear name and add it to a dashboard for easy access and a consolidated view.

ServiceNow offers diverse report types for visualizing data, ranging from simple List Reports to complex charts like bar, line, pie, funnel, heat maps, and pivot tables, plus advanced options like bubble charts, gauges, and histograms, all designed to show trends, comparisons, or parts-to-whole relationships, easily added to dashboards for at-a-glance insights.

Some common report types are as follows:

- **List**: A simple, filterable list of records from a table (e.g., all open incidents).
- **Bar/Column**: Compares quantities across categories (e.g., incidents by assignment group).
- **Pie/Donut**: Shows parts of a whole (e.g., incident states: New, In Progress, Resolved).
- **Line tracks**: Trends over time (e.g., tickets closed per week).
- **Pivot**: Summarizes data by grouping across multiple fields (e.g., grouping incidents by priority and category).
- **Gauge/Speedometer**: Displays a single metric, often with color-coded thresholds for performance.

Some advanced and specialized types are as follows:

- **Heat map**: Uses color intensity to show data density in a matrix.
- **Bubble chart**: Shows relationships between three data points (X, Y, size).
- **Funnel /Pyramid**: Visualizes stages in a process (e.g., lead conversion).
- **Histogram**: Displays data distribution (e.g., resolution times).
- **Time series**: Focuses on temporal patterns, often with projections.

They are used as follows:

- **Dashboards**: Reports are placed on dashboards for consolidated views, allowing for drill-downs to see underlying data.

- **Scheduling**: Reports can be automatically sent via email (PDF, CSV).
- **Interactivity**: Users can click data points to explore records or related reports.

ServiceNow Reporting shows a snapshot of current data, like open incidents, while Performance Analytics provides historical trends, predictions, and targets by taking regular data snapshots over time, answering questions about improvement and forecasting future performance.

The ServiceNow Reporting includes the following:

- **Focus**: Current state or specific point-in-time data.
- **Data**: Queries live data from tables directly.
- **Answers**: How many incidents are open right now?
- **Use case**: Quick checks, simple lists, single-question answers, present conditions.

The **Performance Analytics** (**PA**) includes the following:

- **Focus**: Trends, historical performance, forecasts, and targets.
- **Data**: Collects periodic snapshots (e.g., daily) and stores them as scores, enabling trend analysis.
- **Answers**: Are incidents increasing weekly? Or are we hitting our resolution time goals?
- **Use case**: Measuring improvement, setting goals, proactive issue identification, and strategic insights.

The key differences are summarized as follows:

- **Time**: Reports = Now; PA = Over time.
- **Data source**: Reports = Live table data; PA = Stored historical scores.
- **Functionality**: Reports = Static views; PA = Trends, forecasts, thresholds, benchmarks.

Enabling PA involves specific plugin requirements and subscription tiers that dictate feature access. ServiceNow provides a baseline Complimentary version for all customers, while more advanced capabilities require a Premium subscription. Subscription tiers and constraints for enabling PA is detailed as follows:

- **Subscription tiers and constraints**: The main constraint for PA is the distinction between the free baseline version and the paid Premium version.
  - **Complimentary (free) version**:
    - **Scope**: Restricted specifically to incident management.
    - **Data retention**: Limited to 180 days of historical data.
    - **Features**: Provides a fixed set of roughly 15 KPIs (e.g., New/Open/Closed/Backlog growth) and specific dashboards.

        - **Constraint**: You cannot create custom indicators, breakdowns, or collect data for other applications like problem or change management.

    - **Premium version**:

        - **Scope**: Provides unlimited KPIs and data collection across all subscribed applications (incident, problem, change, HR, etc.).

        - **Data retention**: Unlimited historical data collection.

        - **Features**: Full access to create custom KPIs, automated breakdowns, and advanced visualization tools.

        - **Activation**: Requires a paid subscription, often bundled with Professional or Enterprise application suites (e.g., ITSM Pro).

- **Required plugins**: Plugin names vary depending on whether you are activating the core engine or specific industry content packs.

    - **Core plugin**: `com.snc.pa` is the primary plugin to enable the engine.

    - **Complimentary plugin**: `com.snc.pa.incident` is the plugin for the free incident-specific version.

    - **Content packs**: These are pre-built dashboards and KPIs for specific applications. Examples include:

        - ITSM: `com.snc.pa.premium.it_service_management`.

        - CSM: `com.snc.pa.customer_service_management`.

        - HR: `com.snc.pa.hr_service_delivery`.

- **Environment and deployment constraints**:

    - **Non-production vs. production**: Plugins can generally be activated on **personal developer instances (PDIs)** or sub-production environments for testing and demo purposes without an immediate purchase. However, activation on a production instance requires a verified entitlement and purchase.

    - **Entitlement verification**: ServiceNow uses the subscription management application to track your licenses. Before activating PA Premium in Production, an administrator must typically verify that the instance is entitled through the ServiceNow Store or an account manager.

    - **Role requirements**: Activation requires the admin role. Configuration and management typically require the **pa_adm**in or **pa_power_user** roles once the plugin is active.

- **How to enable**:

    1. **Identify entitlement**: Check your order form or the subscription management module in your instance to confirm if PA Premium is included in your package.

2. **Activate plugin**: Navigate to **System Definition | Plugins**, search for the desired plugin (e.g., **Performance Analytics Premium**), and click **Activate**.
3. **Run data collection**: After activation, you must configure and execute data collection jobs to begin gathering historical and daily snapshots of your data.

Notifications

In ServiceNow Notifications are used to inform users about events or actions within the platform. This can be configured to be triggered by various events like record changes, scheduled tasks, or user actions. This is done via email and text notifications. Text notifications are done for mobile.

Navigate to the following path to access the notifications:

1. **All**
2. **System Notification**
3. **Email | Notifications**

ServiceNow Notifications are automated alerts (email, SMS, push) triggered by system events (record changes, escalations) to inform users about critical updates, tasks, or approvals, configured via the Notification module (defining triggers, conditions, recipients, content) and managed with system properties (like `glide.email.smtp.send`) for mail server settings, ensuring timely communication and workflow automation within the platform.

The details about notifications are as follows:

- **Definition**: Automated messages sent to users or groups when specific events occur in ServiceNow, keeping them informed about system activities.
- **Types**: Primarily email, but also SMS and push notifications.
- **Purpose**: Provide timely updates, reminders, alerts for critical incidents, approvals, or changes, reducing manual checks and improving response times.

The configuration is as follows:

- **Navigate**: Go to **System Notification | Email | Notifications** (or **Notifications | Email | Notifications**).
- **Create/Edit**: Click **New** or open an existing notification.
- **Table**: Select the table (e.g., **Incident, Task**) the notification applies to.
- **When to send (triggers)**: Define when it fires (e.g., Record Inserted, Updated, Deleted) and specific conditions (e.g., [State] [changes to] [In Progress]).
- **Who will receive**: Specify recipients (users, groups, roles) using fields or specific lists.
- **What will it contain**: Compose the message (Subject, Body) using variables like `${number}` or `${assigned_to}` to personalize content.

- **Save**: Save the notification to activate it.

Core scripting objects

When writing an email script, you have access to several global variables:

- **Current**: The **GlideRecord** of the record triggering the notification (e.g., an incident or request).
- **Template**: Used to print content to the email body using a **template.print("your text")**.
- **Email**: The **EmailOutbound** object, used to set the subject, add recipients (**CC**/**BCC**), or set the **Reply To** address.
- **Event**: Represents the event that triggered the notification (useful for accessing event parameters like **event.parm1**).

Let us look at some common scripting examples:

- **Print record details**:

```
javascript
template.print("Incident Number: " + current.number + "<br />");
template.print("Priority: " + current.priority.getDisplayValue());
```

- **Add CC recipients**:

```
javascript
email.addAddress("cc", "manager@example.com", "Manager Name");
```

- **Dynamic links**:

```
javascript
var url = gs.getProperty('glide.servlet.uri') + 'nav_to.do?uri=incident.
do?sys_id=' + current.sys_id;
template.print('<a href="' + url + '">View Incident</a>');
```
```

- **Conditional formatting (CSS)**:

```
javascript
template.print(' URGENT: ACTION
REQUIRED ');
```
```

The best practices are as follows:

- **Avoid complex logic**: If a script becomes too long, move the logic to a Script Include and call it from the email script.

- **Use HTML for layouts**: Use `template.print()` to output HTML tags like `<table>`, `<tr>`, and `<td>` for structured data.
- **Test previews**: Use the **Preview Notification** button in the notification record to see the script's output before going live.

The following figure shows the email notifications configuration:

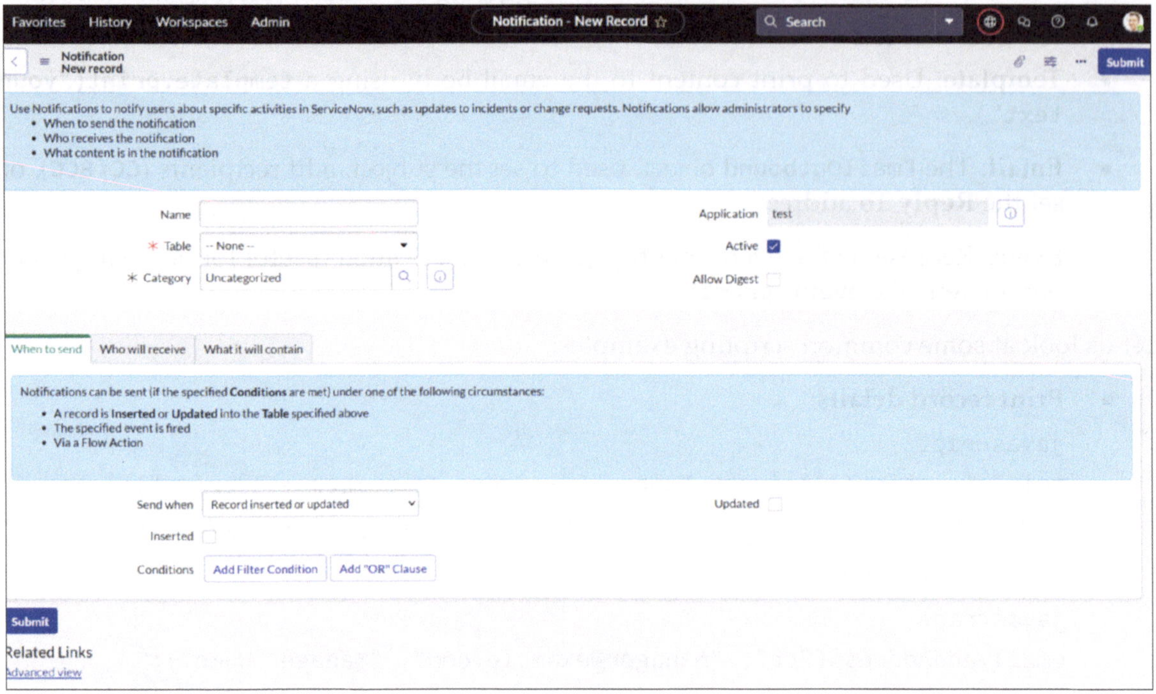

Figure 3.25: Email notifications

Predefined notification layouts can be viewed using the following steps. Navigate to:

All | System Policy | Email | Layouts

Predefined notification template layouts can be viewed by navigating to:

All | System Policy | Email | Templates

In ServiceNow email notifications, the watermark symbol is a unique identifier (a string) added to the email footer. This is to match incoming replies with the original record, enabling the update of the correct record.

The default length of a ServiceNow email watermark notification is 31 characters. This consists of "Ref:", a customizable prefix (default "MSG"), an underscore, and a 20-character random string.

The backend configuration is done within the email notifications module in ServiceNow. An administrator defines *when* the email is sent, *who* receives it, and *what* it will contain. Configuration steps of email notifications are detailed here:

1. **Navigate to notifications**: In the filter navigator, type **System Notifications | Email | Notifications.**
2. **Create new**: Click the **New** button to create a new notification.
3. **Fill in the form (Example: "Incident Assigned"):**
   a. **Name: Incident Assigned Notification**
   b. **Table: Incident**
   c. **Active: Checked**
4. **Configure "When to send":**
   a. Select the conditions that trigger the notification. For this example, we would configure it to send when an incident record is updated and the **Assignment Group** changes or is filled.
   b. **Screenshot description (backend)**: A screen showing the **When to send** tab with conditions like **Update** checked, and a filter condition [Assignment group] [changes] and [Assigned To] [is empty].
5. **Configure "Who will receive":**
   a. Define the recipients.
   b. **Screenshot description (backend)**: A screen showing the **Who will receive** tab, with the **Users** field containing dynamic values like [Assignment group] [Group email] or by referencing a specific user field on the incident record like [Assigned To].
6. **Configure "What it will contain":**
   a. This is where the email content is defined, often using a combination of plain text, HTML, and dynamic variables.
   b. **Subject**: Incident **`INC${number}`** assigned to your group
7. **Message HTML**: Message in HTML is stated as follows:

```
<p>Hello,</p>
<p>Incident ${number} has been assigned to your group. Please review the details.</p>
<p><b>Short Description:</b> ${short_description}</p>
html
<p><b>Priority:</b> ${priority}</p>
<p>You can view the incident here: ${URI_REF}</p>
```

The frontend view to the receiver is detailed as follows.

When an incident record is updated with an assignment group that matches the trigger condition, the user in that group receives an email.

An example of how the received email looks in a typical email client (e.g., *Outlook, Gmail*) is provided as follows:

```
From:  "ServiceNow Helpdesk" <instance@service-now.com>
Subject:     Incident INC1234567 assigned to your group
Body:
 Hello,
Incident INC0009005 has been assigned to your group. Please review the
details.
Short Description : Email server is down
Priority: 1 Critical
```

HealthScan

HealthScan is ServiceNow's comprehensive, external, expert-driven health check for deep platform assessment (performance, security, config), while Instance Scan is an internal, customer-activated, rule-based tool for ongoing quality control, development governance, and finding specific issues (code quality, hardcoded IDs) within your instance, both aiming to reduce tech debt but with different scopes and activation methods.

Here is a breakdown of their differences:

- **HealthScan**:
  - o **Nature**: An external application run by ServiceNow personnel.
  - o **Scope**: A holistic full-body assessment of your instance's overall health, encompassing performance, customizations, security, and data quality against best practices.
  - o **Activation**: Can only be activated by ServiceNow personnel.
  - o **Goal**: Provides broad insights for major optimization and stability.
- **Instance Scan**:
  - o **Nature**: An internal platform capability running within your instance.
  - o **Scope**: More targeted, rule-based scanning for specific issues like security violations, bad code (hardcoded **sys_ids**), upgrade risks, and developer best practices.
  - o **Activation**: Can be activated by customers themselves.

- o **Goal**: Continuous quality control, development governance (linting, security checks before deployment), and fixing specific technical debt.

The key distinctions are as follows:

- **Who runs it**: HealthScan (ServiceNow), Instance Scan (Customer).
- **Depth vs. breadth**: HealthScan (broad, deep health), Instance Scan (targeted, code/config issues).
- **Use case**: HealthScan (major health check), Instance Scan (DevOps, pre-release quality.

Instance Scan

In ServiceNow's Instance Scan checks, the categories assess different aspects of your instance's health, with performance focusing on system responsiveness, security on vulnerabilities and best practices, upgradeability on smooth upgrades, manageability on ease of administration, user experience on usability, and overall summarizing the instance's health across all categories.

The steps to access the Instance Scan menu are as follows:

1. Navigate to **All | Instance Scan**.
2. Instance Scan checks your existing configurations and helps you avoid creating future configuration issues. Instance Scan is a tool that can be used as a part of your development operations, release management, as well as pre- and post-upgrades.

The types of checks are as follows:

- Table check
- Script only check
- Column type check
- Linter check

The following figure shows Instance Scan:

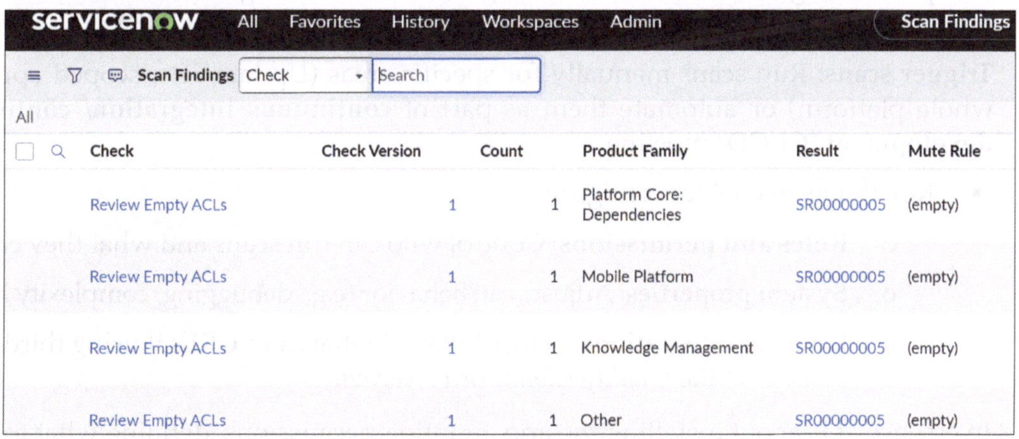

Figure 3.26: *Instance Scan*

To enable ServiceNow Instance Scan, you generally need to activate the **Instance Troubleshooter plugin (com.sn_troubleshooter)**, setup a dedicated service account with API access and proper roles (like **itil**, **admin** or specific scan roles), configure scan checks and suites for your specific needs (platform health, security, best practices), and potentially integrate with external tools using API keys, ensuring your instance URL and credentials are correctly configured for the scanning entity.

The core requirements and steps are as follows:

1. **Install plugin**: Activate the **Instance Troubleshooter plugin (ID: com.sn_troubleshooter)** in your instance via the plugin list or available Applications.
2. **Create service account**:
   a. Create a user with local authentication (not SSO-only).
   b. Assign necessary roles (e.g., **security_admin**, **itil**, or custom roles for specific scans) and API permissions.
3. **Configure scan checks**:
   a. Use built-in checks or create custom ones (script or condition builder) for areas like security, performance, or custom best practices.
   b. Organize checks into suites for focused scans (e.g., Security Suite, Performance Suite).
4. **Enable SecureCheck (for security focus)**:
   a. If using Quality Clouds or similar, enable the certificate and provide instance details.
   b. For native security, ensure the SecureCheck view is enabled on the findings form (**Context Menu | View | SecureCheck View**).
5. **Setup task integration (optional)**: Configure scan task configurations to automatically create tasks for findings in specific product categories (e.g., ITSM, HR).
6. **Trigger scans**: Run scans manually for specific areas (Update Sets, scoped apps, the whole platform) or automate them as part of **continuous integration/ continuous development** (**CI/CD**) pipeline.
   - Key things to enable/configure:
     - **Roles and permissions**: Control who can run scans and what they can see.
     - **System properties**: Adjust scan behavior (e.g., debugging, complexity limits).
     - **External integrations**: Setup API credentials and URLs if using third-party scanners (like *Quality Clouds* or *Forcepoint*).

In essence, it is about installing the app, granting permissions, defining what to check (checks/suites), and how to report/resolve findings (tasks/integrations).

Upgrade Center

This is the module to plan and manage upgrades. The following figure shows the **Upgrade Center**:

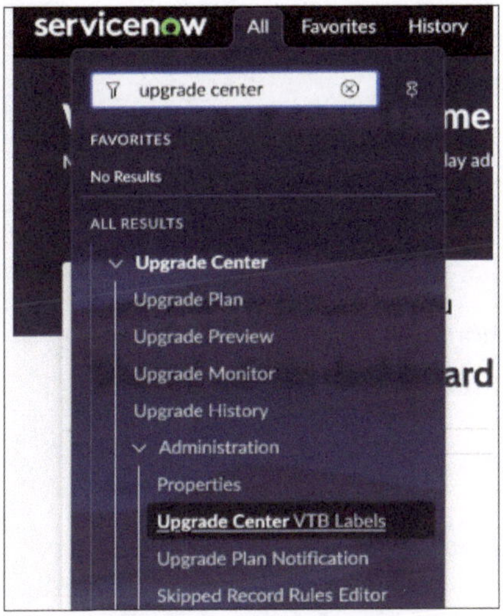

Figure 3.27: Upgrade Center

Upgrade preview

The following figure shows the upgrade preview in **Upgrade Center**:

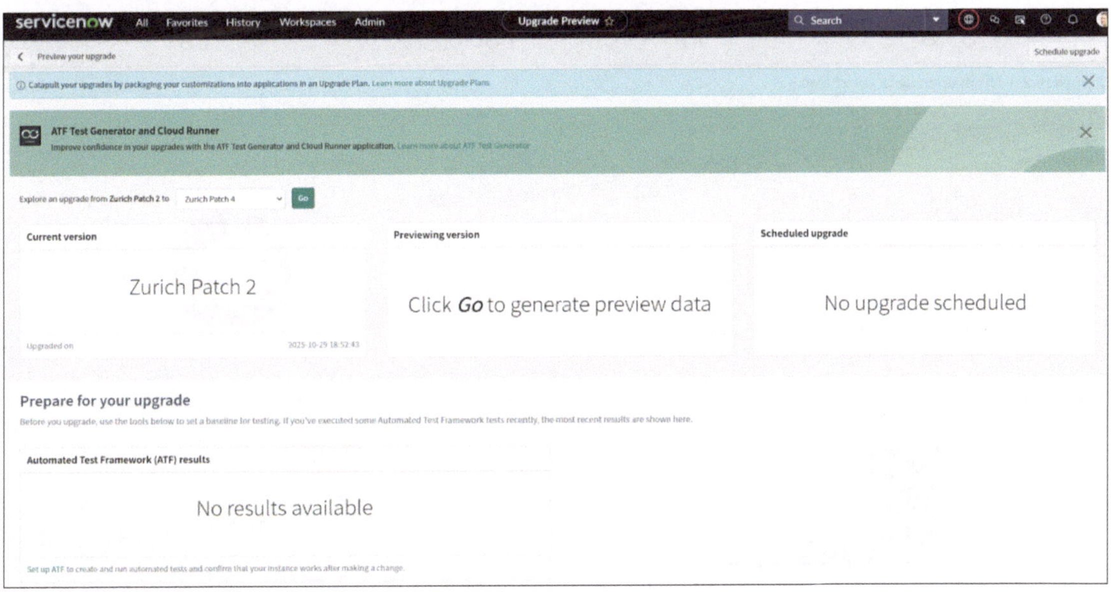

Figure 3.28: Upgrade preview in Upgrade Center

The following figure shows upgrade activity monitoring in **Upgrade Center**:

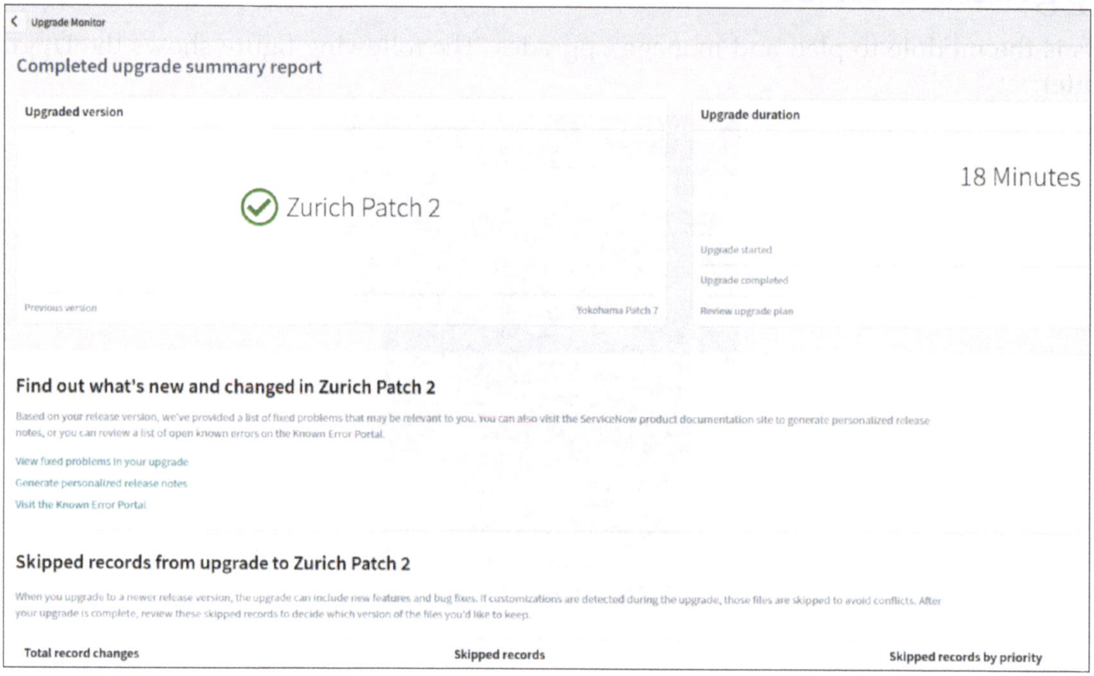

Figure 3.29: Upgrade activity monitoring in Upgrade Center

Skipped records

The following figure shows the skipped records upgrade monitor in the **Upgrade Center**:

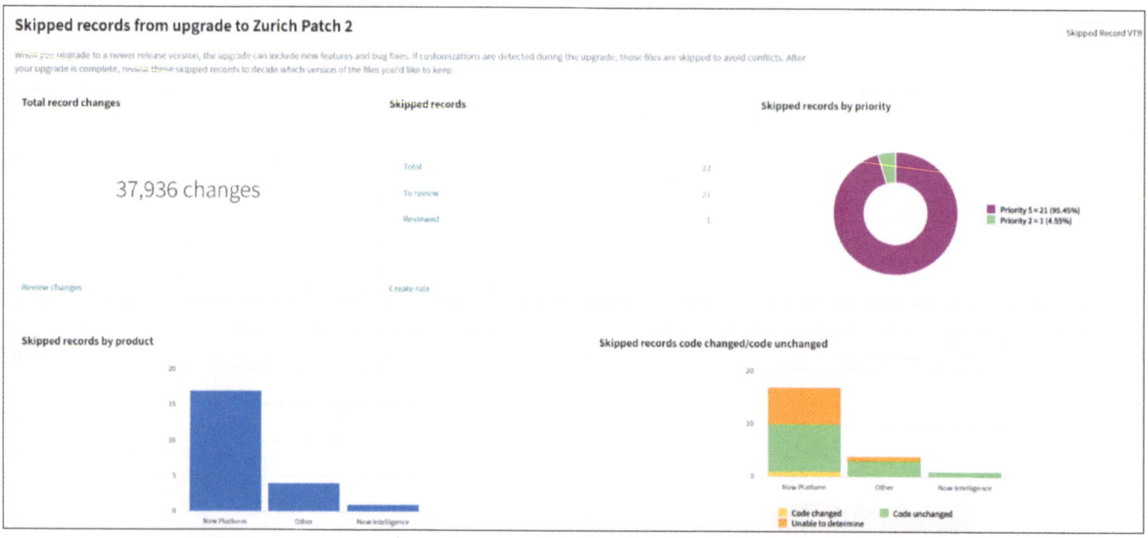

Figure 3.30: Skipped records in Upgrade Center

Skipped records upgrade monitor helps the upgrade process as follows:

- **Centralization**: Acts as a single source for upgrade-related activities.
- **Conflict management**: Highlights skipped changes and integration issues caused by customizations.
- **Efficiency**: Reduces manual effort by automating conflict resolution via Update Sets.
- **Visibility**: Provides insights into plugin status and estimated upgrade duration.
- **Best practices**: Encourages testing in non-production first and guides best practices.

Skipped records upgrade Monitor is mostly used by the below user groups.

- **ServiceNow administrators (admins)**: For day-to-day management, scheduling, and technical issue resolution.
- **Platform owners/IT managers**: For overall planning, risk assessment, and stakeholder communication.
- **Technical consultants/architects**: To perform configuration reviews, address complex customization issues, and ensure alignment with best practices.
- **Developers**: To understand changes affecting their work and resolve code conflicts.

It is used in the following cases:

- **Before upgrade**: To plan, review release notes, assess instance health (config review), and create upgrade plans.
- **During upgrade**: To schedule, monitor progress, and handle the automated upgrade process in non-production environments first.
- **After upgrade**: To resolve skipped changes, perform post-upgrade testing (smoke tests, UAT), and manage post-upgrade tasks.

ServiceNow Learning URL is provided as follows:

Home | ServiceNow University | ServiceNow

This is termed as **ServiceNow University**. ServiceNow offers numerous on-demand courses through Now Learning. Include fundamentals like ServiceNow fundamentals, ITSM Fundamentals, HR fundamentals, and CMDB fundamentals, alongside advanced topics in application development, Performance Analytics, Asset Management (SAM/HAM), and specific areas like **security operations (SecOps)**.

A new learner needs to register here and can use this library of resources. This will also be useful for the preparation of the CSA certification.

The following figure shows the **ServiceNow University** page for learning:

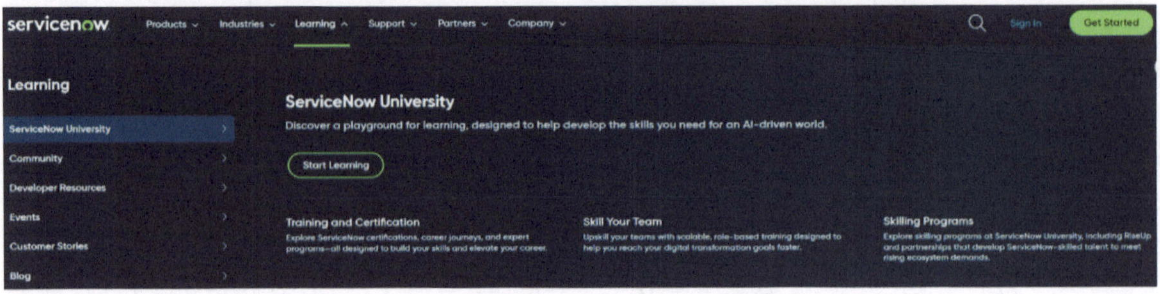

Figure 3.31: ServiceNow University

Conclusion

This chapter covered the concepts of ServiceNow for configuring applications for collaboration. This provided a good understanding of the configuration of lists, filters, tags, form configuration, form templates, VTBs, Reporting, and Dashboards.

The next chapter will cover the ServiceNow self-service and automation, which will cover 20% of the questions towards the CSA certification.

Join our Discord space

Join our Discord workspace for latest updates, offers, tech happenings around the world, new releases, and sessions with the authors:

https://discord.bpbonline.com

CHAPTER 4
Self-service and Automation

Introduction

ServiceNow self-service and automation refers to the process of configuring Knowledge Management, Service Catalog, Flow Designer, and Virtual Agent.

This includes the customization of the unique needs of the organization using these ServiceNow features. This section covers these related concepts, covering 20% of CSA questions.

Structure

This chapter covers the following topics:

- Knowledge Management
- Service Catalog
- Flow Designer
- Virtual Agent

Objectives

This chapter provides insights about ServiceNow regarding configurations of Knowledge Management, Service Catalog, Flow Designer, Virtual Agent, and customizing the instance for the needs of the organization. This chapter will provide users with the skills to configure ServiceNow for these aspects for the unique needs of the organization.

Knowledge Management

Knowledge Management is a feature that provides the systematic creation, organization, and sharing of knowledge within an organization. It functions as a central library of known solutions and resolutions to issues. These can be accessed through knowledge articles. This was aimed at improving self-service and the sharing of knowledge. In these ways, Knowledge Management improves the overall efficiency of the services of the organization.

Knowledge bases are collections of information that can be organized into groups or according to needs, and which can be categorized according to the needs of the organization. Knowledge bases are managed through the knowledge application.

Roles **admin** and **knowledge_admin** allow users to maintain and manage knowledge bases.

To access **Knowledge** in ServiceNow, navigate to **Knowledge** under the **All** menu, or use the global search bar to find relevant articles.

The following figure shows **Knowledge Base** creation:

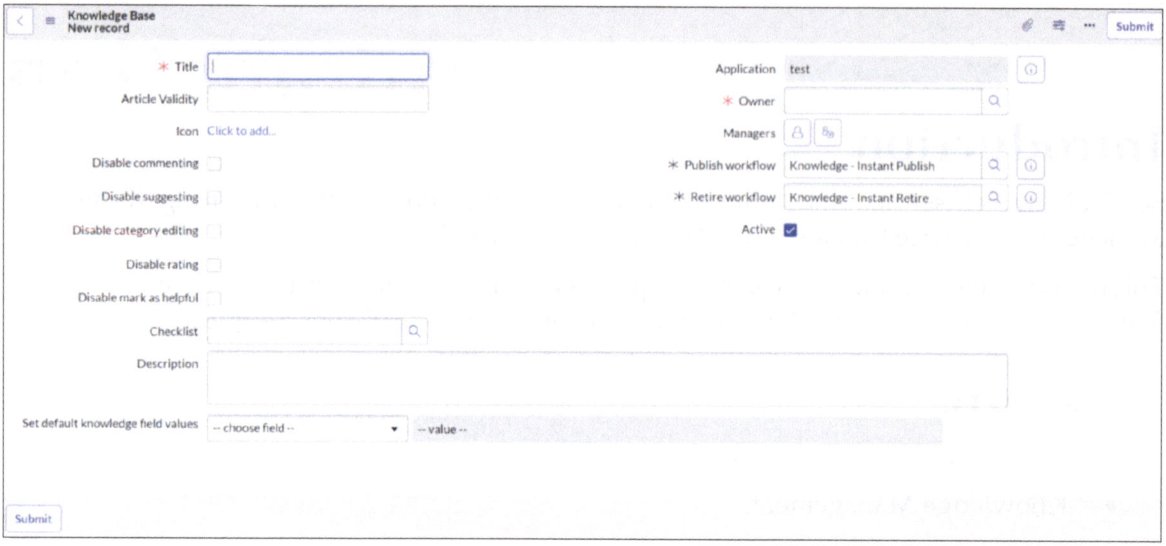

Figure 4.1: Knowledge Base creation

The following figure shows a detailed list of knowledge bases:

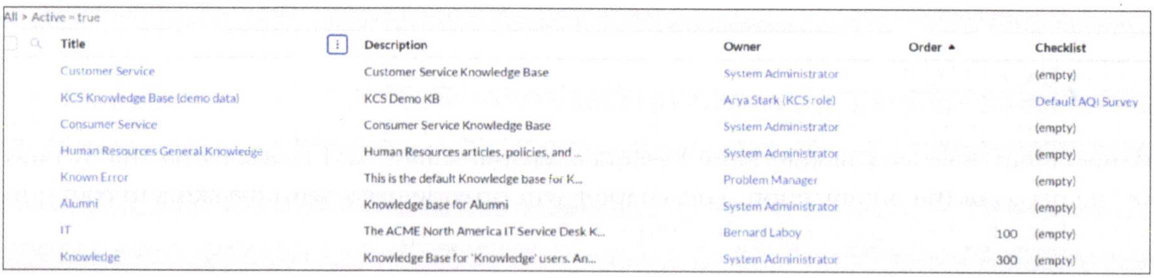

All > Active = true

Title	Description	Owner	Order ▲	Checklist
Customer Service	Customer Service Knowledge Base	System Administrator		(empty)
KCS Knowledge Base (demo data)	KCS Demo KB	Arya Stark (KCS role)		Default AQI Survey
Consumer Service	Consumer Service Knowledge Base	System Administrator		(empty)
Human Resources General Knowledge	Human Resources articles, policies, and ...	System Administrator		(empty)
Known Error	This is the default Knowledge base for K...	Problem Manager		(empty)
Alumni	Knowledge base for Alumni	System Administrator		(empty)
IT	The ACME North America IT Service Desk K...	Bernard Laboy	100	(empty)
Knowledge	Knowledge Base for 'Knowledge' users. An...	System Administrator	300	(empty)

Figure 4.2: List of knowledge bases

In ServiceNow, the Guided Setup for Knowledge Management guides administrators through the configuration process for the Knowledge Management application, ensuring smooth and efficient implementation.

This path in the **All** menu brings up Guided Setup for Knowledge Management. Navigate to **All | Knowledge | Administration | Guided Setup**.

This path in the **All** menu is used to administrate knowledge bases. Go to **All | Knowledge | Administration | Knowledge Base**.

In Knowledge Management, user criteria are sets of conditions used to control access to knowledge bases and articles. They define which users or groups can view and/or contribute to specific knowledge resources. These criteria can be based on various factors like roles, groups, departments, locations, or custom fields. Based on this, users can create, read, write, and retire articles.

In ServiceNow, User criteria define who Can Read (view) and Contribute (create/edit/retire) knowledge articles and catalog items, acting as granular conditions (like roles, groups, locations) applied at the Knowledge Base or catalog item level, separate from roles, allowing fine-tuned access; for knowledge, you link user criteria to Can Read or Can Contribute lists on a Knowledge Base to control audience and creators.

The key concepts of user criteria in Knowledge Management are as follows:

- **Can Read**: Defines users allowed to view articles in a Knowledge Base.
- **Can Contribute**: Defines users allowed to create, edit, and retire articles in a Knowledge Base.
- **Cannot Read / Cannot Contribute**: Exclusions to prevent specific users/groups from reading or contributing.
- **Application**: Set on the Knowledge Base record via the Can Read and Can Contribute related lists.
- **Conditions**: Defined using fields like roles, groups, locations, departments, and can use **Match All** (AND) or **Match Any** (OR) logic.

The working is as follows:

1. **Define criteria**: Create user criteria records specifying conditions (e.g., **ITIL Users, Database Admins**).
2. **Assign to Knowledge Base**: Go to a **Knowledge Base**, select a **Knowledge Base**, and add your **User Criteria** to the "Can Read" list for viewing access or "Can Contribute" for editing access.
3. **Access control**: A user must meet the conditions (or be excluded) to gain the defined permission (read or contribute) for that **Knowledge Base**.

The example scenario is as follows:

- **Goal**: Allow all employees to read IT **frequently asked questions** (**FAQs**), but only IT Support can add/edit articles.
- **Solution**: Create one user criteria for **All Employees** and add it to the "Can Read" list of the IT FAQ Knowledge Base. Create another for **IT Support** and add it to the "Can Contribute" list.

The role required to administer Knowledge Bases depends on the specific tasks involved. For overall management and control of the entire Knowledge Management system, the **knowledge_admin** role is needed. For managing individual knowledge bases and their content, the **knowledge_manager** role is provided.

The publishing and retirement processes for a knowledge article are controlled by predefined workflows for approval and retirement. Custom publishing and retirement processes. Custom Workflows for different types of knowledge can be created as well. Standard and instant Workflows are stated as follows:

- **Approval publish**: Requests approval from a manager of the **Knowledge Base** before moving the article to the published state.
- **Approval retire**: Requests approval from a manager of the **Knowledge Base** before a knowledge article is retired.
- **Instant publish**: Immediately publishes a draft article without requiring approval. The workflow is canceled, and the article remains in the draft state if any manager rejects the request.
- **Instant retire**: Immediately retires a published article without requiring approval.
- **Retire knowledge**: moves a knowledge article to the retired state.

The following figure shows details of workflow selection in Knowledge Management:

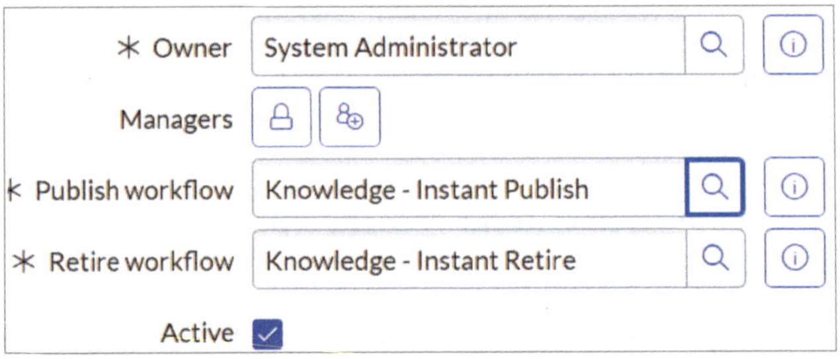

***Figure 4.3:** Workflow selection, Knowledge Management*

The two other key workflows are the **Publish workflow** and **Retire workflow**, explained as follows:

- **Publish knowledge**: This subflow is used within other workflows to move an article to the published state.
- **Retire knowledge**: This subflow is used within other workflows to move an article to the published state.

User criteria allow for granular control over who can interact with knowledge content, ensuring that sensitive or specialized information is only accessible to those who need it. These user criteria are applied to knowledge bases or individual articles to restrict access accordingly. User criteria can control read and contribute to knowledge articles.

The following figure shows an example of **User Criteria Records** in a **Knowledge Base**:

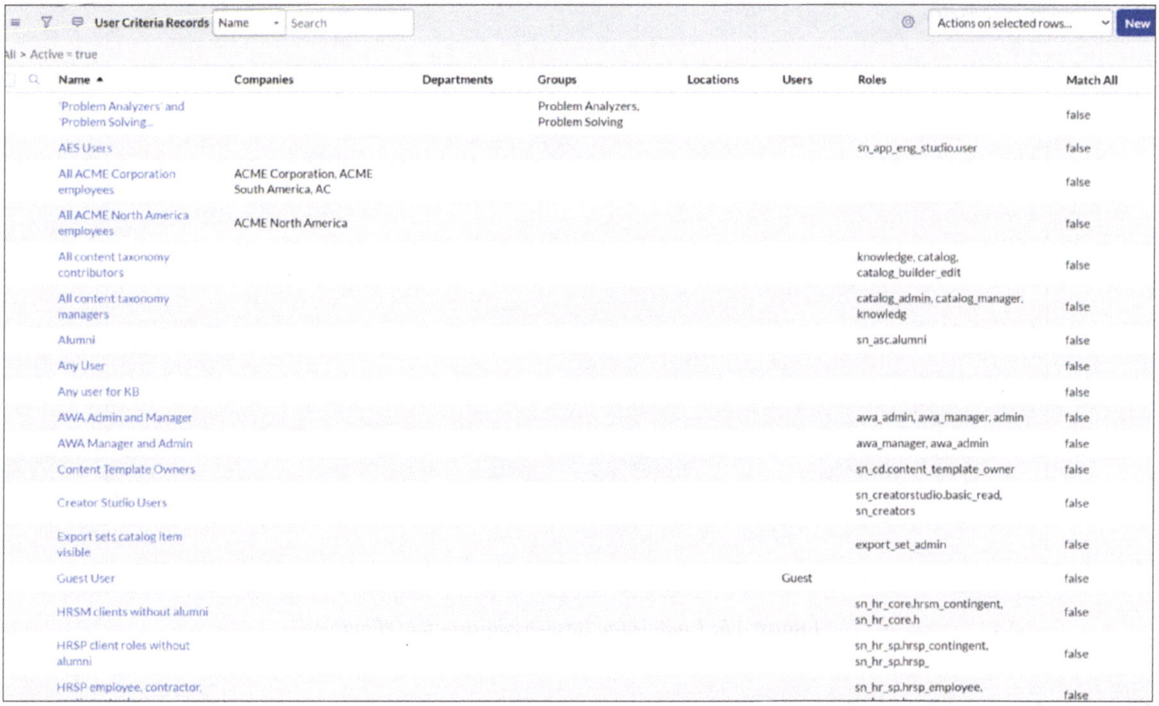

User Criteria Records | Name | Search | Actions on selected rows... | New

All > Active = true

Name	Companies	Departments	Groups	Locations	Users	Roles	Match All
'Problem Analyzers' and 'Problem Solving...			Problem Analyzers, Problem Solving				false
AES Users						sn_app_eng_studio.user	false
All ACME Corporation employees	ACME Corporation, ACME South America, AC						false
All ACME North America employees	ACME North America						false
All content taxonomy contributors						knowledge, catalog, catalog_builder_edit	false
All content taxonomy managers						catalog_admin, catalog_manager, knowledg	false
Alumni						sn_asc.alumni	false
Any User							false
Any user for KB							false
AWA Admin and Manager						awa_admin, awa_manager, admin	false
AWA Manager and Admin						awa_manager, awa_admin	false
Content Template Owners						sn_cd.content_template_owner	false
Creator Studio Users						sn_creatorstudio.basic_read, sn_creators	false
Export sets catalog item visible						export_set_admin	false
Guest User					Guest		false
HRSM clients without alumni						sn_hr_core.hrsm_contingent, sn_hr_core.h	false
HRSP client roles without alumni						sn_hr_sp.hrsp_contingent, sn_hr_sp.hrsp_	false
HRSP employee, contractor,						sn_hr_sp.hrsp_employee,	false

***Figure 4.4**: User Criteria Roles, Knowledge Base*

To setup knowledge base workflow approvals and user criteria in ServiceNow, first, you need to configure workflows to manage article submissions and updates, ensuring they go through designated approval processes. Then, we need to define user criteria to control which users have access to specific knowledge bases and articles based on roles, groups, departments, or other conditions. Sample steps are defined as follows:

1. Create the **Knowledge Base**.
2. Create a group to manage the **Knowledge Base** for approvals.
3. Assign the roles to the group **knowledge_manager** and **approver_user**.
4. Update the owner for the **Publish workflow** and the **Retire workflow**.
5. Add the group under Can Contribute for the **Knowledge Base**.
6. Create **User Criteria**.
7. Apply **User Criteria** to Can Read for **Knowledge Base**.

The following figure shows an example of assigning workflows to a **Knowledge Base**:

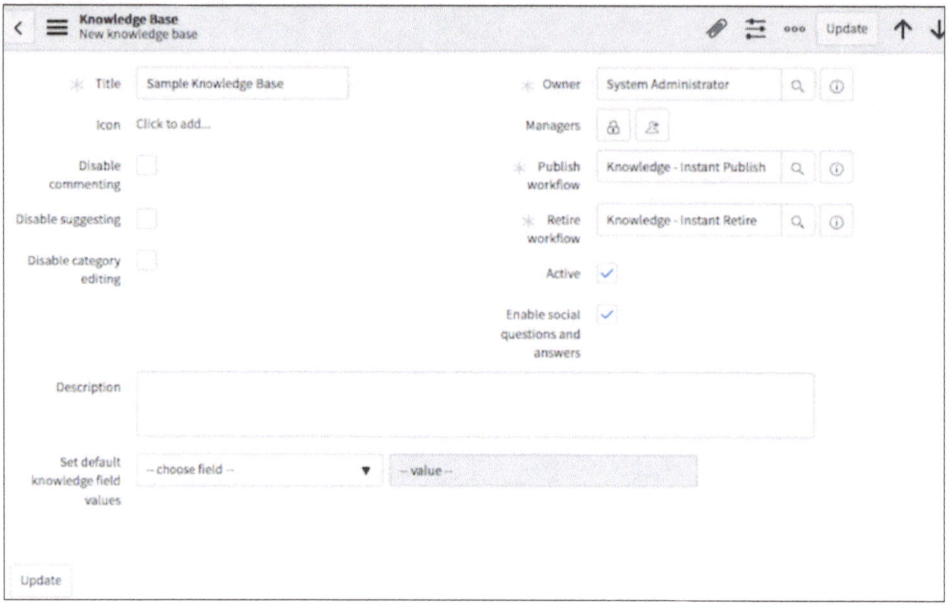

Figure 4.5: Knowledge Base–assigning workflows

Service Catalog

A **Service Catalog** is a UI for requesting services or products. The **Service Catalog** UI is for users of all skill levels and is familiar to anyone who has ordered online.

The following figure shows a **Service Catalog**:

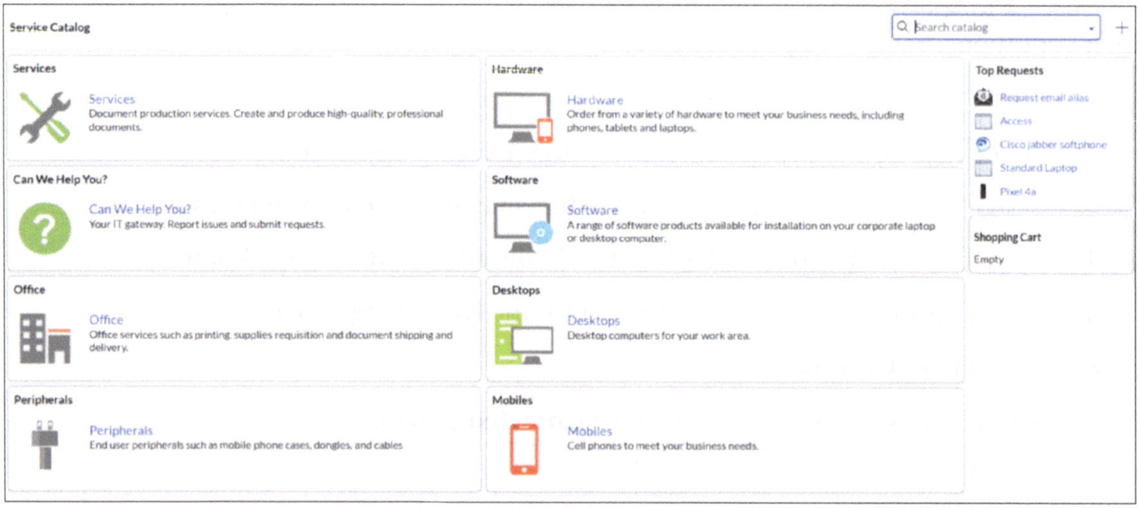

Figure 4.6: Service Catalog

The ServiceNow **Service Catalog** major components include catalog items, record producers, and order guides. Catalog items represent individual services or products users can request, record producers allow creating records like incidents or requests directly from the catalog, and order guides help users create tasks or requests by guiding them through necessary information.

In ServiceNow, a **Service Catalog** request initiates a process in which it generates a **requested item** (**RITM**) and a catalog task (SCTASK). When a user orders a catalog item, a RITM is created, and associated catalog tasks are generated through workflows to handle the fulfillment process.

RITM is a record that contains details about the specific item being ordered (e.g., a specific software or service). Catalog tasks are the individual steps or tasks needed to fulfill an RITM.

The following figure shows a service request:

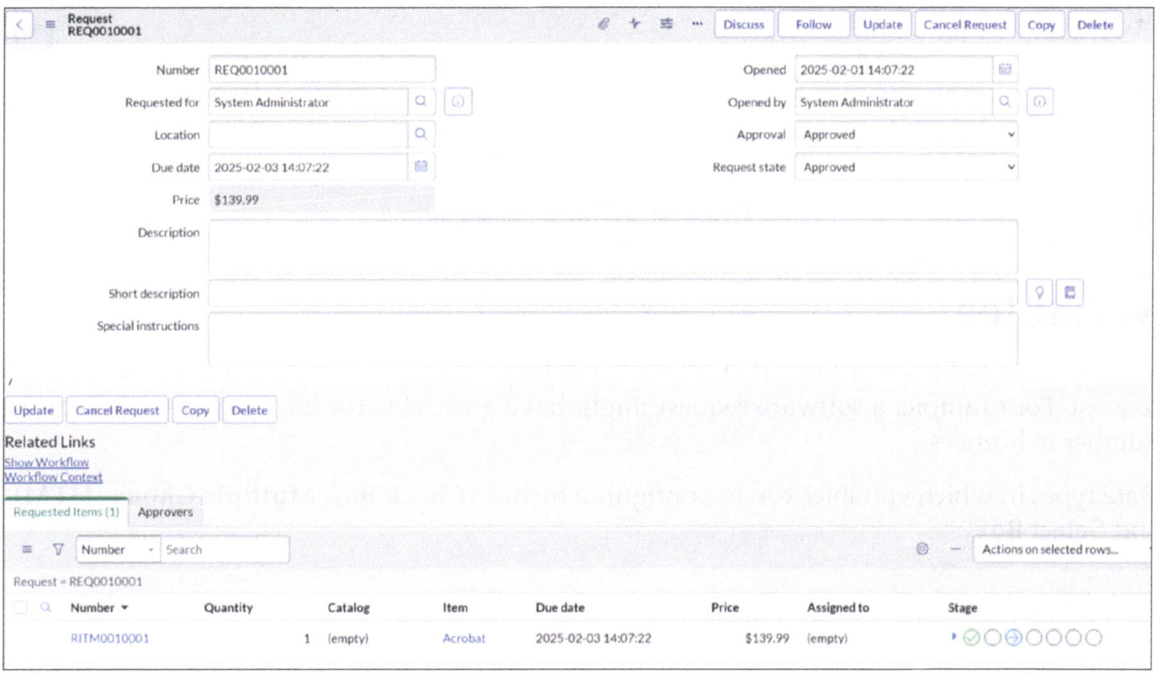

Figure 4.7: *Service request with an RITM*

The following figure shows RITM and **Catalog Tasks**:

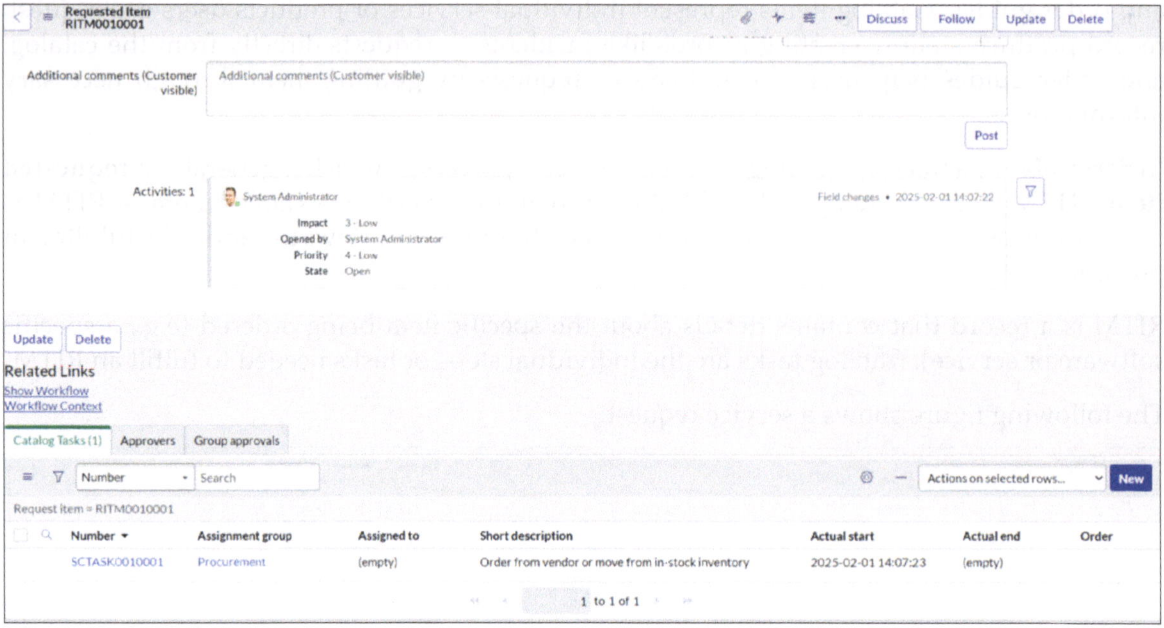

Figure 4.8: RITM and catalog task

Variables

Variables are fields on a form that allow users to provide specific information about their request. For example, a software request might have a variable for the desired version or the number of licenses.

Data types in which variables can be configured include **Check Box**, **Multiple Choice**, **HTML**, and **Select Box**.

The following figure shows different data types for variables used in Service Catalog:

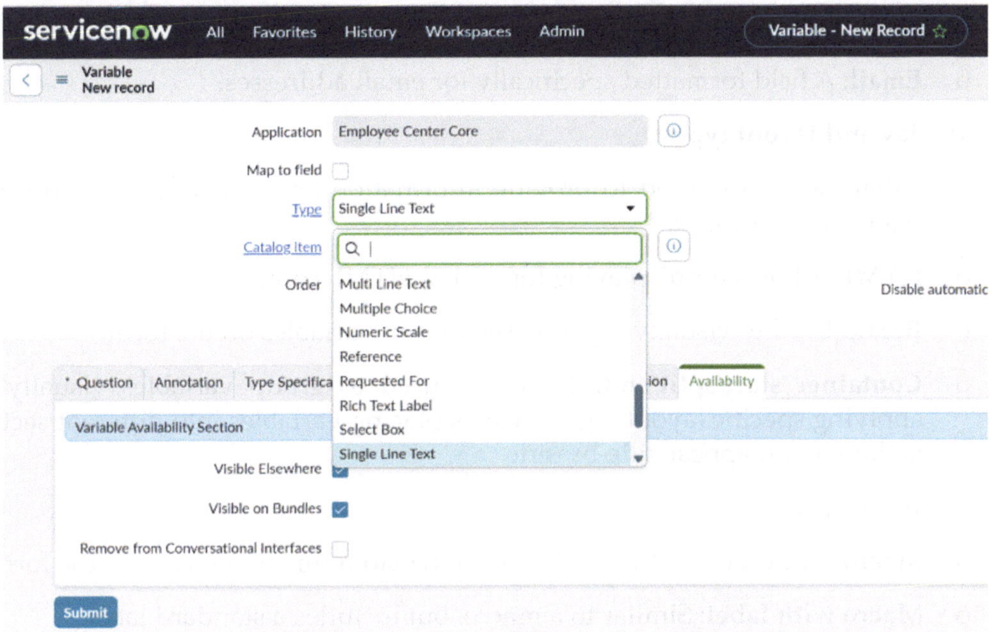

Figure 4.9*: Variables data types for catalog items*

ServiceNow offers a variety of variable types for catalog items, allowing users to provide diverse inputs when ordering services. The specific list of available variable types can be found in the ServiceNow product documentation for the relevant release, but common types generally include:

- **Standard input types**:
  - o **Single Line Text**: A simple text input field for a single line of information.
  - o **Multi Line Text**: A larger text area for longer descriptions or comments.
  - o **Check Box**: A simple true/false or yes/no option.
  - o **Select Box**: A dropdown list where users can select one option from predefined choices.
  - o **Multiple Choice**: A list of radio buttons for selecting a single option from several choices.
  - o **Reference**: Allows users to select a record from another table in ServiceNow (e.g., selecting a user from the **sys_user** table).
  - o **List Collector**: A dual-list interface allowing users to select multiple items from a list and move them to a selected items list.

  - **Date/Time**: Fields for capturing date and time information.
  - **Duration**: Used for entering a length of time.
  - **Email**: A field formatted specifically for email addresses.
- **Display and layout types:**
  - **Label**: Static text used to provide information or context on the form without requiring user input.
  - **HTML**: Allows for displaying formatted HTML content.
  - **Break**: Used to visually separate sections of variables on the form.
  - **Container start/split/end**: These are used to group variables visually or for applying specific layout logic, such as placing variables into different sections or making them appear side-by-side.
- **Advanced types:**
  - **Macro**: Allows embedding a UI macro (custom functionality) into the form.
  - **Macro with label**: Similar to a macro, but includes a standard label.
  - **UI page**: Embeds a custom UI page into the catalog item form.
  - **Lookup Multiple Choice**: Similar to **Multiple Choice**, but the options are populated from a database table lookup.
  - **Lookup Single Line**: Similar to **Select Box**, but the options are populated from a database table lookup.
  - **Masked**: A field where the input is hidden (e.g., for sensitive information like passwords).

Variable sets

A variable set is a collection of variables that can be reused across multiple items. This can save time and effort when creating similar items with the same set of custom fields.

Record producer

A record producer is a specialized form within the Service Catalog that allows users to create new records in a specific table. This is without needing direct access to the table itself. A record producer is used to create new records in application-specific tables within the Service Catalog, offering a simplified user interface for creating task-based records. It is essentially a type of catalog item designed for streamlining the creation of these records, as opposed to standard catalog items, which typically involve more complex workflows and fulfillment processes.

The following figure shows **Record Producer** while being created:

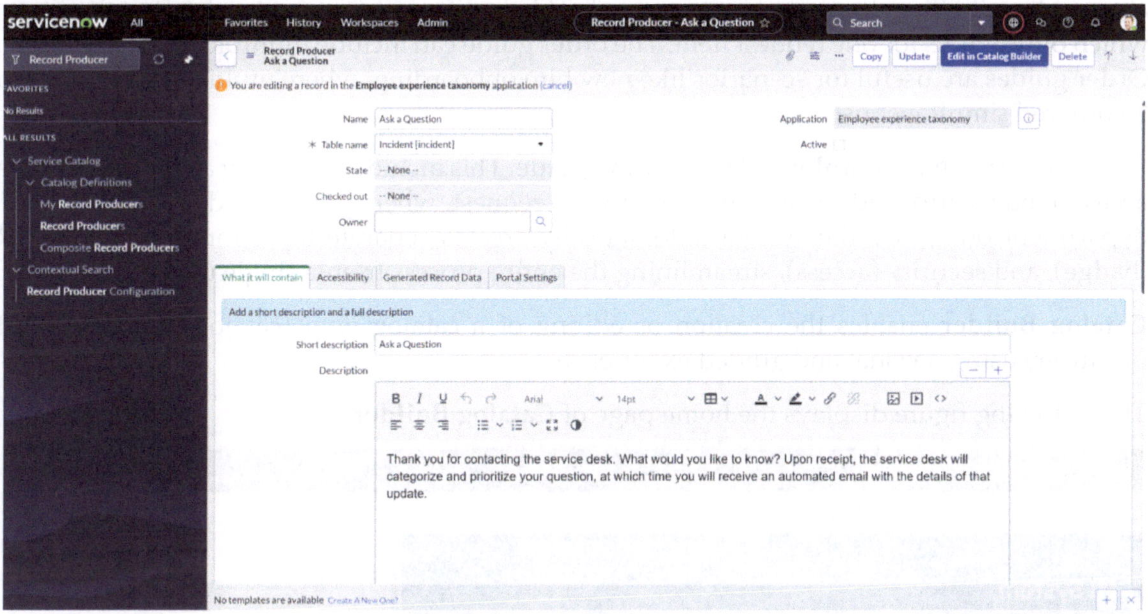

Figure 4.10: *Creation of Record Producer*

The following figure shows the **Record Producer** | **Variables** details:

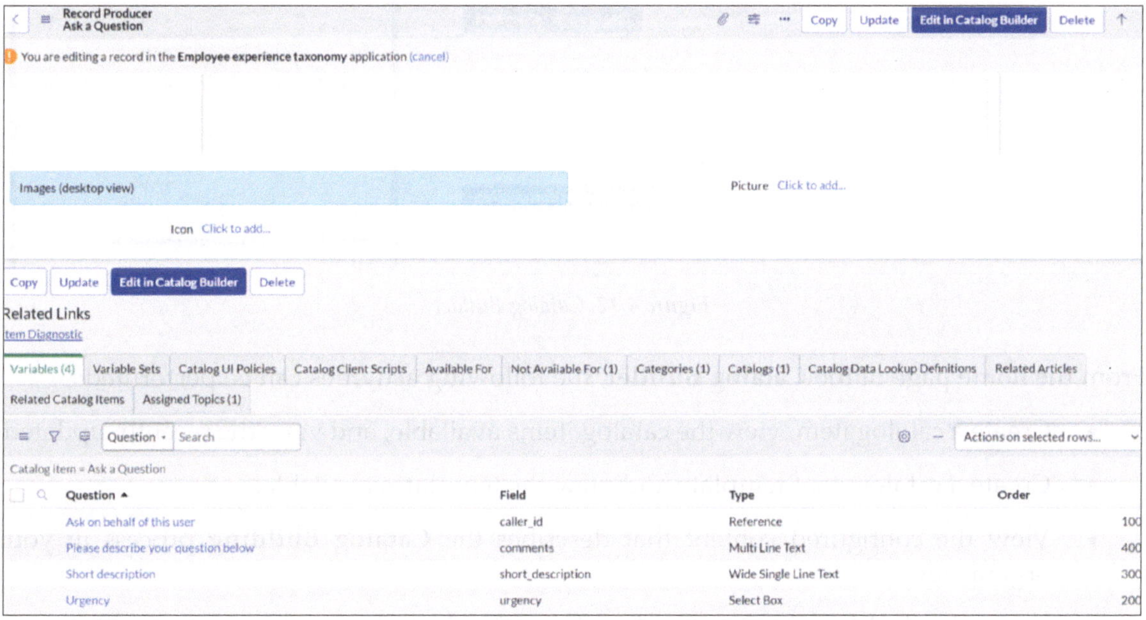

Figure 4.11: *Record Producer* | *Variables*

An order guide is a type of catalog item that allows users to request multiple catalog items at once, bundled together as a single request. This is different from a standard catalog item, which only allows for one request item. The order guide can include multiple requested items. Order guides are useful for scenarios like new hire onboarding, where multiple items need to be ordered simultaneously.

An example is a **New Employee Onboarding** guide. This includes bundling a laptop, software access, email setup, and security badge into one request, where you enter details like name/department once, and the system automatically creates separate tasks for IT (laptop), HR (badge), and security (access), streamlining the entire process from a single user entry.

Catalog Builder enables the creation or editing of a catalog item (catalog item or record producer) using a visual and guided experience.

The following figure displays the home page of **Catalog Builder**:

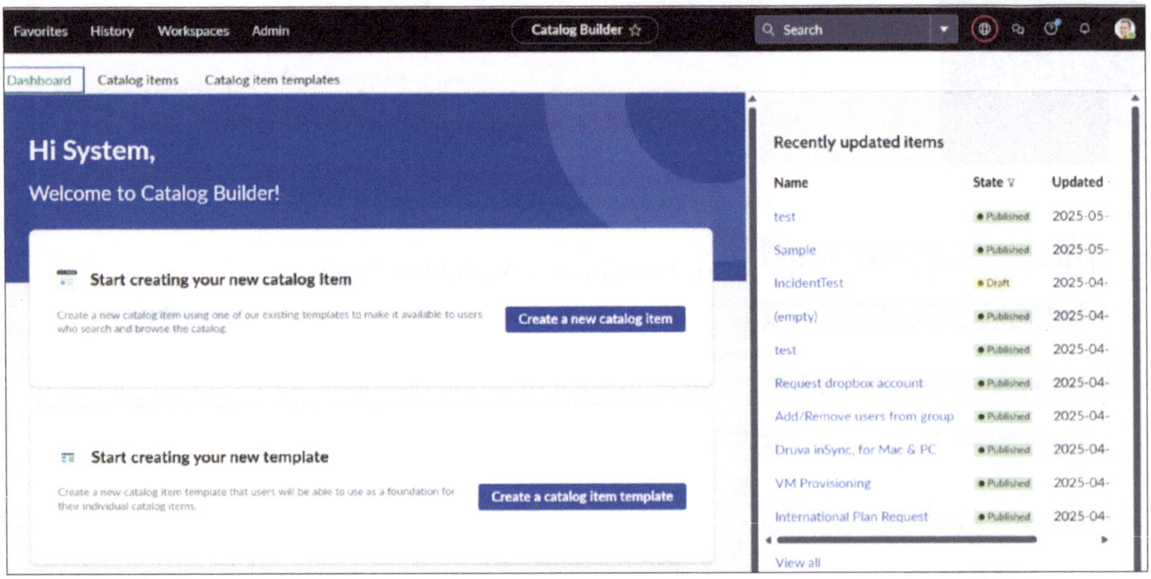

***Figure 4.12**: Catalog Builder*

From the home page of the **Catalog Builder**, the following activities can be performed:

- Create a catalog item, view the catalog items available, and view the recently updated.
- Create a catalog item template and view the templates available.
- View the configured content that describes the **Catalog Building** process in your organization.

To manage a ServiceNow Service Catalog, key roles include **Catalog_manager**, **Catalog_editor**, **Catalog**, and **ITIL**. These roles provide different levels of access to manage catalog items, categories, and workflows:

- **Catalog**: This role grants access to the Service Catalog module itself.
- **ITIL**: This role is associated with IT operations and may be needed for certain catalog-related tasks.
- **Catalog_manager**: This role allows users to manage the catalog, including creating, editing, and deleting catalog items, categories, and workflows.
- **Catalog_editor**: This role allows users to make modifications to existing catalog items within a sub-production instance.
- **Catalog_admin**: This role provides broader administrative capabilities within the Service Catalog, including setting up service templates, **service level agreements** (**SLAs**), and fulfillment workflows.

The main components of the Service Catalog are request items, variables, variable sets, record producers, and flows.

Flow Designer

Flow Designer is a platform for building automated processes. It is a powerful tool that allows users to automate business processes without writing code.

The following figure shows Flow Designer and its components:

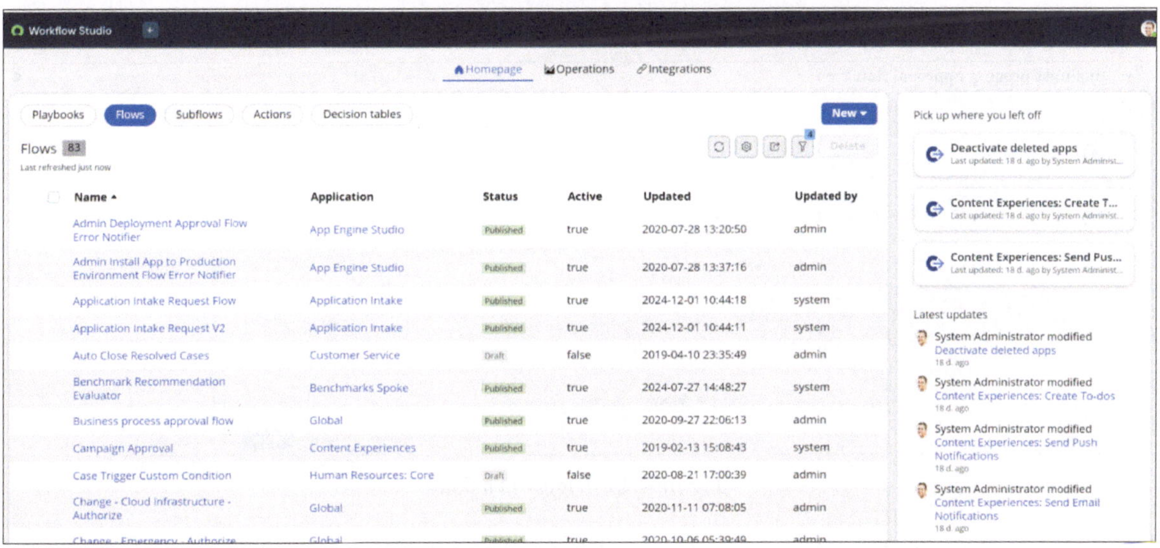

***Figure 4.13**: Flow Designer*

The main components of Flow Designer are **Flows**, **Subflows**, **Actions**, and **Triggers**. **Flows** are the main building blocks that define a process. **Subflows** are reusable units of logic. **Actions** are the operations performed within a flow. **Triggers** are determined when a flow is executed.

The following figure shows a sample flow that includes **Trigger**, **Actions**, and **ERROR HANDLER**:

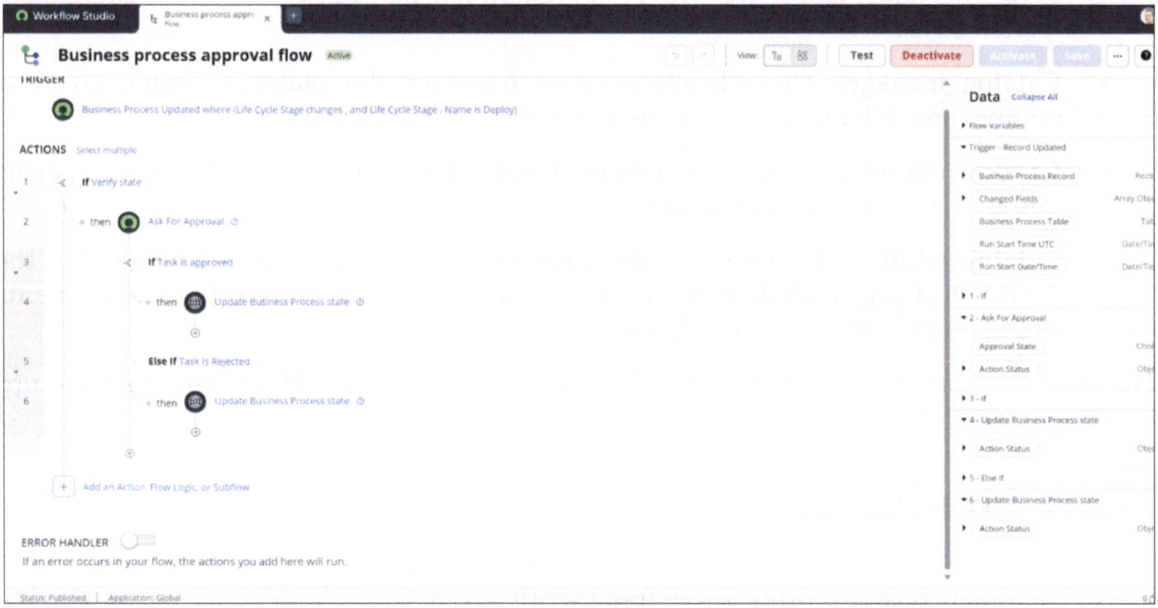

Figure 4.14: Flow with Trigger, Actions, and ERROR HANDLER

The following figure shows details of a **Trigger** in a flow:

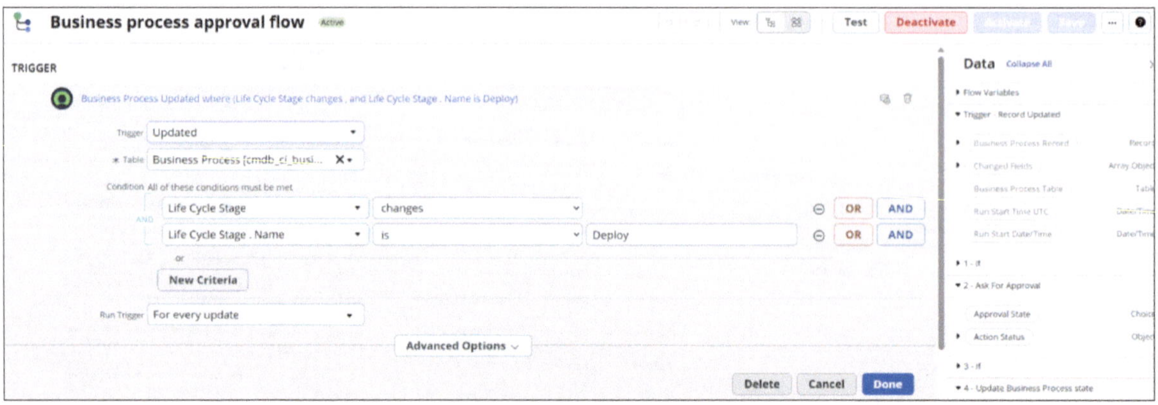

Figure 4.15: Trigger in a flow

A flow consists of a **Trigger** and a sequence of actions. **Subflows** are reusable units of logic that can be used within multiple flows. **Actions** are the operations that a flow performs.

In ServiceNow Flow Designer, there are three main types of triggers: record, date, and application. These triggers determine when a flow's logic is executed.

The elaboration is as follows:

- **Record**: This trigger executes the flow when a record is created or updated on a specific table. Conditions that must be met for the flow to run, such as a specific field value or the creation of a new record.
- **Date**: This trigger executes the flow at a specific date and time or on a recurring schedule (e.g., daily, weekly, monthly). This is useful for automating tasks that need to be performed at regular intervals.
- **Application**: This trigger executes the flow when a specific event or action occurs within the ServiceNow instance. Examples include receiving an email, a notification from a different application, or a button click within an application.

To access Flow Designer in ServiceNow, navigate to the application navigator and search for **Flow Designer**.

The path to access Flow Designer can be reached by navigating to **All | Process Automation | Flow Designer**.

In **Flow Designer**, three main roles grant different levels of access, listed as follows:

- **flow_designer** (for creating and editing flows).
- **flow_operator** (for viewing execution details, dashboards, and logs).
- **action_designer** (for creating and editing custom actions).
- **fd_read** role provides read-only access to flows, actions, and execution details.

The **Flow Designer** consists of three types of triggers, listed here:

- **Record**: Execute the flow when a record is created or updated on a table.
- **Date**: Execute the flow at a specific time or interval.
- **Application**: Execute the flow from an application.

ServiceNow Flow Designer offers a wide variety of actions to automate processes. The core actions include **Ask for Approval**, **Create Record**, **Delete Record**, **Look Up Record**, and **Wait for Condition**, alongside others like **Log**, **Send Email**, **Update Record**, and more. These actions allow users to build workflows that handle various tasks within ServiceNow, from managing tasks to sending notifications and handling approvals.

To pull data into Flow Designer using the Data Pill Picker icon and dot walking, first locate the desired data pill in the Data panel. Then, click the Data Pill Picker icon (a small icon that looks like a small square with an arrow pointing out of it) next to the field where you want to insert the data. Select the data pill and, if necessary, expand it using the expand icon to access fields within a related record. Then use dot walking to access fields on referenced tables by expanding the data pill and navigating through the related fields.

For example, to get the user's email address from the user record in a flow, follow these steps:

1. Find the data pill representing the user record in the **Data** panel.
2. Click the Data Pill Picker icon for the field in your flow where it is needed to insert the user's email.
3. Expand the data pill to show its fields, including the username and email fields.
4. Select **user.email** to insert the user's email address into the field.

The following figure shows the Data Pill Pillar icon in a flow:

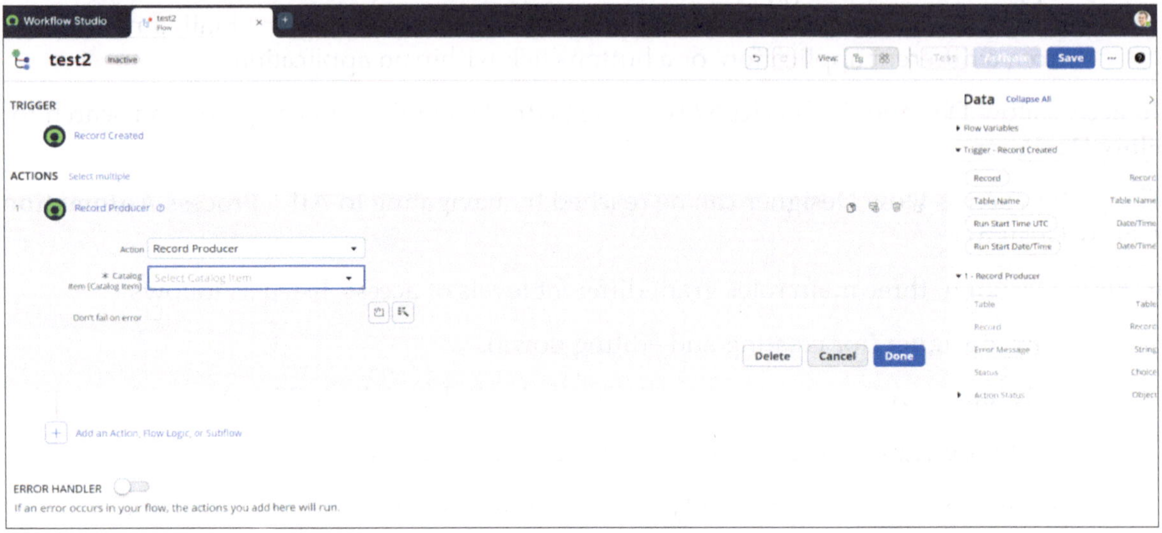

Figure 4.16: Data Pill Pillar in a flow

Process Automation Designer (**PAD**) in ServiceNow allows process owners to build, manage, and visualize cross-enterprise workflows without writing code. It leverages the power of Flow Designer but provides a broader, more user-friendly interface for organizing and visualizing workflows for business users. PAD enables users to create, manage, and visualize end-to-end business processes, ultimately improving efficiency and customer experience.

Flow Designer has surpassed the legacy Workflow Editor primarily because it provides a modern, low-code/no-code, and user-friendly platform designed for a wider range of users, including business analysts and citizen developers. The Workflow Editor, while still operational, is in maintenance mode and receives no new features.

Key reasons for the shift to Flow Designer include:

- **Accessibility and usability**: Flow Designer utilizes a visual, drag-and-drop interface with natural language descriptions, making it much more intuitive and accessible to non-technical users compared to the Workflow Editor, which often requires extensive scripting for complex logic.

- **Integration capabilities**: It is tightly integrated with the Integration Hub, allowing for seamless, low-code connections with external systems (like Slack, SAP, Salesforce) through pre-built connectors called **spokes**. This was a major limitation of the legacy Workflow Editor, which needed custom scripting for integrations.
- **Modularity and reusability**: Flow Designer emphasizes the creation of reusable components like actions and subflows, which promotes a more efficient and modular approach to automation and reduces development costs. The Workflow Editor had limited reusability, with logic often tied to specific processes.
- **Improved performance and maintenance**: Flows are more lightweight, perform well with asynchronous processing, and offer better logging, debugging, and error handling capabilities, reducing technical debt and simplifying troubleshooting.
- **Strategic focus**: ServiceNow has ceased new development for the Workflow Editor and is focusing all future investment and new features (including generative AI innovations) on Flow Designer and the broader Workflow Studio, future-proofing development efforts.

In essence, while the Workflow Editor is still functional and used for legacy processes (such as certain SLA timers or existing Service Catalog items), Flow Designer is the strategic path forward for all new automation development on the Now Platform.

Virtual Agent

Virtual Agent is an automated chatbot for employees and customers to resolve common requests.

A Virtual Agent is an **artificial intelligence** (**AI**) powered conversational platform (chatbot) that simulates human conversation through natural language processing, **machine learning** (**ML**), and **large language model** (**LLM**). It can communicate with users through various interfaces, such as text messaging. Virtual Agent can be integrated into multiple communication channels such as *Teams*, *Slack*, *User Messaging*, etc.

The following figure shows **Virtual Agent Designer** and **Topics**:

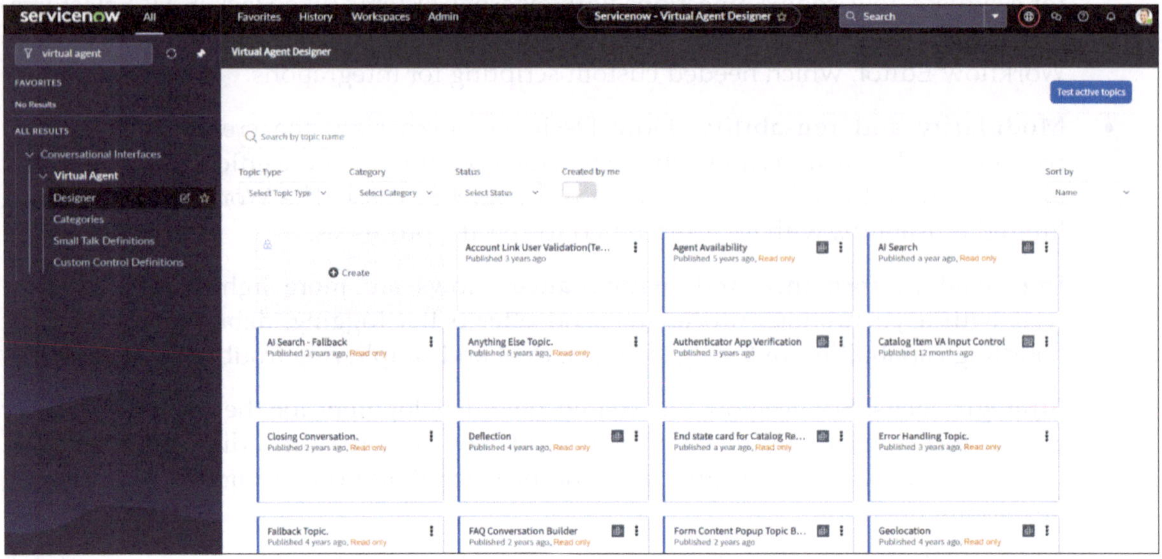

Figure 4.17: Virtual Agent Designer and Topics

The Virtual Agent accesses the following components:

- Knowledge Bases
- System Records
- Service Catalog

The following figure shows **Virtual Agent Designer**:

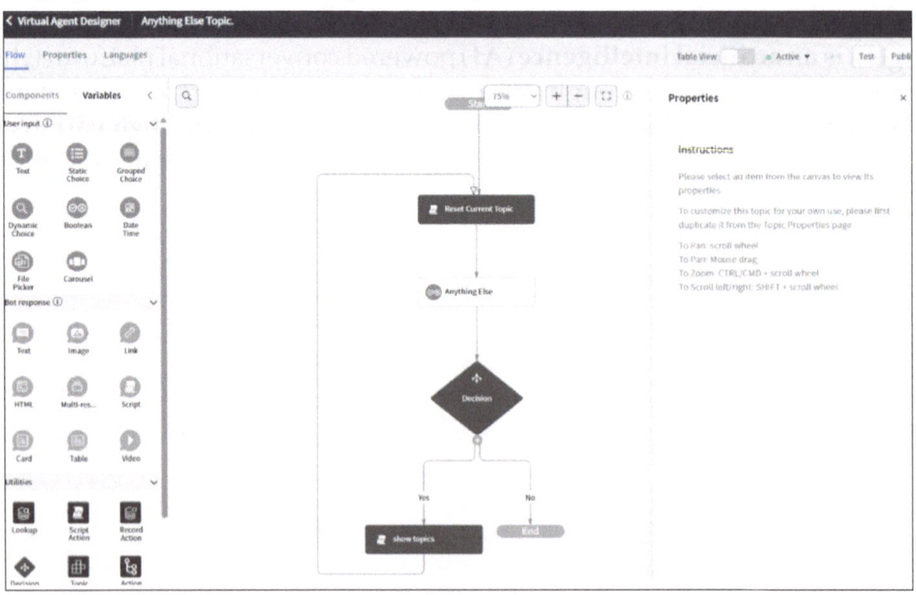

Figure 4.18: Virtual Agent Designer

ServiceNow's Virtual Agent can automate a wide range of tasks. This includes answering frequently asked questions, resolving simple issues, and guiding users through self-service processes like password resets and incident submissions. It can also trigger workflows, create tickets automatically, and even escalate complex issues to human agents when necessary.

The following figure shows the Virtual Agent chatbot and how it looks to the end user:

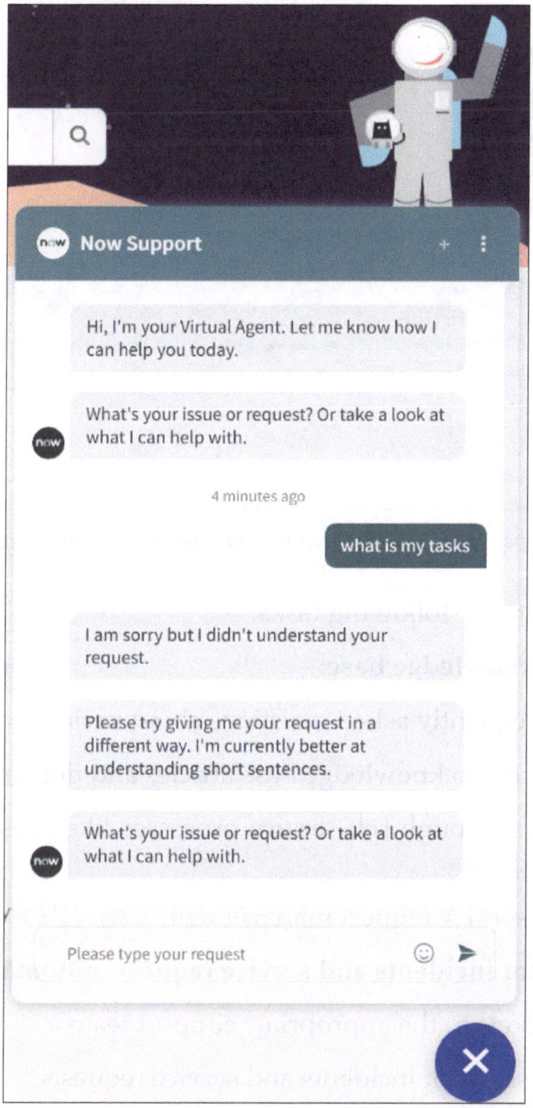

***Figure 4.19**: Virtual Agent looks for the end user*

The following figure shows that the Virtual Agent chat icon is part of the Employee Center page. The chat agent icon is to be clicked to start the Virtual Agent chat:

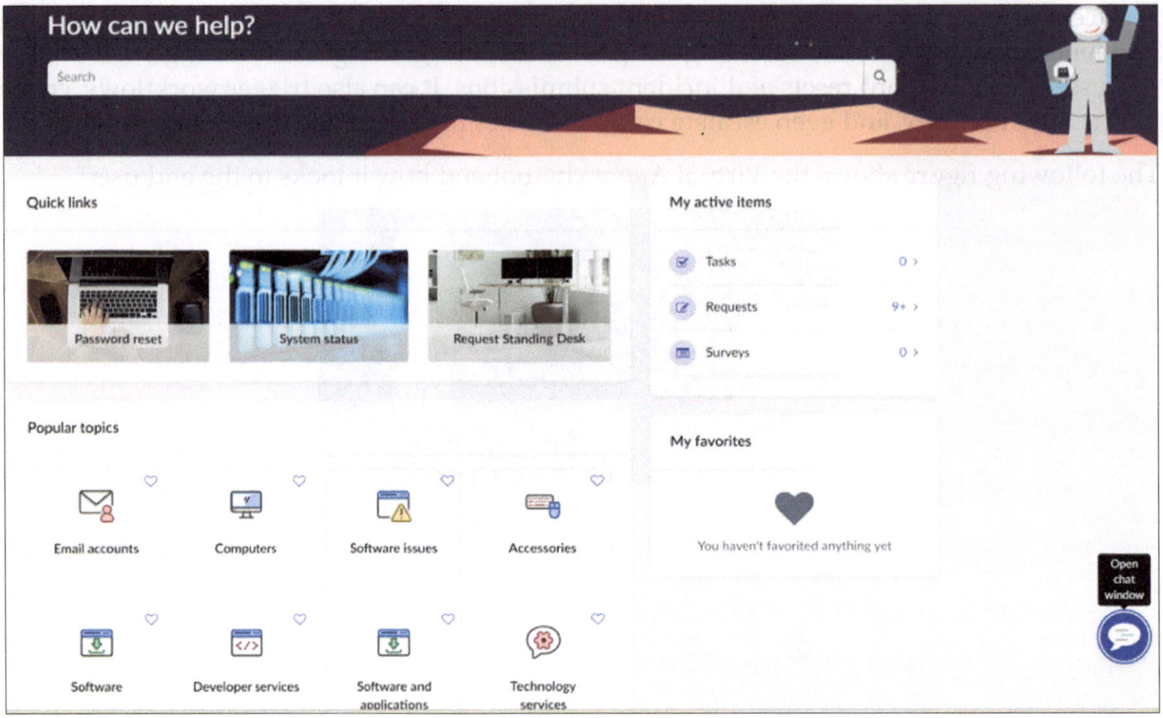

***Figure 4.20**: Open chat Virtual Agent icon in Employee Service Center (ESC) page*

Virtual Agent can automate the following tasks:

- **Self-service and knowledge base**:
  - o Answering frequently asked questions about various topics.
  - o Providing access to knowledge base articles and documents.
  - o Guiding users through self-service processes like password resets, onboarding, and access requests.
  - o Incident and service request management.
- **Creating tickets for incidents and service requests automatically**:
  - o Assigning tickets to the appropriate support teams.
  - o Tracking the status of incidents and service requests.
  - o Providing updates and notifications to users.
- **Workflow automation**:
  - o Triggering workflows for various business processes, such as onboarding, offboarding, or change management.

  - Integrating with other systems to automate tasks across different departments.
  - Automating approvals and notifications within workflows.
- **IT service management (ITSM)**:
  - Automating common IT tasks like software installation, hardware requests, and software deployment.
  - Performing system diagnostics and troubleshooting.
- **HR Service Delivery (HRSD)**:
  - Automating HR-related tasks like leave requests, benefits enrollment, and payroll inquiries.
  - Creating Cases, providing information about HR policies and procedures.
  - Handling employee data and records.
- **Customer service management (CSM)**:
  - Answering customer inquiries and resolving customer issues, providing support for products and services, and handling customer feedback and complaints.

In essence, Virtual Agent acts as a digital assistant that can handle a variety of tasks, freeing up human agents to focus on more complex issues and strategic initiatives.

Now Assist for Virtual Agent uses LLMs, replacing traditional **natural language processing** (**NLP**) systems for better accuracy and search results.

Now, Assist in Virtual Agent can be used as follows:

- Use the wizard to choose your portals, channels, and mobile options where the Virtual Agent will appear (e.g., Employee Center).
- Select between the enhanced chat experience and the standard chat.

Conclusion

This chapter covered the concepts of ServiceNow, including configuring features, Knowledge Management, Service Catalog, Flow Designer, and Virtual Agent for automation. This provided a good understanding of configuring these features.

The next chapter will cover database management, which will cover 27% of the questions towards the CSA certification.

Chapter 5
Database Management

Introduction

ServiceNow database management refers to the process of knowing and configuring data schema, application/access control, importing data, **configuration management database (CMDB)**, and **Common Service Data Model (CSDM)**.

This includes the customization of the unique needs of the organization using these ServiceNow features. This section covers these related concepts, covering 27% of CSA questions. Data and effective management on ServiceNow are crucial for transforming disparate info into unified, actionable insights, enabling better risk mitigation, automated workflows (ITSM, CSM, HR), improved decision-making, and streamlined operations, leading to cost savings and enhanced service delivery by ensuring data quality, security, and compliance across the platform. Without it, businesses face siloed data, poor processes, and increased risk, making agility impossible.

Data breaks down silos by connecting data from IT, HR, customer service, etc., providing a single source of truth for operations and risks. Real-time analytics and data-driven insights support strategic choices, from talent planning to service improvements.

Data in ServiceNow proactively identifies and manages risks by giving context to critical assets and services, reducing disruption impact. It improves incident resolution, customer satisfaction, and employee experience through better data access and management.

Additionally, it acts as a Workflow Data Fabric connecting data repositories for a holistic view of risk and assets. Policies for data growth, archiving, and storage visualization are provided by Data Management Console.

In essence, managing data effectively on ServiceNow is not just about storage; it is about unlocking the platform's full potential to create agile, intelligent, and resilient digital workflows.

Structure

This chapter covers the following topics:

- Data schema
- Application/Access control
- Importing data

- CMDB and CSDM

Objectives

This chapter provides insights about ServiceNow, including configurations of data schema, application/access control, importing data, CMDB, CSDM, and customizing the instance for the needs of the organization. This chapter will provide users with the skills to configure ServiceNow for these aspects for the unique needs of the organization.

Data schema

In ServiceNow, a data schema refers to the organization and structure of the database tables, how they relate to each other, and how the data is stored and accessed. It essentially defines the logical blueprint of the database, including the tables, fields, and relationships. ServiceNow uses a relational database model, meaning data is organized into tables with rows and columns, and these tables are linked to each other through relationships.

In ServiceNow, **Tables** can be accessed by **System Definition | Tables.**

The following figure shows **Tables**:

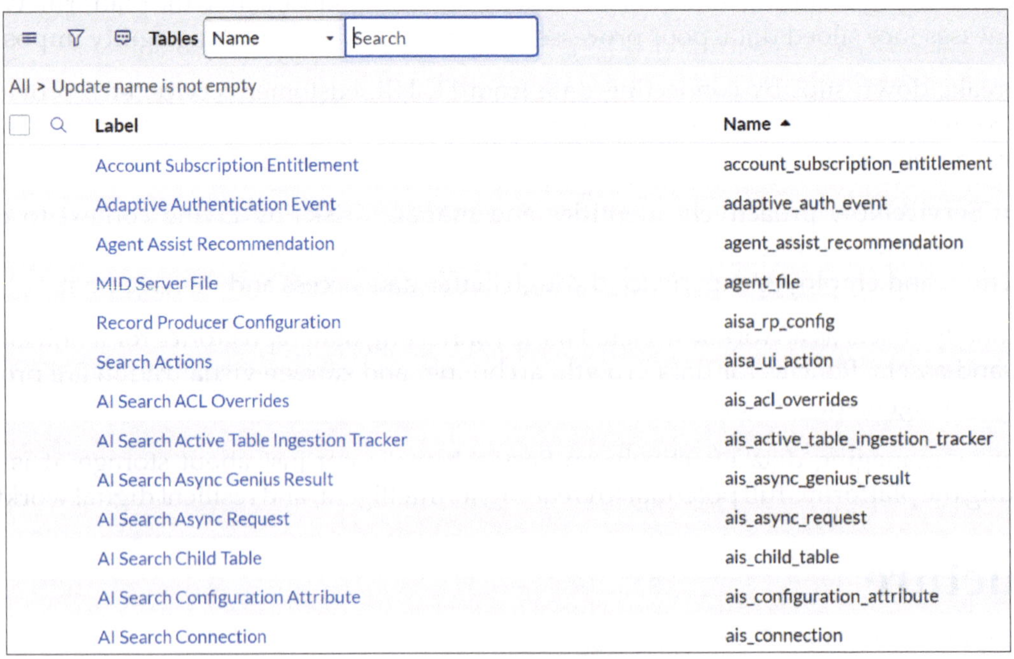

***Figure 5.1**: Tables*

An admin's role is needed to view the column name for the field. The column can be viewed by right-clicking on the field and clicking on **Configure Dictionary**.

The following figure shows the **Table** columns:

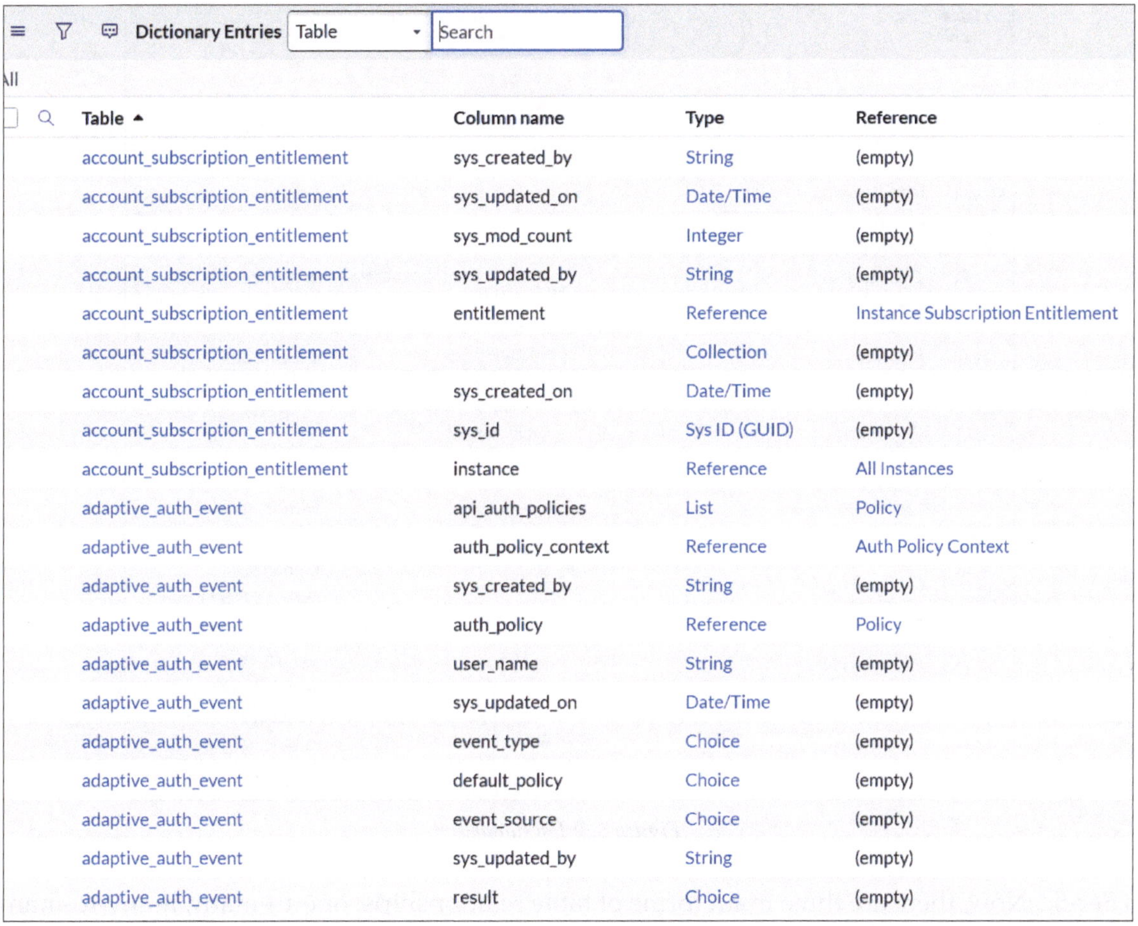

Dictionary Entries | Table | Search

All

Table ▲	Column name	Type	Reference
account_subscription_entitlement	sys_created_by	String	(empty)
account_subscription_entitlement	sys_updated_on	Date/Time	(empty)
account_subscription_entitlement	sys_mod_count	Integer	(empty)
account_subscription_entitlement	sys_updated_by	String	(empty)
account_subscription_entitlement	entitlement	Reference	Instance Subscription Entitlement
account_subscription_entitlement		Collection	(empty)
account_subscription_entitlement	sys_created_on	Date/Time	(empty)
account_subscription_entitlement	sys_id	Sys ID (GUID)	(empty)
account_subscription_entitlement	instance	Reference	All Instances
adaptive_auth_event	api_auth_policies	List	Policy
adaptive_auth_event	auth_policy_context	Reference	Auth Policy Context
adaptive_auth_event	sys_created_by	String	(empty)
adaptive_auth_event	auth_policy	Reference	Policy
adaptive_auth_event	user_name	String	(empty)
adaptive_auth_event	sys_updated_on	Date/Time	(empty)
adaptive_auth_event	event_type	Choice	(empty)
adaptive_auth_event	default_policy	Choice	(empty)
adaptive_auth_event	event_source	Choice	(empty)
adaptive_auth_event	sys_updated_by	String	(empty)
adaptive_auth_event	result	Choice	(empty)

***Figure 5.2:** Table columns*

In ServiceNow, three key attributes for a field are its **Label**, **Name**, and **Value**. The **Label** is a user-friendly term displayed in the UI, the **Name** is a unique identifier used by the system in scripts and business processes, and the **Value** is the actual data stored in the field.

In ServiceNow, a reference field in a table links records in that table to records in another table. It essentially creates a relationship between the two tables, allowing you to select records from the linked table when filling in the field.

In ServiceNow, the system dictionary, a table with label **Dictionary Entry** and named **sys_dictionary**, stores details about each table and its columns. To access it, navigate to **System Definition | Dictionary** from the left navigation panel. Records within ServiceNow are uniquely identified by their **sys_id**, a unique identifier assigned to each record.

The following figure shows the **Dictionary**:

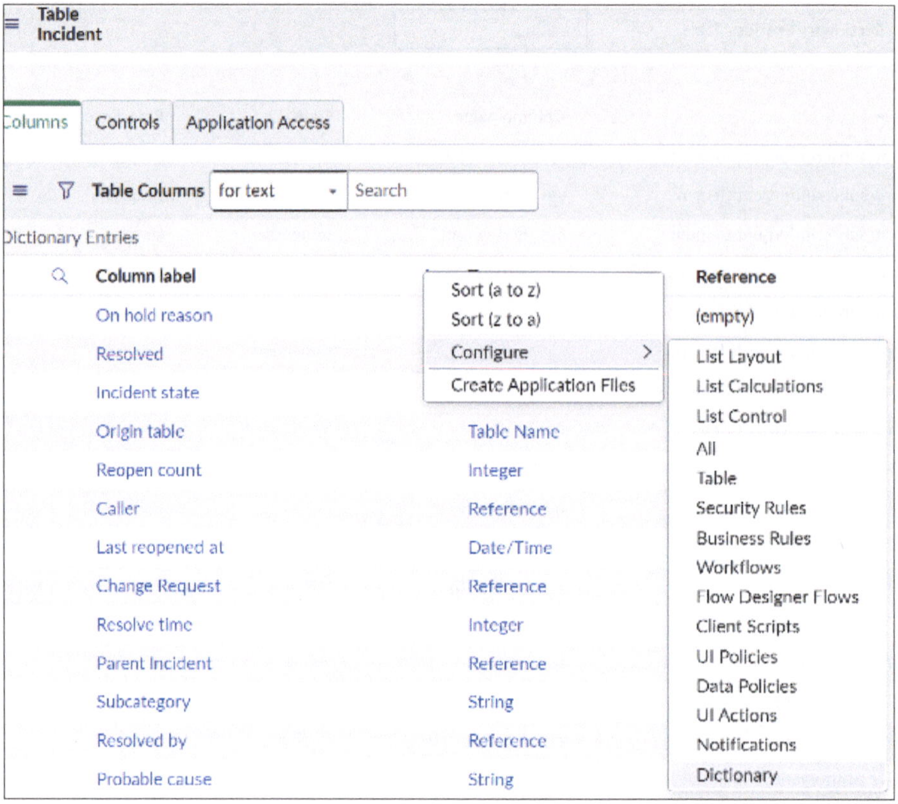

Figure 5.3: Dictionary

In ServiceNow, there are three main forms of table relationships: one-to-many, many-to-many, and extension. A fourth form, one-to-one, is less common.

Here is a breakdown of them all:

- **One-to-many**: This is the most prevalent relationship, where one record in a parent table can be associated with multiple records in a child table. For example, a single user (parent table) might have many incidents (child table) assigned to them.
- **Many-to-many**: This allows a record in one table to be linked to multiple records in another table, and vice versa. ServiceNow uses the **sys_m2m** table to manage these relationships. For instance, a project can have multiple tasks, and each task can belong to multiple projects.
- **Extension**: A table can extend another table, inheriting all fields of the parent table and adding its own. This creates a hierarchy where the child table is a specialized version of the parent table. For example, an **Incident** table extends the **Task** table, inheriting **Task** fields and adding incident-specific fields.

- **One-to-one**: This is less common, where a single record in one table is related to only one record in another table. An example might be a user account related to a user profile.

In ServiceNow, one-to-many, an example is incident to work notes is most common, linking one parent to many children via reference fields. For many-to-many an example is user to role uses a linking table for complex connections. A common one-to-one example is user to user Profile.

These relationships are fundamental to ServiceNow's data model, enabling efficient management of data and workflows across different tables.

The ServiceNow infrastructure includes applications, a database, and a developer environment. These three elements work together to provide a platform for managing IT workflows, automating tasks, and enabling digital transformation.

Here is a more detailed breakdown:

- **Applications**: ServiceNow offers a suite of applications tailored for various IT processes like incident management, problem management, change management, and more. These applications are designed to streamline workflows and provide users with the tools they need to perform their tasks efficiently.
- **Database**: The ServiceNow platform uses a database to store all the information related to the applications and their users. This database is crucial for managing data, ensuring data integrity, and enabling the platform to track and report on various aspects of IT processes.
- **Developer environment**: ServiceNow provides a developer environment that allows users to create custom applications and integrate the platform with other systems. This flexibility enables organizations to tailor the platform to their specific needs and automate processes that may not be covered by the out-of-the-box applications.
- **Base table**: A base table is a foundational table in the ServiceNow schema that other tables inherit from. It is a parent table that does not extend from any other table itself. For example, the task table is a base table because many other tables, like incident, problem, and change request, extend from it.
- **Core table**: Core tables are the tables that are included with the ServiceNow platform when it is initially installed. These are the tables that provide the core functionality of ServiceNow, like the **cmdb_ci** (**configuration item** (**CI**)) table or the incident table. They are part of the baseline instance and are not created by users.
- **Custom table**: Custom tables are tables that are created by users (administrators or developers) to store specific data that is not covered by the core tables. These tables are not part of the original ServiceNow installation and are created to meet specific business needs or requirements. For example, a company might create a custom table to track employee training records or specific project details.

- **Namespace**: In the ServiceNow database, a namespace essentially acts as a container that logically groups related database components like tables within a specific scope.
- **Scoped application example**: If one creates a scoped application named **MyApp** and creates a custom table labeled **Project Requests**, the table name will be prefixed with the scoped application's identifier, for instance, **x_myapp_project_requests**.
- **Global application example**: If one creates a custom table labeled **Employee Records** in the global application, the system will automatically name it **u_employee_records**.

In ServiceNow, parent and child table relationships, also known as inheritance, enable child tables to inherit fields and business logic from their parent tables. This structure mirrors object-oriented programming concepts, promoting code reusability and simplifying data management. When a child table extends a parent table, it does not create physical copies of the parent's fields; instead, it gains access to them through dot walking notation. This means the child table can both directly access inherited fields as if they were its own and also use dot walking to access them through the parent table's name.

The key aspects of parent-child relationships and inheritance are as follows:

- **Inheritance**: Child tables inherit fields, business rules, UI policies, and other configurations from their parent tables.
- **dot walking**: Inherited fields are accessed via dot walking notation (e.g., **child_table.parent_field**).

The following figure shows dot walking:

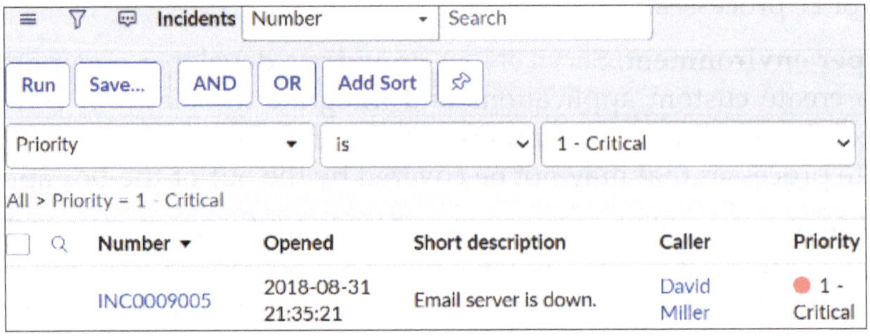

Figure 5.4: Dot walkimg

- **Example**: Consider the **Incident** table extending the **Task** table. The **Incident** table inherits all fields from the **Task** table. For example, if the **Task** table has a field called **priority**, the **Incident** table can access it directly as **priority** or using dot walking as **task.priority**. However, the priority field is physically stored only in the **Task** table.

In ServiceNow, a schema map is a visual representation of a table and its relationships with other tables. It helps users understand how data is structured and connected within the database. To access the schema map for a table, navigate to **System Definition | Tables and Columns**, select the desired table, and then click on the **Show Schema Map** related link.

The following figure shows the **Show Shema Map** link:

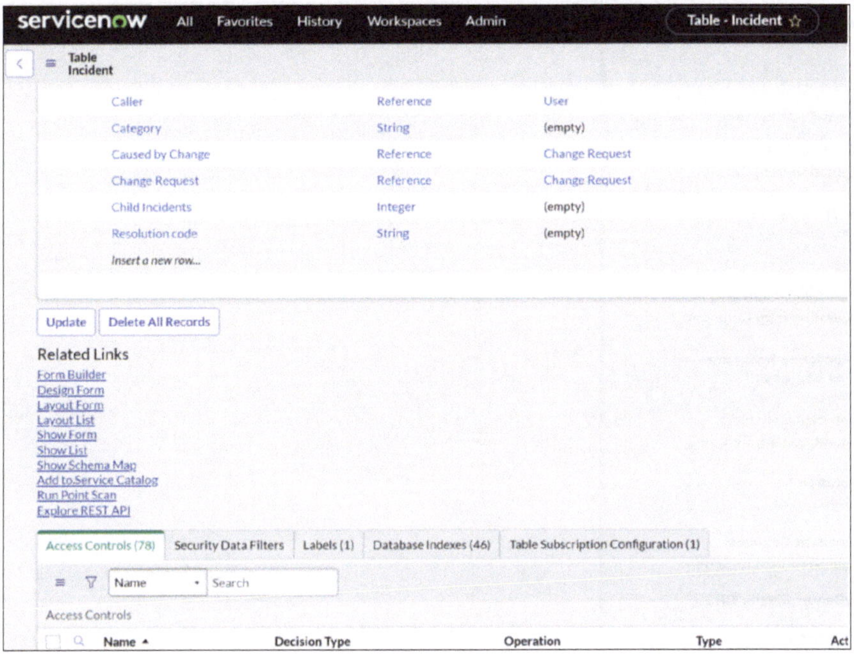

***Figure 5.5**: Show Schema Map link*

The following figure shows the schema:

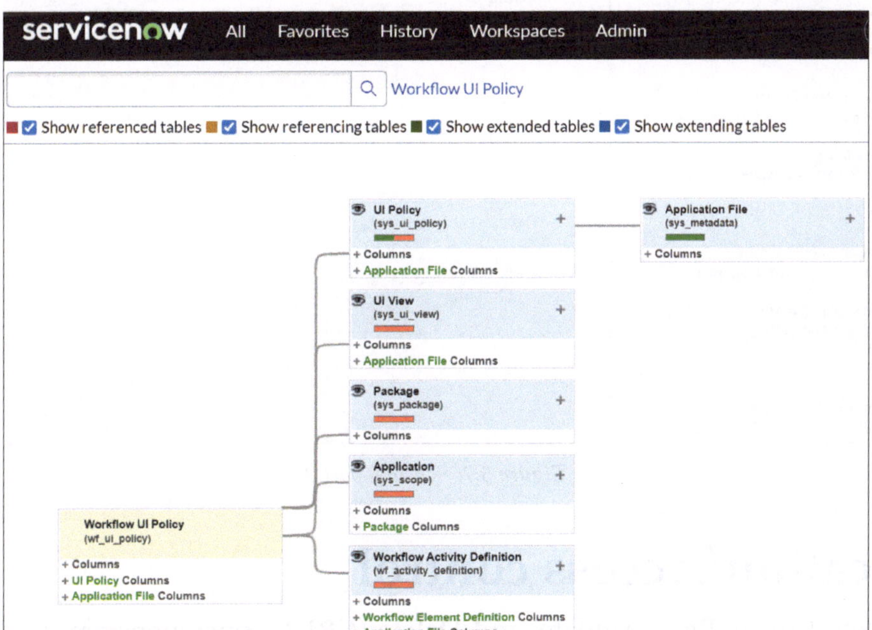

***Figure 5.6**: Schema–part 1*

The following figure shows the schema:

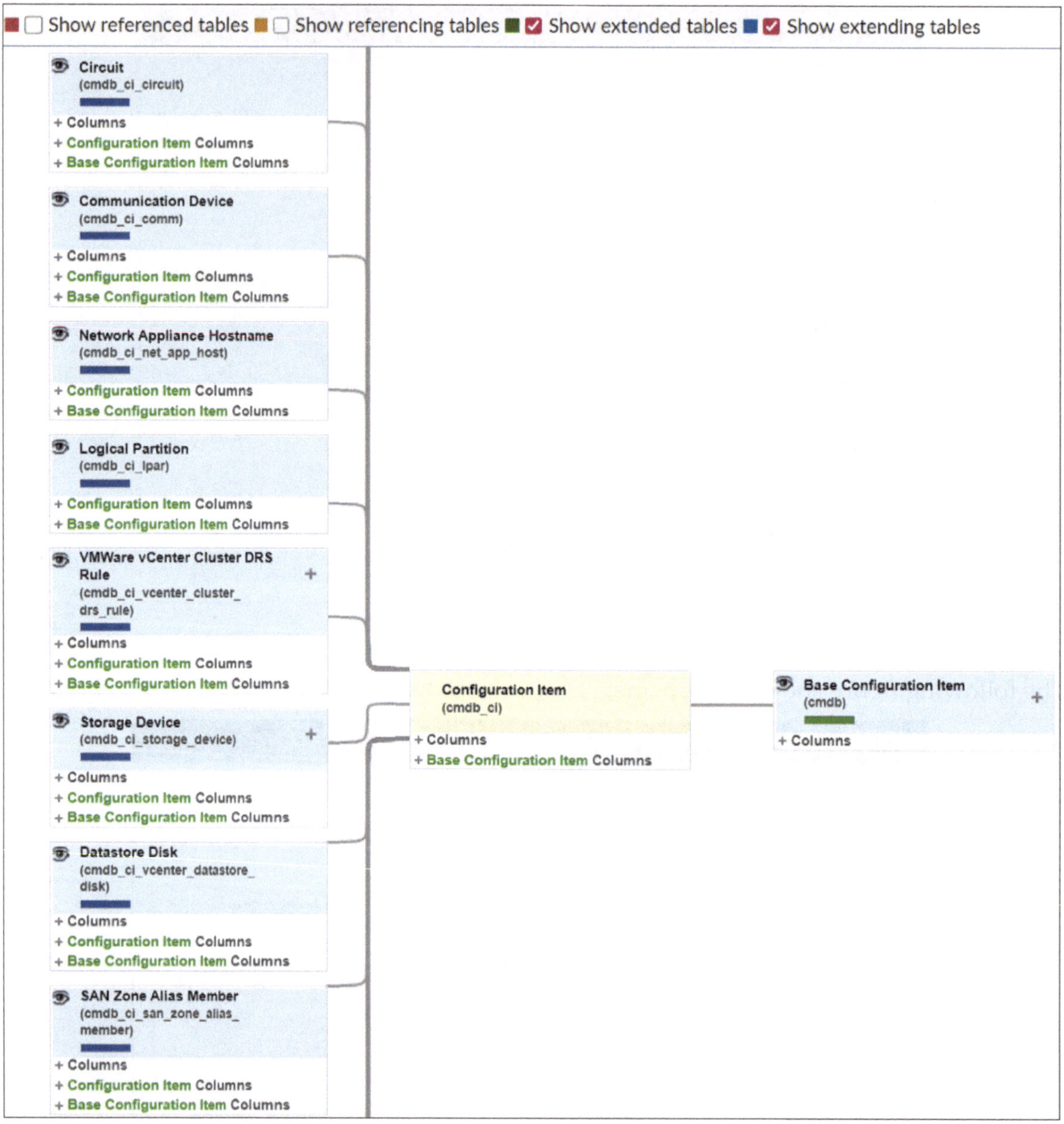

Figure 5.7: Schema–part 2

Application/Access control

In ServiceNow **Create, Read, Update, and Delete** (**CRUD**) operations are fundamental for managing data within the platform. In ServiceNow, three levels of security control user access to perform CURD operations on tables: user authentication/login, application and module access, and database access. These levels ensure that only authorized users can interact with specific tables and perform operations like create, read, update, and delete:

- **User authentication/login**: This initial layer verifies the user's identity before granting access to the platform. ServiceNow supports various authentication methods, including **single sign-on** (**SSO**) for common access and **multi-factor authentication** (**MFA**) to enhance security. These methods can be used independently or in combination to create a robust identity and access management strategy.
- **Application and module access**: ServiceNow uses roles to define permissions for accessing specific applications and modules. This level controls which features and functionalities a user can access within the platform.

  The following figure shows the **Modules**:

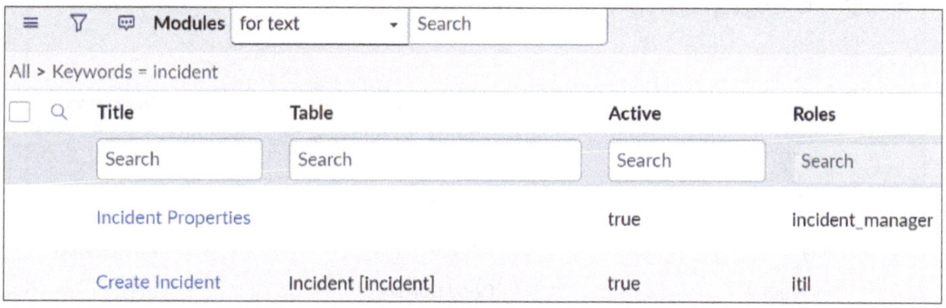

***Figure 5.8:** Modules*

- **Database access**: This layer uses **access control lists** (**ACLs**) to define permissions for accessing specific tables, fields, and records. ACLs dictate which users can perform CRUD operations on particular data within the database.

ServiceNow security modules, especially those utilized by system administrators, are essential for maintaining a secure and compliant environment. These modules include ACLs, system properties (security), and high security settings, along with password management (security questions).

The ServiceNow Instance Security Dashboard provides a centralized view to monitor the instance's security health. This includes detecting misconfigurations, tracking compliance, and managing security posture by consolidating metrics, alerts, and best practices into one place, helping admins quickly find and fix vulnerabilities.

Here is a more detailed look:

- **ACLs**: Define who can access specific data and functionality within ServiceNow.
- **System Security | Security**: This module allows administrators to manage overall security settings, including the hardening of the instance and other security-related configurations.

- **High Security Settings**: Controls specific security features like session timeouts and advanced security options.
- **Password Management | Security Questions**: Enhances password security by requiring users to answer security questions in addition to their password.

These modules work together to ensure that the ServiceNow instance is properly secured, access is controlled, and compliance requirements are met.

ACLs are the process by which ServiceNow provides granular security for its data and can be applied to individual records, as well as fields within those records.

The following figure shows **Access Controls**:

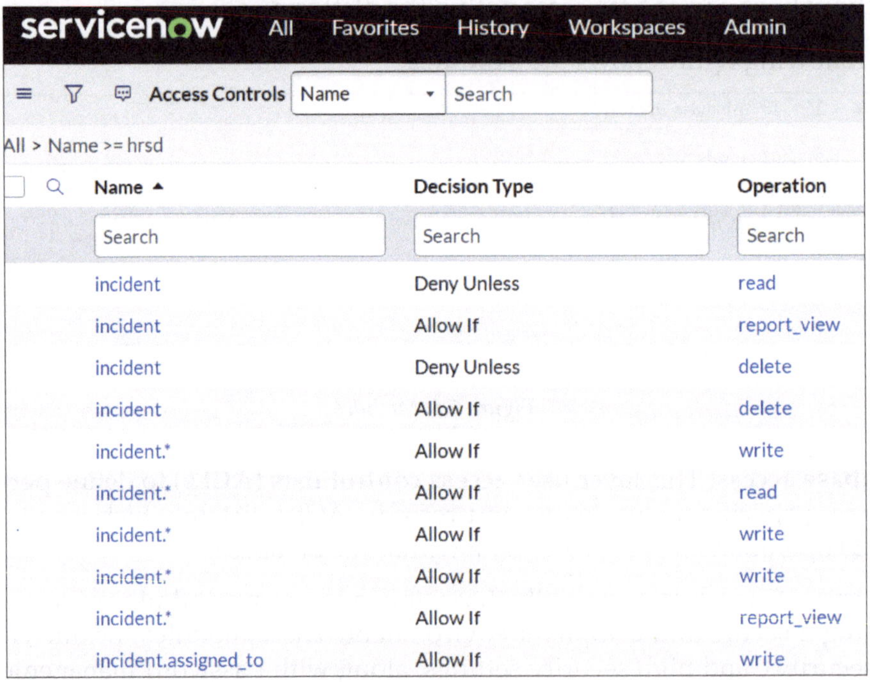

Figure 5.9: Access Controls

The following figure shows **Access Control** record configurations:

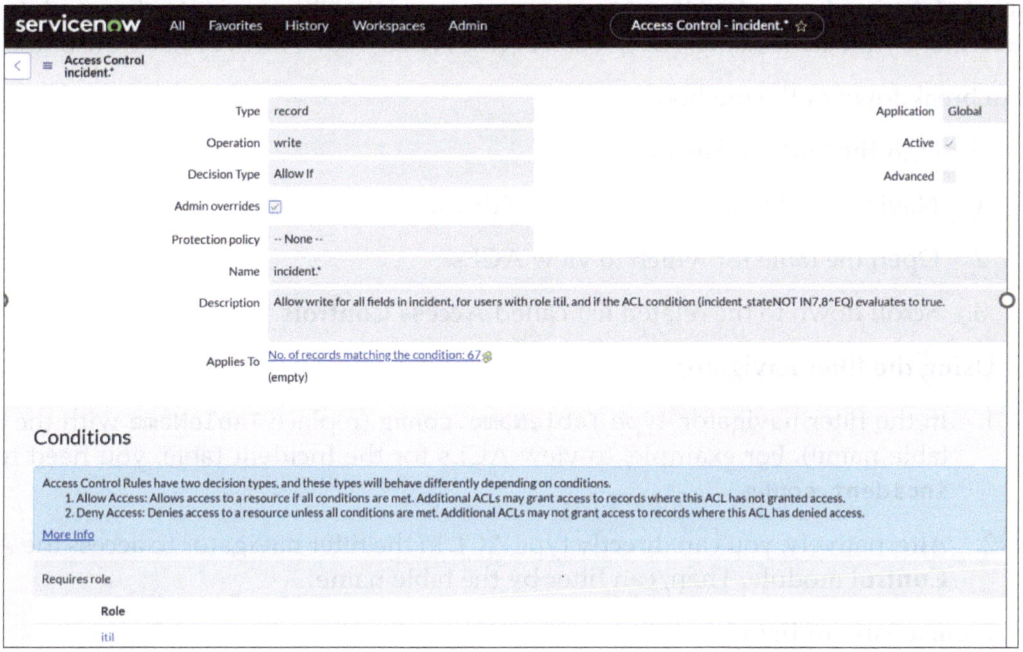

***Figure 5.10**: Access Control record configurations*

The following figure shows the **Access Controls** tab:

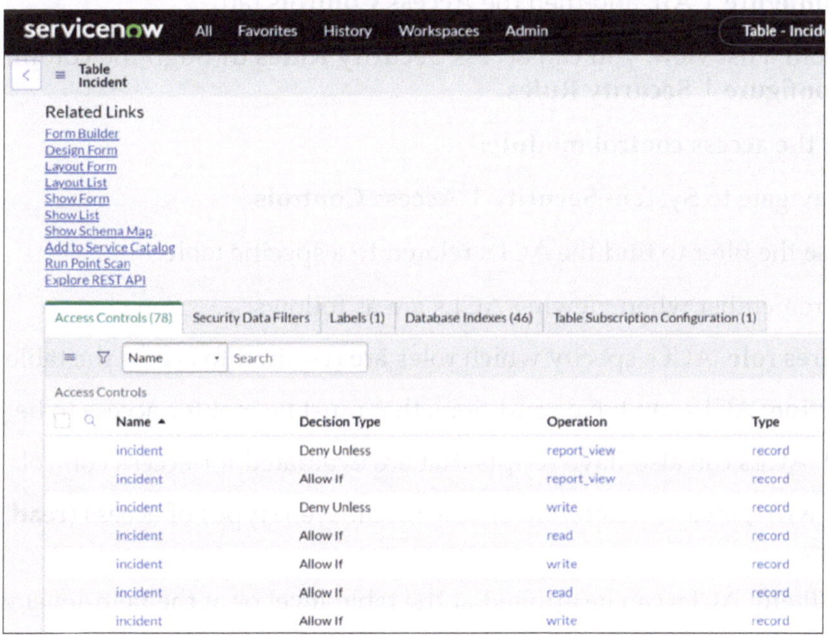

***Figure 5.11**: Access Controls tab*

To view ACLs for a table in ServiceNow, navigate to the table definition and then access the related list of **Access Controls**. Alternatively, you can use the filter navigator to search for *ACL* and then filter by the table name. Also, it can access ACLs from a form or list view of the table.

Here is a breakdown of the methods:

- **Through the table definition**:
    1. Navigate to **System Definition | Tables**.
    2. Open the table for which to view ACLs.
    3. Scroll down to the related list called **Access Controls**.
- **Using the filter navigator**:
    1. In the filter navigator, type `TableName.config` (replace `TableName` with the actual table name). For example, to view ACLs for the Incident table, you need to type `incident.config`.
    2. Alternatively, you can directly type ACL in the filter navigator to access the **Access Control** module. Then, can filter by the table name.
- **From a form or list view**:
    1. Open a form or list view of the table.
    2. From the form, you can find **Security Rules** under **Configure | Security Rules** or **Configure | All**, and then the **Access Controls** tab.
    3. From a list view, you can access **Security Rules** through the column menu under **Configure | Security Rules**.
- **Using the access control module**:
    1. Navigate to **System Security | Access Controls**.
    2. Use the filter to find the ACLs related to a specific table.

Key things to remember when viewing ACLs are as follows:

- **Requires role**: ACLs specify which roles are required to access the table or its fields.
- **Condition**: ACLs can have conditions that must be met for access to be granted.
- **Script**: ACLs can also have scripts that are evaluated for access control.
- **Read, write, create, delete**: ACLs control different types of access (**read, write, create, delete**).
- **Table/Field**: ACLs can be applied at the table-level or at the field-level within a table.
- *** (All fields)**: An ACL with * means access is granted to all fields on the table.

- **None**: An ACL with **None** means access is granted to the table itself but not to its fields.

ACLs are the process by which ServiceNow provides granular security for its data and can be applied to individual records, as well as fields within those records.

While working with ACLs, one should know the types of ACLs. The types are as follows:

- Row-level ACL or table-level ACL.
- Column-level ACL or field-level ACL.

ACLs can be created for different operations on the table, like **read**, **write**, **create**, and **delete**. ACLs can be created for client-callable script includes, UI pages, REST endpoints, etc.

Application access can be controlled through the scope. Each application has a scope associated with it. There is a global scope that can access all applications.

Update sets that are getting created for configuration changes are aligned to a particular scope. These are applicable to out-of-the-box applications and to customized applications.

To navigate to and manage the ACL in ServiceNow, need the **security_admin** role. This role grants elevated security privileges, allowing the creation, editing, and deletion of ACLs. While the admin role can view ACLs, it cannot make changes to modify an ACL. Admin role to be elevated to the **security_admin** role.

ServiceNow ACLs follow a specific execution order: they first check **Roles**, then the **Condition**, and finally the **Script**, moving from general (table-level) to specific (field-level), and a grant at any specific rule stops further evaluation, with the user needing to pass relevant rules at both table and field-levels to gain access. This hierarchical approach ensures efficient access control, denying access early if roles or conditions fail.

ACL execution flow

ACL execution order is detailed as follows:

- **Table-level ACLs (general)**: ServiceNow first checks ACLs that apply to the entire table (e.g., incident).
- **Field-level ACLs (specific)**: If table access is granted, it then checks more specific ACLs for individual fields (e.g., **incident.priority**).
- **Within each ACL (rule order)**: For any given table or field ACL, the evaluation is:
    1. **Roles**: Does the user have any required roles? (If not, access denied immediately).
    2. **Condition**: Does the ACL's condition filter (e.g., **state=1**) evaluate to true? (If false, stops).
    3. **Script**: Does the script (if present) return true? (If false, stops).

- **Granting access**: A user must pass both a table-level rule and a field-level rule for a specific field to have full access to that field, but only one matching rule (e.g., a table-level one) is needed to access the table generally.
- **First true wins**: Once an ACL rule evaluates to true and grants access for a given level (table / field), that evaluation stops for that object, preventing broader rules from being checked unnecessarily.

This process ensures granular control, checking permissions from broad table access down to specific field restrictions, only progressing if previous checks are passed.

Importing data

In ServiceNow, an import set is a tool that allows administrators to import data from various external sources into the platform. It acts as a staging area, temporarily storing the imported data before it is transformed and loaded into the target ServiceNow tables. To manage import sets, users typically need the **admin** or **import_admin** roles, with specific roles like **import_set_loader** granting access to load data.

Here is a breakdown:

- **Staging area**: Import sets provide a temporary storage space (import set tables) for data extracted from external sources (like **comma-separated values** (**CSV**) files, **Java Database Connectivity** (**JDBC**), or web services).
- **Transformation**: The data in the import set table is then mapped and transformed into the appropriate format for the target ServiceNow tables using transform maps.
- **Data source**: An import set is linked to a data source record, which specifies where the data is coming from.

The roles required and provided out of the box for managing import sets are as follows:

- **Admin role**: This role is required to create and manage data sources, which are essential for importing data.
- **import_set_loader**: This role allows users to load data into import set tables using the **Load Data** module.
- **import_admin_role**: Provides comprehensive control over import sets, including creating, configuring, and managing transform maps and data sources.
- **Import_transformer**: This role is necessary for creating and managing transform maps, which are crucial for mapping data from import sets to target tables.
- **Permissions for specific tables**: In some cases, users may need specific permissions (like READ) for the target tables they are importing data into.

Load data into staging table

The following table shows a sample file for file import processing:

user id	first name	last name	email	active
jsmith	John	Smith	jsmith@example.com	TRUE
amayer	Anna	Mayer	amayer@example.com	TRUE
bwayne	Brian	Wayne	bwayne@example.com	FALSE

***Table 5.1**:Sample file*

The following figure shows the file import processing:

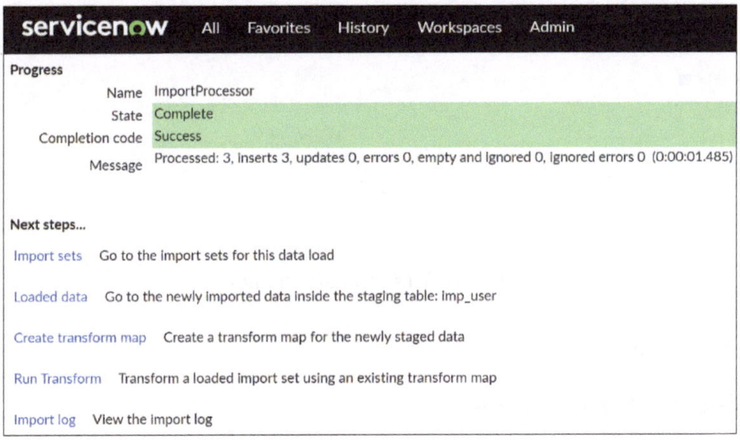

***Figure 5.12**: Import processing*

The following figure shows the **Load Data** into staging table:

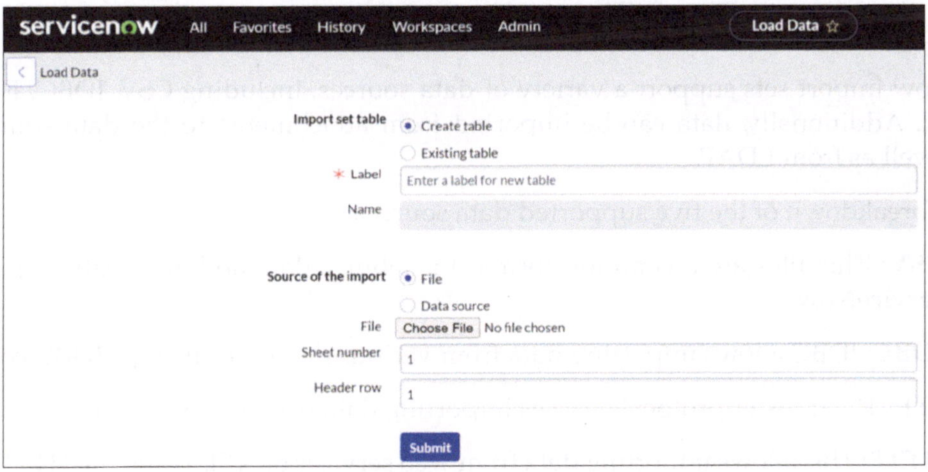

***Figure 5.13**: Load Data into staging table*

A ServiceNow transform map is needed whenever importing data from an external source into a ServiceNow table, and it needs to define how that data maps, transforms, and lands in specific fields, especially for complex data. A staging table is introduced so that it can hold raw data from external source and using transform map that data is mapped into needed table of ServiceNow.

The next step in the loading date is the transform map. Transform map is a map that stages the table (sourcing table) and its fields to the **Target table** and its fields. The following figure shows the **Table Transform Map**:

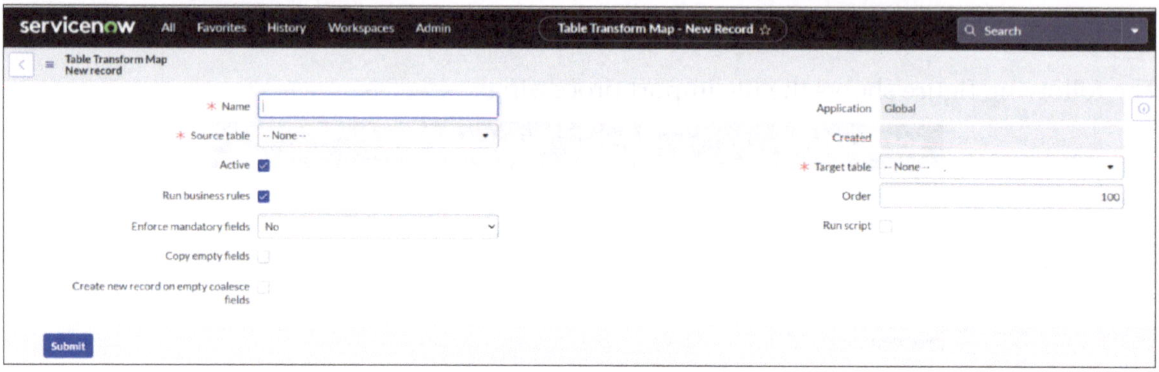

Figure 5.14: Transform map

An example is as follows:

- **Source table**: **u_staging_users**
- **Target table**: **User [sys_user]**

Run transform

The source table and its field contents are transformed and added to the destination table.

ServiceNow import sets support a variety of data sources, including CSV, JDBC, FTP, HTTP, and XML. Additionally, data can be imported from attachments to the data source record itself, as well as from LDAP.

Here is a breakdown of the five supported data sources:

- **CSV**: This files are a common format for tabular data and are easily imported into ServiceNow.
- **JDBC**: JDBC allows importing data from various databases using a JDBC connection.
- **FTP**: The transfer protocol enables importing data from remote servers.
- **HTTP**: This allows importing data from web services or APIs using the HTTP protocol.

- **XML**: It is a structured data format commonly used for data exchange.

In ServiceNow, the automatic mapping utility and mapping assist utility are tools used during data transformation processes, specifically when importing data into ServiceNow tables. The automatic mapping utility simplifies the process by automatically matching fields between an import set and a target table based on identical field names. The mapping assist utility provides a visual interface for manually mapping fields, allowing for more complex mappings and the ability to map a single source field to multiple destination fields.

In essence, the automatic mapping utility is a quick and easy solution for simple field mappings, while the mapping assist utility offers more advanced features for complex or non-standard mappings.

Here is a breakdown of each utility:

- **Automatic mapping utility**:
  - **Function**: Automatically matches fields in an import set with corresponding fields in the target table based on matching names.
  - **How it works**: If the field names in the respective import set exactly match the field names in the target table, you can use the **Auto map matching fields** option within the transform map.
  - **Purpose**: Streamlines the mapping process when there is a direct correspondence between the source and destination fields.
- **Mapping assist utility**:
  - **Function**: Provides a visual interface to manually map fields, offering flexibility and control over the mapping process.
  - **Key features**:
    - **Visual mapping**: Allows to drag-and-drop fields from the import set onto the corresponding fields in the target table.
    - **Multiple field mapping**: Enables mapping a single source field to multiple destination fields.
    - **Complex logic**: Supports the use of advanced logic and scripting for more complex mapping scenarios.
  - **Purpose**: Useful when the automatic mapping does not suffice, or when more complex relationships need to be established between source and destination fields.

The following figure shows the links for **Auto Map Matching Fields, Mapping Assist** in **Table Transform Map**:

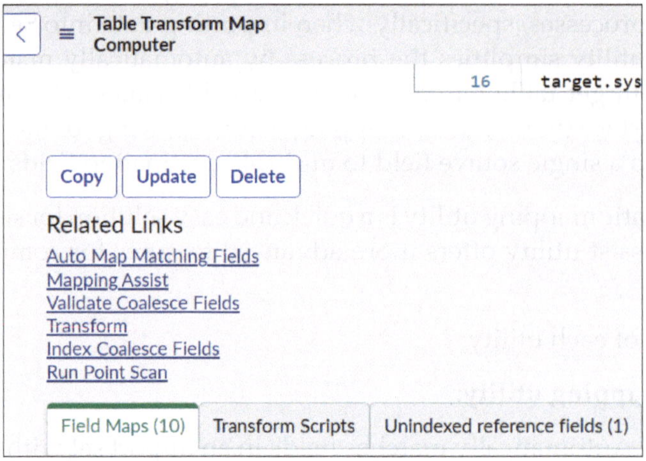

***Figure 5.15**: Links Auto Map Matching Fields, Mapping Assist*

The following figure shows the **Mapping Assist**:

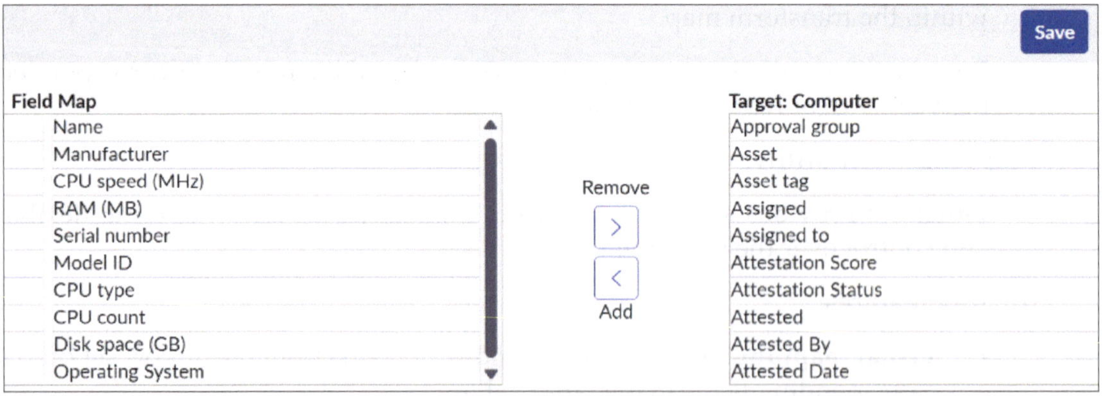

***Figure 5.16**: Mapping Assist*

In essence, the automatic mapping utility is a quick and easy solution for simple field mappings, while the **Mapping Assist** utility offers more advanced features for complex or non-standard mappings.

In ServiceNow, when importing data using transform maps, the coalesce option allows you to determine how records are matched between the respective import set (staging table) and the target table. This is crucial for preventing duplicate records and updating existing ones.

Based on the provided search results, there are four main ways to configure coalesce in ServiceNow:

- **No coalesce**: When no field is set to coalesce, all imported rows are treated as new records, and no existing records are updated. This results in the creation of duplicate records if the import is executed again.
- **Single field coalesce**: Can designate a single field as the unique identifier. If a target table record with the same value in that field as the staging table record exists, the target record is updated. Otherwise, a new record is inserted.
- **Multiple-field coalesce**: This configuration involves setting multiple fields to coalesce. For an update to occur, all coalesce fields in the staging table record must match the corresponding fields in the target table record. If a match is found, the existing record is updated; otherwise, a new record is inserted.
- **Conditional coalesce**: This is a more advanced configuration that uses a script to determine if a record should coalesce. The script can return the **sys_id** of the target record to be updated if a match is found. If the script does not return a matching **sys_id**, a new record will be inserted.

The following figure shows an example of **Coalesce** fields:

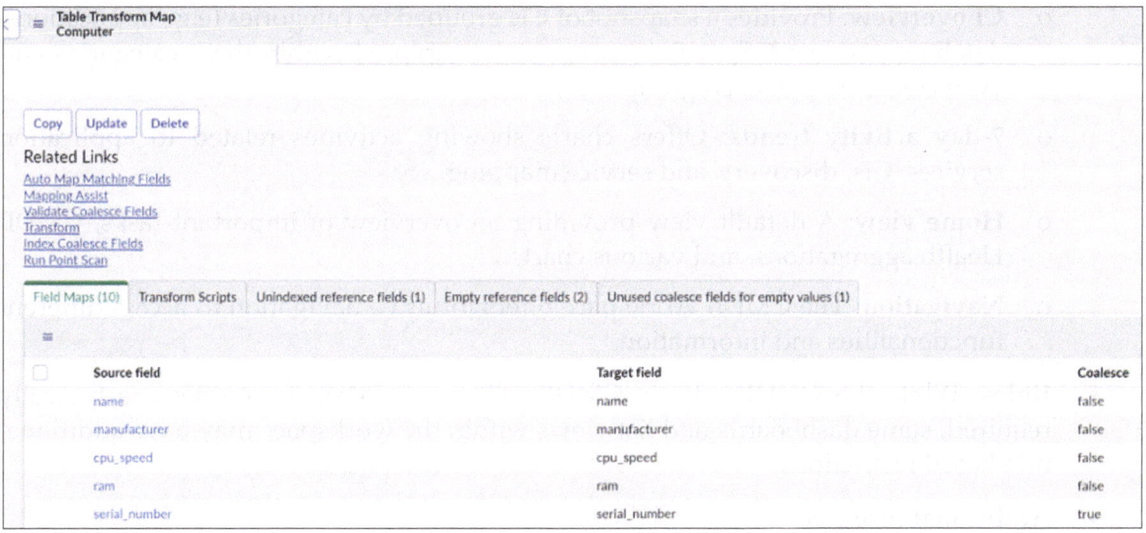

Figure 5.17: Coalesce fields

CMDB and CSDM

To access the CMDB Workspace in ServiceNow, navigate to **Workspaces | CMDB Workspace** from the application navigator. Within the workspace, you can search for CIs, view CMDB Health metrics, and access various CMDB dashboards and tools.

Here is a more detailed breakdown:

- **Accessing the workspace**:
  - o Open the ServiceNow application navigator (usually on the left side of the screen).
  - o Locate and click on the **Workspaces** menu.
  - o Select **CMDB Workspace** to open the workspace in a new browser tab.
- **Key features and information**:
  - o **CI search**: Allows searching for CIs based on specific criteria (attributes) within a selected CI Class or across all classes. Search can be refined using up to five conditions.
  - o **CMDB Health**: Displays health metrics for CIs and their relationships, including correctness, compliance, and completeness. CMDB Health can be drilled down into and CMDB Relationship Health dashboards by clicking on the percentage numbers.
  - o **CI overview**: Provides a snapshot of CIs grouped by categories (e.g., applications, databases, servers). Specific classes can be explored within these categories and even create custom class groups.
  - o **7-day activity trends**: Offers charts showing activities related to application services, CIs, discovery, and service mapping.
  - o **Home view**: A default view providing an overview of important tasks, CMDB Health aggregations, and various charts.
  - o **Navigation**: The CMDB Workspace offers intuitive navigation to access different functionalities and information.
- **Roles**: While the CMDB admin, CMDB editor, or CMDB user roles are typically required, some dashboards and list views within the workspace may have additional role-based restrictions.
- **Additional resources**:
  - o The ServiceNow basics learning module **Home | ServiceNow University | ServiceNow** provides information on lists, forms, and navigation within ServiceNow, which can be helpful for using the **CMDB Workspace.**
  - o The CI Class Manager (accessible through the application navigator) allows you to view and manage CI Classes, which can be useful for understanding the structure of the CMDB.

The following figure shows **CMDB Workspace**:

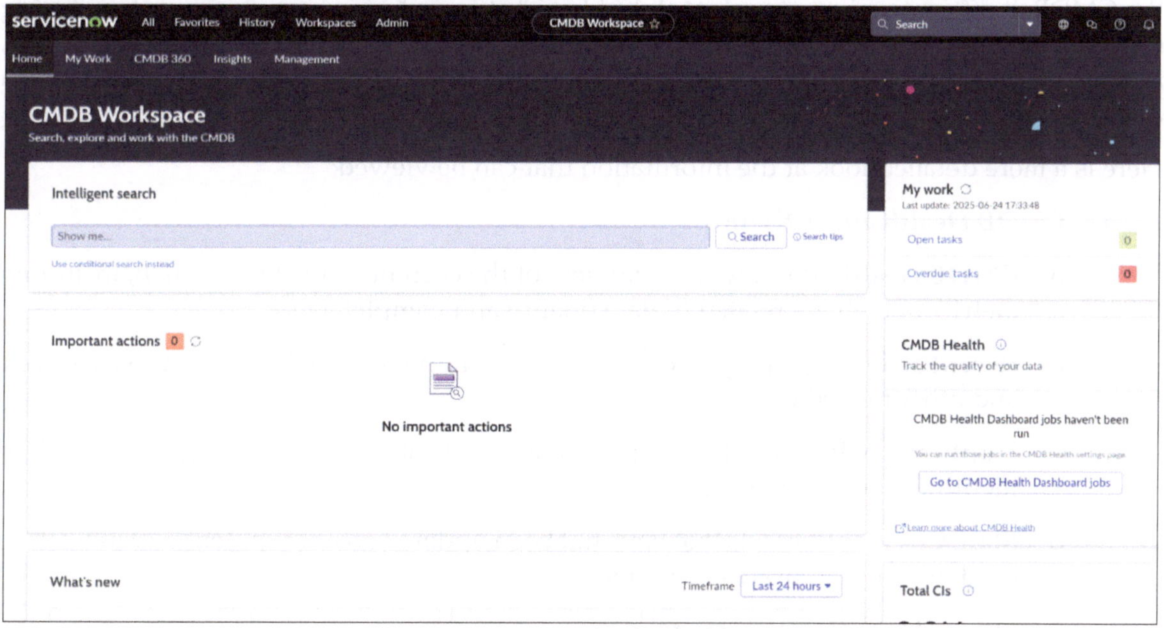

Figure 5.18: CMDB Workspace

The following figure shows the **CI overview** in the **CMDB Workspace**:

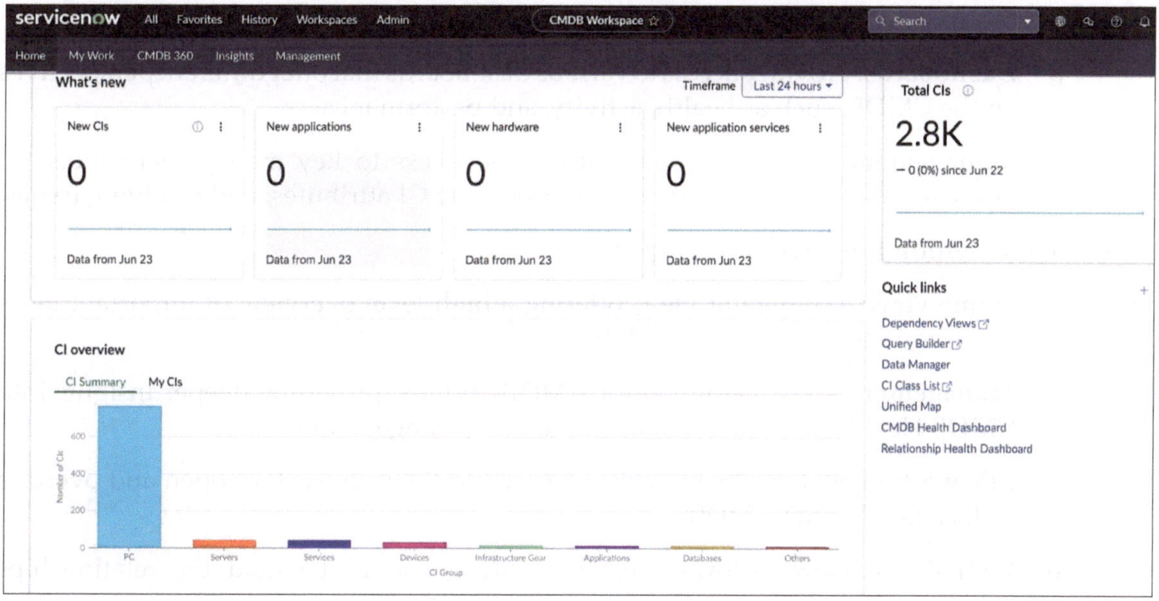

Figure 5.19: CI overview in CMDB Workspace

The ServiceNow **CMDB Workspace** provides a centralized and modernized way to manage the CMDB. It offers a variety of tools and dashboards for exploring, managing, and analyzing CMDB data. Users can view information related to the CIs, application services, discovery, and service mapping, as well as access key management tools and insights into **CMDB Health** and activities.

Here is a more detailed look at the information that can be viewed:

- **CMDB Health and activities**:
  - **CMDB Health**: Provides an overview of the current state of the CMDB, including metrics and charts related to data quality and completeness.
  - **Recent activity**: Displays recent changes and updates to CIs, Application services, and other related components.
  - **Duplicate CIs**: Highlights potential duplicate CIs, allowing for efficient identification and resolution.
  - **Stale CIs**: Identifies CIs that have not been updated recently, potentially indicating outdated or inaccurate information.
- **CMDB exploration and management**:
  - **CI search**: Allows users to easily search and locate specific CIs within the CMDB.
  - **List views**: Presents CIs in a tabular format, allowing for easy browsing and filtering based on various criteria.
  - **Dashboards**: Provides access to various dashboards that offer different perspectives on the CMDB, such as health, activity, and performance.
  - **Management tools**: Gives administrators access to key management tools for tasks like managing CI relationships, updating CI attributes, and resolving issues.
- **Views within the CMDB Workspace**:
  - **Home view**: The default view, offering a high-level overview of important tasks and activities related to the CMDB.
  - **Management view**: Designed for CMDB admins, providing deeper insights into CMDB Health, activities, and access to key management tools.
  - **MY work view**: Focuses on tasks assigned to the user, such as open and overdue tasks related to the CMDB.
  - **CMDB 360 view**: Allows users to analyze and understand the relationships between CIs and their attributes.
- **Unified map**:

- o **Hierarchical map visualization**: This feature provides a visual representation of the hierarchical relationships between CIs, centered on a selected CI.

The **CMDB Workspace** is a powerful tool for managing and understanding the complex relationships and data within the ServiceNow CMDB. It offers a user-friendly interface with various views and dashboards designed to streamline CMDB management tasks.

The following figure shows the **CI Class Manager**:

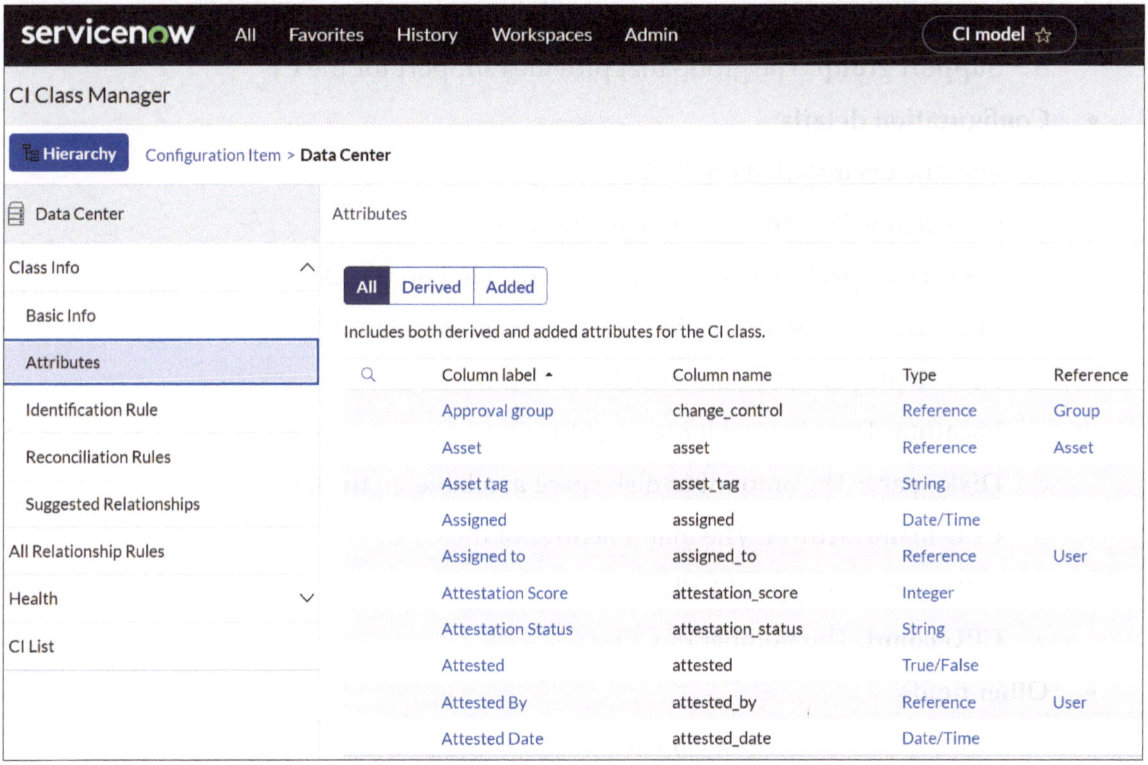

***Figure 5.20**: CI Class Manager*

In ServiceNow, a CI form typically includes fields for identifying information (like name, serial number, model, manufacturer, and description) and configuration details (such as **operating system** (**OS**), location, and resource usage). It is used to manage and track IT components within the CMDB, ensuring accurate information for service management processes.

Here is a more detailed breakdown:

- **Identifying information**:
  - o **Name**: A unique identifier for the CI.
  - o **Asset tag**: If applicable, the asset tag assigned to the physical item.
  - o **Serial number**: The manufacturer's unique serial number.

- **Model ID**: The specific model of the CI.
- **Manufacturer**: The company that manufactured the CI.
- **IP address**: The IP address associated with the CI (if applicable).
- **MAC address**: The MAC address of the CI (if applicable).
- **Description**: A brief explanation of the CI.
- **Owner group**: The group responsible for the CI.
- **Support group**: The group that provides support for the CI.

- **Configuration details**:
  - **OS**: The OS installed on the CI.
  - **OS version**: The specific version of the OS.
  - **OS service pack**: The service pack is installed on the OS.
  - **Manufactured date**: The date the CI was manufactured.
  - **Date deployed**: The date the CI was deployed.
  - **Location**: The physical location of the CI.
  - **Disk space**: The amount of disk space available on the CI.
  - **CPU manufacturer**: The manufacturer of the CPU.
  - **CPU type**: The type of CPU.
  - **CPU count**: The number of CPUs.
- **Other fields**:
  - **Company**: The company that owns the CI.
  - **Assigned to**: The user the CI is assigned to.
  - **Maintenance schedule**: Information about maintenance periods for the CI.
- **CMDB hierarchy**:
  - Each CI belongs to a specific class within the CMDB hierarchy.
  - The hierarchy helps organize CIs based on their type and relationship to other CIs.
- **Usage**:
  - CIs are used to track and manage IT components, such as servers, routers, software, and other service components.
  - They are essential for incident management, change management, and other service management processes.

The following figure shows the CI attributes:

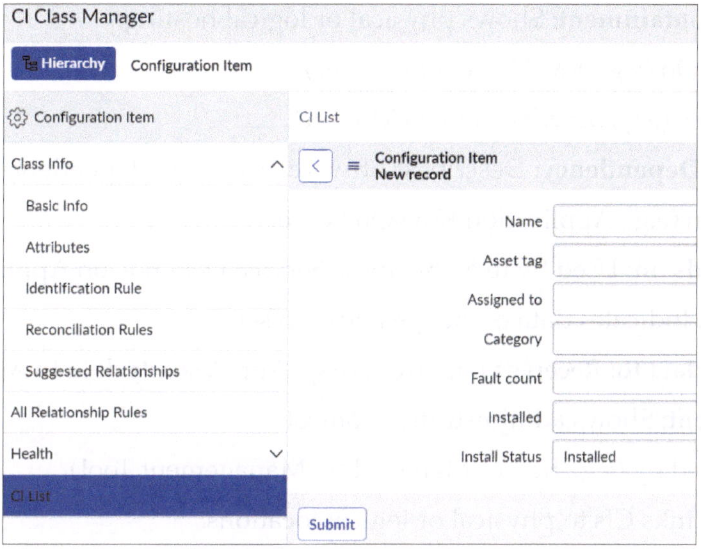

Figure 5.21*: CI attributes*

To access the CI **Relationship Editor** in ServiceNow, you first need to open a specific CI form. Then, locate the CI relations formatter and click the icon within it to launch the **Relationship Editor**. This editor allows to view, create, modify, or delete relationships between CIs.

The following figure shows the **Relationship Editor**:

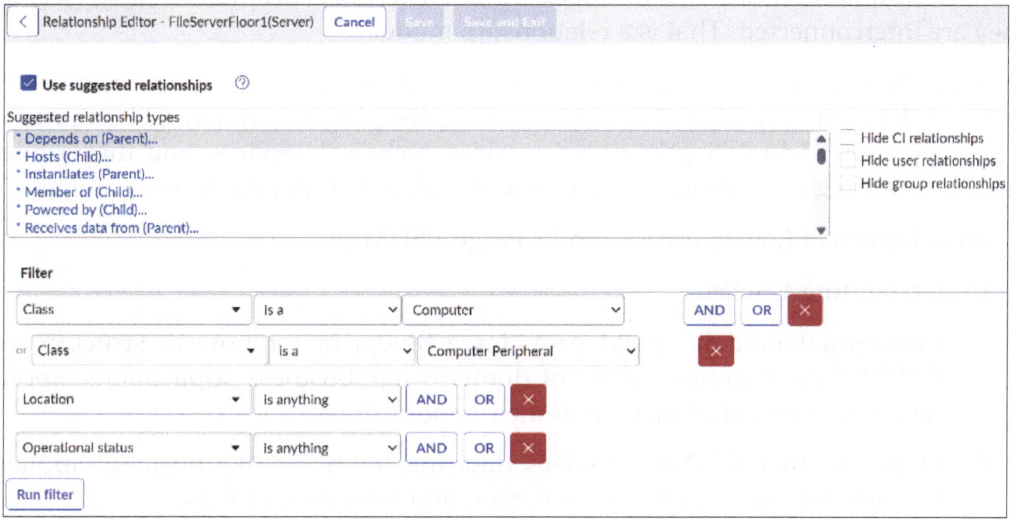

Figure 5.22*: CI Relationship Editor*

The common relationship types are as follows:

- **Hosting/Containment**: Shows physical or logical hosting.
  - HostedOn (e.g., VM HostedOn Server)
  - Contains (e.g., Server Contains Module)
- **Execution/Dependency**: Describes software or process dependencies.
  - RunsOn (e.g., Application RunsOn Server)
  - **Depends on**: Used by (e.g., Business Service Depends on Application)
- **Data Flow**: Indicates data exchange between services.
  - **Sends data to**: Receives data from (e.g., App A sends data to App B)
- **Management**: Shows administrative control.
  - Managed by (e.g., Server Managed by Management Tool)
- **Location**: Links CIs to physical or logical locations.
  - **Located in**: Houses (e.g., Server located in data center)

CIs represent individual components or assets that need to be managed within the CMDB.

Each table consists of rows and columns in a relational model. Tables consist of rows and columns. Data is stored in these tables. The list view can be seen by selecting the **Table**. Select a **Table** and click on **Schema Map** to see the **Schema**.

CSDM is the Common ServiceNow Database Model. This is a concept of what services are and how they are interconnected. That is a relationship model.

The CSDM in ServiceNow is a standardized framework that provides a blueprint for how to organize and structure data related to services across the platform. It defines best practices for defining, managing, and relating business services, technical services, and their underlying components, ensuring consistency and alignment between IT and business strategies.

Here is a breakdown of how to access and leverage CSDM:

- **Understanding CSDM**:
  - **Conceptual model**: CSDM provides a blueprint for how to structure specific CMDB data. It defines different domains like business applications, application services, technical services, and their relationships.
  - **Data domains**: CSDM organizes data into domains like business applications, business services, application services, and technical services.
  - **Relationships**: CSDM defines relationships between these domains, allowing for tracing the impact of changes from a business service down to the underlying infrastructure components.

- **Enabling CSDM in ServiceNow**:
  - o **Activate the CSDM plugin**: If not already enabled, you need to activate the CSDM plugin within the respective ServiceNow instance.
  - o **Access CSDM through the Navigator**: Once enabled, you can access CSDM-related modules through the application navigator by searching for CSDM.
  - o **Roles and permissions**: Ensure that the necessary roles (e.g., **cmdb_librarian, service_admin, business_planner**) are there to access and to manage different aspects of CSDM.
- **Populating and managing CSDM data**:
  - o **Start with business applications**: CSDM recommends beginning with business applications, which align with business needs and can be internal or external.
  - o **Define application services**: Define application services as operational views of business applications.
  - o **Map technical services**: Identify and map technical services that support application and business services.
  - o **Establish relationships**: Use the relationship editor to define relationships between CIs according to CSDM.
  - o **Data quality**: Ensure data accuracy and completeness through data import, monitoring, and audits.
  - o **Leverage dashboards**: Utilize built-in CSDM dashboards to monitor data quality and compliance.
- **Applying CSDM to ServiceNow products**:
  - o **Change management**: Align change processes with CSDM to minimize risks.
  - o **Incident management**: Ensure incidents are recorded in a way that aligns with CSDM.
  - o **Asset management**: CSDM provides a framework for connecting assets and CIs through lifecycle status.

In essence, accessing CSDM involves understanding its data model, enabling the plugin, and then populating and managing data according to its principles, while leveraging the available tools and dashboards within ServiceNow.

What CSDM defines is listed as follows:

- **Standardized service-related terms and relationships**: CSDM provides a common language for describing and linking IT assets to services, users, costs, and other related elements.

- **Best practices for data modeling and management**: It guides how to structure data in the CMDB.
- **Relationship mappings**: CSDM defines how different CIs in the CMDB relate to each other and to services.
- **Service categories/tiers**: It categorizes services into levels like business services, service offerings, and technical services for better alignment between IT and business priorities.
- **Data domains**: CSDM organizes data into specific domains like foundation, design, manage technical services, build, and sell / consume, each supporting different aspects of IT services.

What CSDM does not define are as follows:

- **A one-size-fits-all guide**: While it provides guidance, CSDM needs to be customized to fit an organization's specific needs and services.
- **An automated fix for models in prior implementations**: CSDM will not automatically fix existing data modeling issues; it requires manual effort and adjustments.
- **Code to be installed**: CSDM is a framework, not a piece of software that can be installed.
- **An implementation guide for every ServiceNow product**: It provides guidance on how to use core CMDB tables and relationships, but not detailed implementation steps for every ServiceNow module.

The benefits of CSDM implementation are as follows:

- **Improved data accuracy and consistency**: CSDM's standardized approach ensures consistent and reliable data within the CMDB, reducing issues like duplicates.
- **Better service mapping and visibility**: It enhances the understanding of service dependencies and relationships, improving incident and change management processes.
- **Streamlined IT processes**: By providing a clear framework for managing services and CIs, CSDM improves the efficiency of processes like incident, problem, and change management.
- **Enhanced alignment with business strategies**: It facilitates connecting IT assets and services to business goals, supporting strategic decision-making and digital transformation initiatives.
- **Improved reporting and analysis**: Standardized data enables better reporting and analysis of service performance and utilization.

- **Stronger governance and compliance**: CSDM supports regulatory compliance and data governance through standardized data practices.
- **Reduced costs**: By identifying and eliminating redundant processes, CSDM can help reduce operational overhead and improve resource allocation.
- **Easier upgrades and better utilization of ServiceNow features**: Adhering to CSDM makes it easier to upgrade the ServiceNow platform and leverage new features.

CSDM's latest version 5.0 is a major evolution from 4.0, shifting from an IT-centric to a digital product centric model, expanding scope beyond IT to HR/finance, introducing new product modeling.

CSDM Data Foundations Dashboard provides visibility and monitoring for CMDB data quality and CSDM implementation health.

ServiceNow Discovery uses a multi-phased process to identify devices on a network and update the CMDB with their details. It begins by scanning open ports, classifying devices, identifying them, and then exploring them to gather specific attributes. This process relies on probes, sensors, and patterns, all managed by MID Servers to interact with devices and update the CMDB.

Here is a breakdown of the process:

- **Scanning phase**:
  - o Discovery starts by scanning for open ports on devices in the network using a probe called **Shazzam**.
  - o It identifies potential devices based on the responses received from these ports.
  - o For example, a device responding on port 135 is likely a Windows server.
- **Classification phase**:
  - o Discovery uses information from the scanning phase to determine the device type and OS.
  - o It uses classifiers, which are records specifying which probes to run based on the device type.
  - o For instance, a WMI probe is sent to Windows machines to gather details about the OS.
- **Identification phase**:
  - o This phase determines if a discovered device already exists as a CI in the CMDB.
  - o It uses identification rules to match discovered devices to existing CIs or create new ones if necessary.

- **Exploration phase**:
  - o The exploration phase is launched to gather specific details about the device, such as hardware configuration, installed software, and other attributes.
  - o This information is used to update the corresponding CI in the CMDB.

The key components are as follows:

- **MID Server**: A lightweight application that runs on the target network and acts as a bridge between the ServiceNow instance and the devices being discovered. It executes probes and patterns, sending data back to the instance.
- **Probes**: Scripts that gather data from devices, such as open ports, OS details, and hardware information.
- **Sensors**: Process the data collected by probes and update the CMDB with the information.
- **Patterns**: Used to discover complex applications and their relationships, providing more detailed information than traditional probes.
- **Classifiers**: Determine which probes to run based on the device type and OS.

Overall, ServiceNow Discovery automates the process of identifying devices, gathering their attributes, and updating the CMDB, providing a comprehensive view of the IT infrastructure and its components.

Discovery first takes the Shazzam probe (and then port probes) and places it in a request in the **External Communication Channel** (**ECC**) queue. The MID Server checks the ECC queue, retrieves the discovery request, and runs the probes against the host to discover open ports.

Service Mapping in ServiceNow creates a visual representation of how IT infrastructure components are interconnected to deliver specific business services. It automates the discovery of these components and their relationships, allowing IT teams to understand the dependencies between services, applications, and infrastructure. This helps in troubleshooting, impact analysis, and proactive management of IT services.

Here is a breakdown of how it works:

- **Discovery**:
  - o Service mapping utilizes various discovery techniques (SNMP, WMI, SSH, etc.) to automatically identify and map infrastructure components like servers, databases, and network devices.
  - o It can also discover applications and their relationships to these components.
  - o Discovery can be triggered manually or automatically based on schedules.

- **Identification and mapping**:
  - o Service mapping identifies the relationships between discovered components, such as which server hosts a particular application or which applications connect to a specific database.
  - o It maps these relationships visually, showing how different components contribute to a service.
- **Service definition**:
  - o Users define services by grouping together the relevant infrastructure components and applications.
  - o These services can be modeled from a business perspective (e.g., customer order processing) or a technical perspective (e.g., an application stack).
- **Dependency mapping**:
  - o Service mapping creates a visual representation of the dependencies between the components of a service.
  - o This map shows how changes or issues in one component can impact the overall service.
- **Benefits**:
  - o **Improved troubleshooting**: Quickly identify the root cause of issues by tracing the impact of a problem through the service map.
  - o **Impact analysis**: Assess the potential impact of changes to infrastructure or applications on business services.
  - o **Proactive management**: Identify potential bottlenecks, single points of failure, and other issues before they impact service availability.
  - o **Enhanced visibility**: Gain a comprehensive view of how IT supports business services.
- **Example**:
  - o If there is a service called Online Banking. Service mapping might discover the following: servers hosting the web application, database servers storing customer data, network devices routing traffic, and load balancers distributing traffic.
  - o It would then map these components and show how they are interconnected to deliver the Online Banking service. If a database server fails, service mapping can help identify that the Online Banking service will be impacted.

In ServiceNow, horizontal discovery focuses on identifying and mapping infrastructure components like servers and network devices, while top-down discovery, often facilitated by service mapping, focuses on understanding the relationships between those components and the business services they support. Essentially, horizontal discovery builds the foundation (the what is owned) and top-down discovery reveals how those components work together to deliver specific business services (the how stuff works together).

Here is a more detailed breakdown:

- **Horizontal discovery**:
  - **Focus**: Discovering and mapping infrastructure components such as servers, network devices, storage, and applications within a specific IP range.
  - **Method**: Typically starts with a defined IP range and scans for devices and their configurations.
  - **Output**: Populates the CMDB with CIs and their basic relationships (e.g., runs on relationship between an application and its server).
  - **Example**: Discovering all servers, OSs, and network devices within a given subnet.
- **Top-down discovery (service mapping)**:
  - **Focus**: Mapping the relationships between infrastructure components and the business services they support.
  - **Method**: Starts with a business service (e.g., an email service or a payroll application) and traces the dependencies through the infrastructure to identify all supporting components.
  - **Output**: Creates service maps that show how business services rely on specific infrastructure components, including applications, servers, databases, and network devices.
  - **Example**: Mapping the relationships between a web server, an application server, a database, and a load balancer to understand how they contribute to a website's functionality.

The key differences are as follows:

- **Scope**: Horizontal discovery focuses on the infrastructure, while top-down discovery focuses on the business service layer and its dependencies.
- **Goal**: Horizontal discovery aims to build a comprehensive CMDB inventory, while top-down discovery aims to understand service dependencies and perform impact analysis.
- **Starting point**: Horizontal discovery typically starts with an IP range or network segment, while top-down discovery starts with a business service or entry point.
- **Complexity**: Top-down discovery can be more complex, especially for large and intricate business services, as it requires understanding the relationships between various components.

Upstream and downstream relationships

In essence, horizontal discovery is about finding what is in infrastructure, while top-down discovery is about understanding how that infrastructure supports business services.

The ServiceNow Dependency View offers a powerful graphical representation of the relationships and dependencies between CIs in IT infrastructure. This allows to visually understand how different components interact, and how changes or incidents in one area might impact others.

Within the Dependency View, you can visualize both upstream and downstream dependencies from a selected CI, which serves as the root CI:

- **Upstream**: These are the CIs or services that the root CI relies on. For example, a web server might be dependent on an upstream database or application server. Changes or issues in an upstream component can significantly impact the downstream components.
- **Downstream**: These are the CIs or services that depend on the root CI. For example, a web application might be a downstream dependency of a web server, using its services to function.

The Dependency View typically displays relationships up to a configurable number of levels, both upstream and downstream, providing a comprehensive understanding of the service topology.

Example: For **CI Java Application Server FLX**, the Dependency View is shown as follows. This is termed a tree layout as well.

The following figure shows the CI in a tree layout:

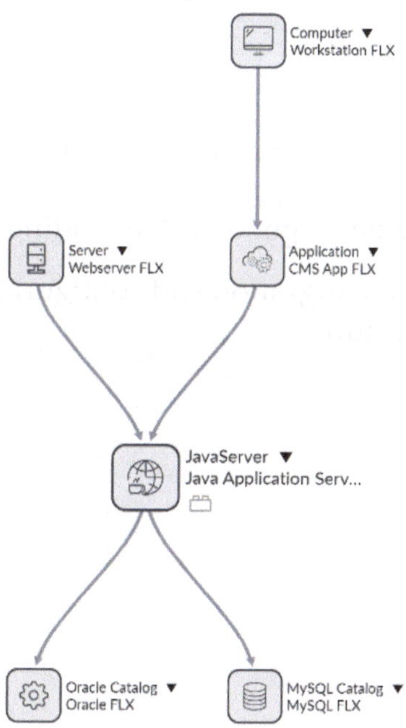

Figure 5.23: CI in tree layout

Different layouts, like flat or tree, can be customized to select how these relationships can be viewed.

The following figure shows the CI in flat layout:

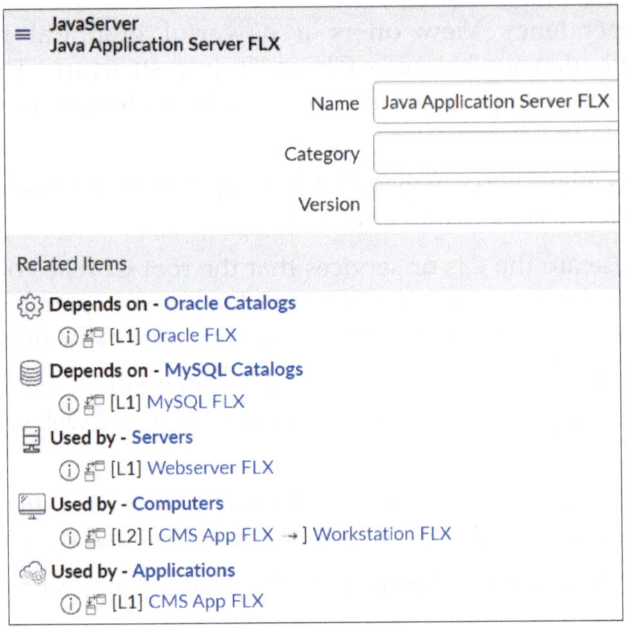

Figure 5.24: CI in flat layout

Conclusion

This chapter covered the concepts of ServiceNow for configuring features of database management, focusing on data schema, application or access control, importing data, CMDB, CSDM, and Dictionary. This provided a good understanding of configuring these features.

The next chapter will cover the data migration and configuration, which will cover 15% of the questions towards the CSA certification.

CHAPTER 6
Data Migration and Integration

Introduction

ServiceNow self-service and automation refers to the process of configuring UI policies, business rules, system update sets, and scripting. UI policy is a client-side rule, business rule is a server-side script based on database operation, system Update Sets are a group of configuration changes that move between instances, and Scripting is using scripts that enhance out-of-the-box capabilities.

This includes the customization of the unique needs of the organization using these ServiceNow features. This section covers these related concepts, covering 15% of CSA questions.

Structure

The chapter covers the following topics:

- UI policies
- Business rules
- Update sets
- Scripting

Objectives

This chapter provides insights about ServiceNow regarding configurations of UI policies, business rules, system update sets, and scripting and customizing the instance for the needs of the organization. This chapter will provide users with the skills to configure ServiceNow for these aspects for the unique needs of the organization.

UI policies

In ServiceNow, a UI policy is a client-side script that dynamically changes the behavior of fields and form sections on a form. It allows administrators to control the visibility, read-only status, and mandatory status of fields based on specific conditions. This helps in enhancing user experience and maintaining data consistency.

The key aspects of UI policies are as follows:

- **Client-side execution**: UI policies run in the user's browser, allowing for real-time updates to the form as users interact with it.
- **Conditions**: UI policies are triggered when specific conditions are met, such as a field value changing or a form loading.
- **Actions**: When the conditions are met, UI policies can perform actions like making fields mandatory, read-only, or hidden.
- **Order of execution**: UI policies execute after client scripts, and their logic overrides conflicting client script logic.

UI policy actions

These actions are the core of UI policies, allowing for setting field attributes like mandatory, visible, and read-only. UI policies primarily control the behavior of form fields (visibility, mandatory, read-only) based on conditions.

UI policy scripts

UI policies can also execute scripts (both client-side) to handle more complex logic.

Reverse if false: This option allows specifying what happens when the conditions of the UI policy are no longer met.

For example, imagine a scenario where one wants the **Resolution Notes** field on an incident form to be mandatory only when the incident state is set to **Resolved**. For this, create a UI policy with the following:

- **Table**: Incident.
- **Condition**: When the **State** field is **Resolved**.
- **UI Policy Action**: Make the **Resolution Notes** field mandatory.

With this UI policy, the **Resolution Notes** field will only be mandatory when the incident is in the **Resolved** state.

To access UI policies in ServiceNow, navigate to **System UI | UI Policies** in the application navigator. Alternatively, can open a record, right-click, go to **Configure**, and select **UI Policies**.

The detailed steps are as follows:

1. Navigate through the application navigator:
    a. Go to **All** (or the appropriate application menu).
    b. Navigate to **System UI**.
    c. Select **UI Policies**.

2. Accessing from a form:
   a. Open any record in a table.
   b. Right-click on the form header.
   c. Go to **Configure**, then select **UI Policies**.
3. Creating a new **UI Policy**:
   a. Follow the navigation steps as outlined above.
   b. Click the **New** button. This will open the **UI Policy form**.
   c. Configure the form:
      i. **Table**: Select the table where the UI policy will apply.
      ii. **Short description**: Provide a clear and concise description of the policy.
      iii. **When to apply**: Define the conditions for when the policy should trigger.
      iv. **UI Policy Actions**: Add actions to specify what should happen when the policy is triggered (e.g., make a field mandatory, read-only, or hidden).
4. Save the UI policy.

The following figure shows **UI Policies**:

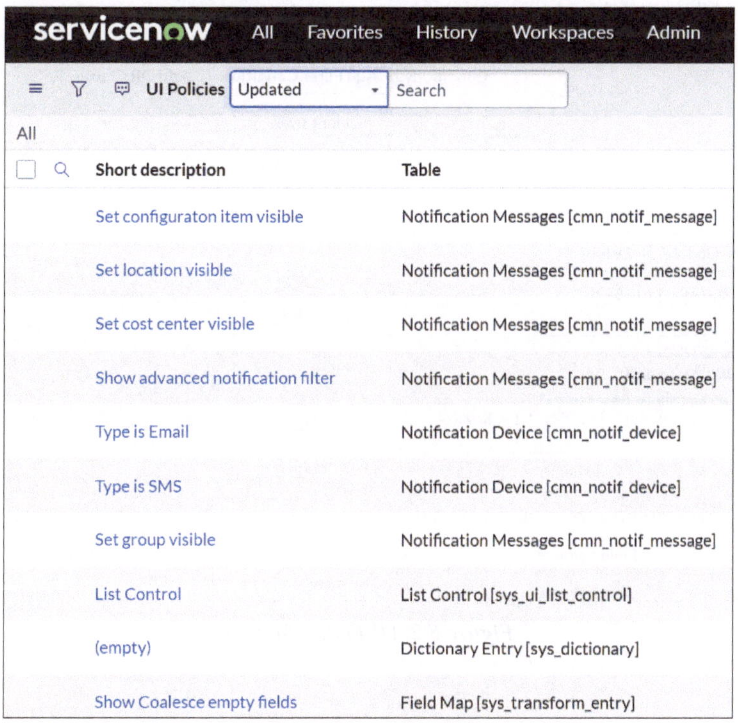

***Figure 6.1**: UI Policies*

UI Policies change fields on a form based on a set of conditions. Use **UI Policies** to show or hide fields, or to make fields mandatory or read-only based on these conditions. A UI policy specifies one or more actions to take when the policy is triggered. First, create the policy. Then add as many actions as necessary. UI policy actions are applied only if all of the following conditions are met:

- The **UI Policy** is **Active**.
- The items in the **Conditions** field evaluate to true.
- The field specified in the **UI Policy Actions** is present on the specified form.

The following figure shows **UI Policy Actions**:

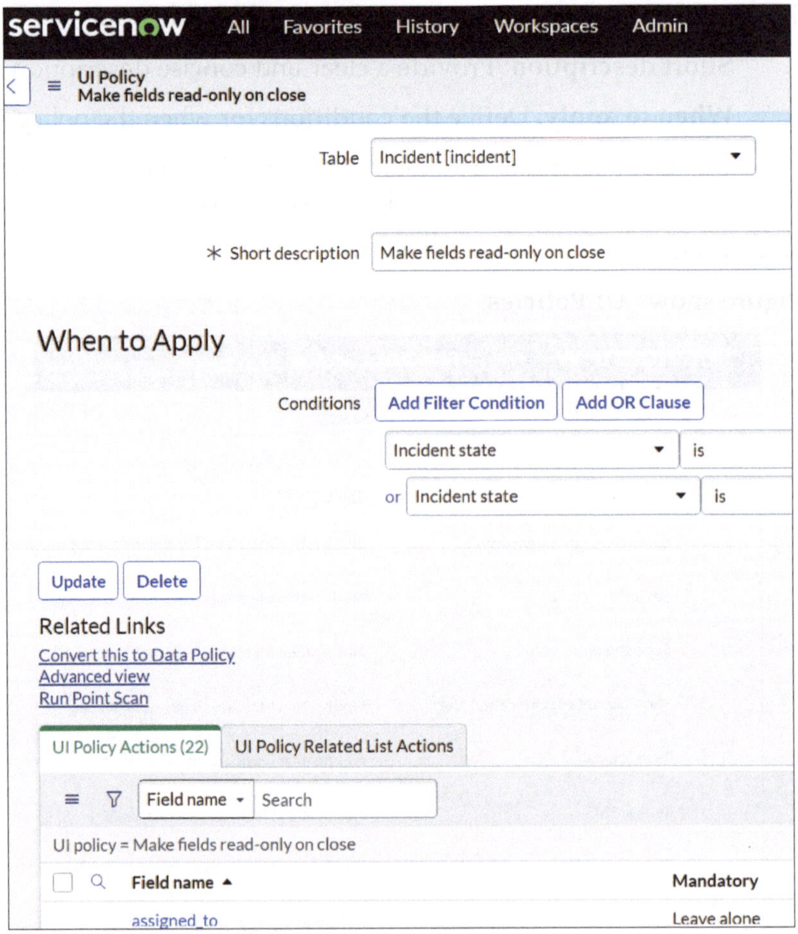

Figure 6.2: UI Policy Actions

The following figures shows creating a **UI policy**:

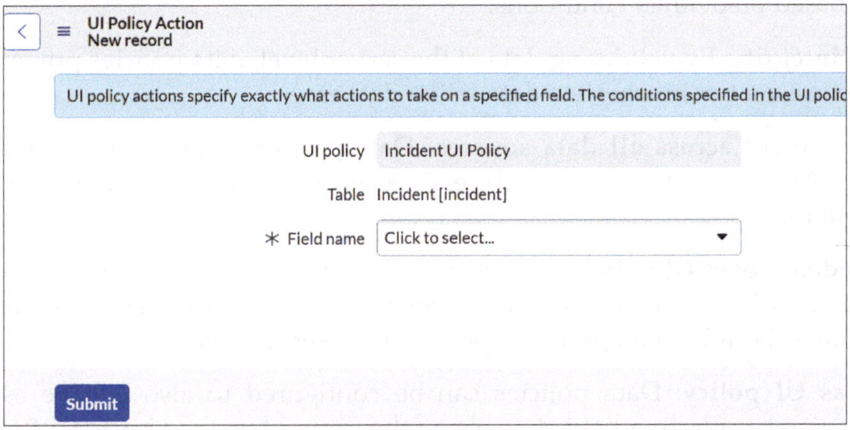

***Figure 6.3**: UI Policy Actions creation*

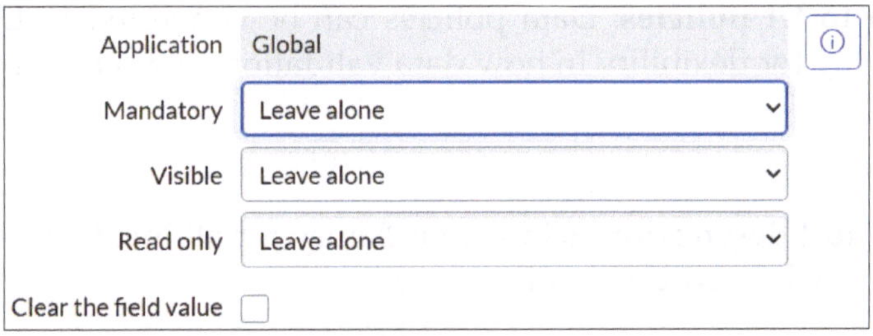

***Figure 6.4**: UI Policy Actions creation -field values set*

The following UI policies can be set for a field:

- **Mandatory** or optional.
- **Visible** or hidden.
- **Read only** or editable.
- **Clearing the field value**.

Checkbox **Clear the field value** is designed to clear the value of the associated field/variable when the main UI policy condition evaluates to true.

Data policy

In ServiceNow, a data policy is a server-side rule that enforces data consistency by validating field values during all table operations, regardless of how the data is entered (UI, APIs, imports). It ensures data integrity by setting fields as mandatory or read-only, and unlike UI policies, it operates at the database level, not just the UI.

The key aspects of data policies in ServiceNow are as follows:

- **Server-side enforcement**: Data policies run on the server, ensuring consistent data validation regardless of the data source or method of entry.

- **Mandatory and read-only fields**: They can make specific fields mandatory or read-only based on defined conditions.
- **Data integrity**: By validating data at the server level, data policies prevent the storage of inconsistent or incomplete data in the database.
- **Enforcement across all data sources**: Data policies apply to data entered through forms, APIs, import sets, and web services, ensuring consistent data validation across the platform.
- **Precedence over UI policies**: When both a data policy and a UI policy apply to a field, the data policy's settings take precedence, especially for mandatory and read-only attributes, because data policies operate at the server level.
- **Use as UI policy**: Data policies can be configured to also behave as UI policies, immediately reflecting field changes on the form when the **Use as UI Policy on client** option is selected, according to ServiceNow developers.
- **Conversion to UI policies**: Data policies can be converted to UI policies, and vice versa, allowing for flexibility in how data validation rules are applied.

Example

Ensuring that the **Short description** field is mandatory for all incident records, regardless of how they are created (UI, import set, API).

In essence, data policies in ServiceNow are crucial for maintaining data quality and consistency across all data entry points by enforcing rules at the server level.

The following figure shows data policy examples:

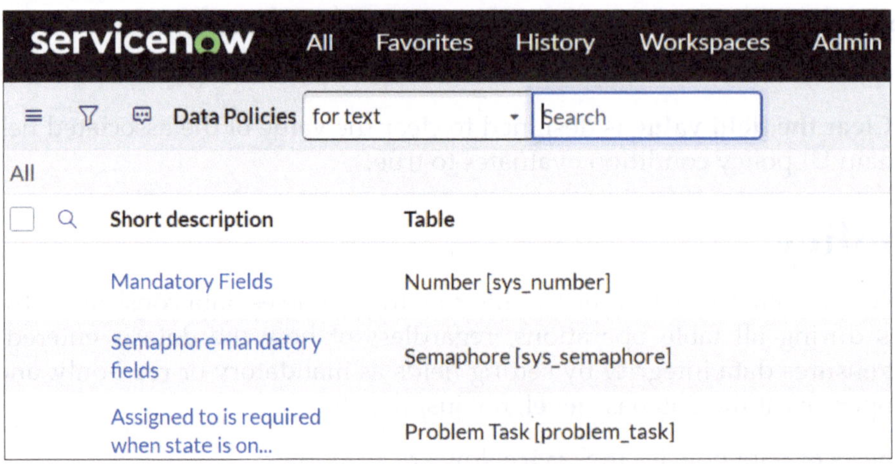

Figure 6.5: Data policy examples

The following figures show **Data Policy**:

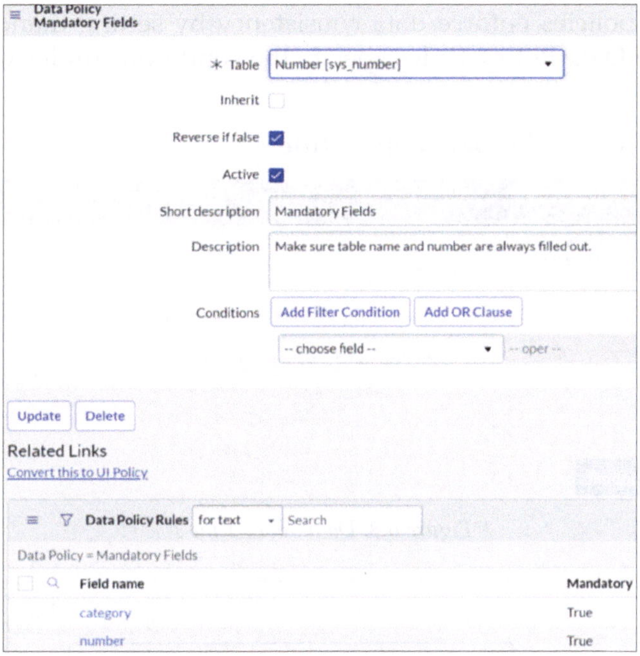

Figure 6.6*: Data Policy 1*

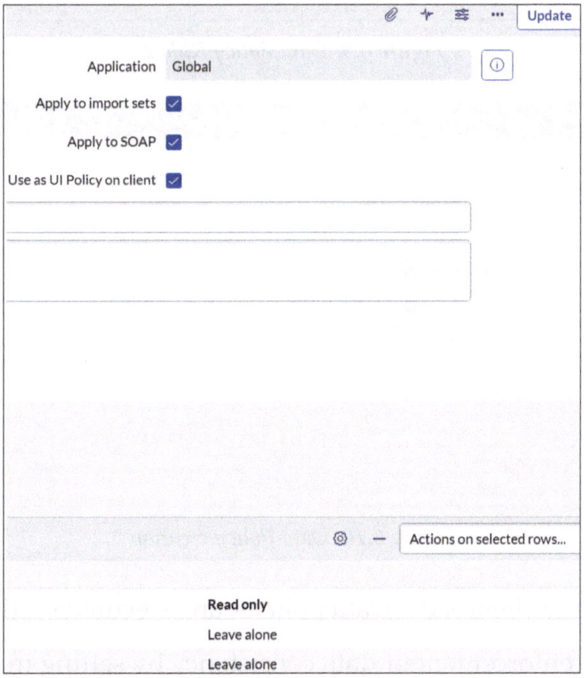

Figure 6.7*: Data Policy 2*

Data policies apply to import set, web services, and form UI.

In ServiceNow, data policies enforce data consistency by setting mandatory and read-only field attributes, while **Data Policy Rules** specify the conditions under which these attributes are applied.

The following figures shows the **Data Policy Rule**:

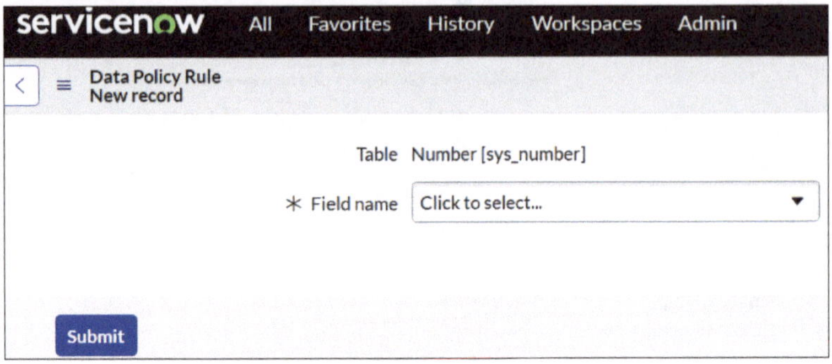

Figure 6.8: Data Policy Rule 1

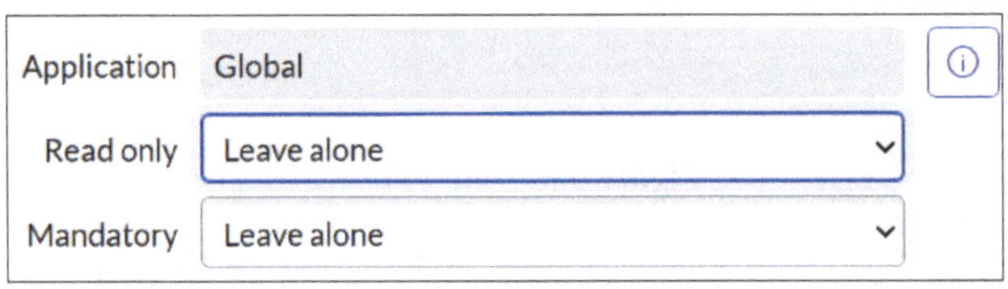

Figure 6.9: Data Policy Rule 2

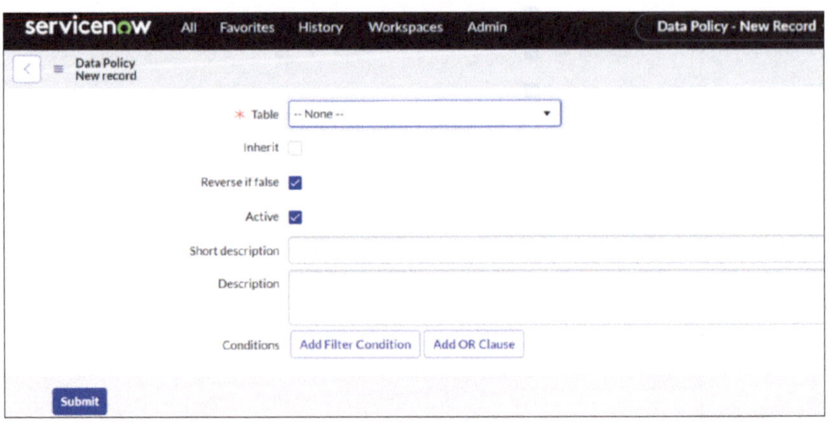

Figure 6.10: Data Policy creation

UI policies are done on the client-side. Data policies are executed on the server-side.

Data policies enable the enforcement of data consistency by setting mandatory and read-only states for fields.

UI action

A UI action allows adding buttons, links, and context menu items on forms and lists, making it possible to create custom on-click actions. The UI action condition is an optional field used to define specific criteria determining when the UI action is visible to the user, via server-side JavaScript code.

In ServiceNow, UI actions are custom actions users can perform on records, appearing as buttons, links, or context menu items on forms and lists. They allow users to trigger specific operations, like creating records, updating fields, or navigating to related pages, directly from the UI. UI actions can be configured to execute either client-side or server-side scripts, or even a combination of both, to perform the desired actions.

UI action types are listed as follows:

- **On forms**: Header left. Header right. Burger menu. Field label context menu. Link. Bottom.
- **On lists**: Header left. Header right. Burger menu. Kebab menu. Column header context menu. Row context menu. Link. Bottom.
- **Other**: Button context menu. Dependency map context menu.

The following figures shows the **UI Action** form:

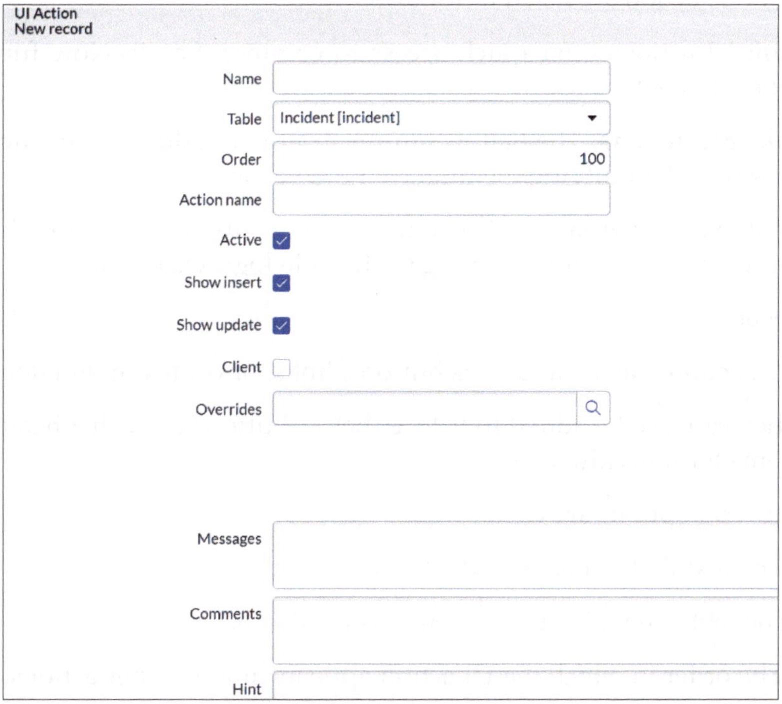

***Figure 6.11**: UI Action form 1*

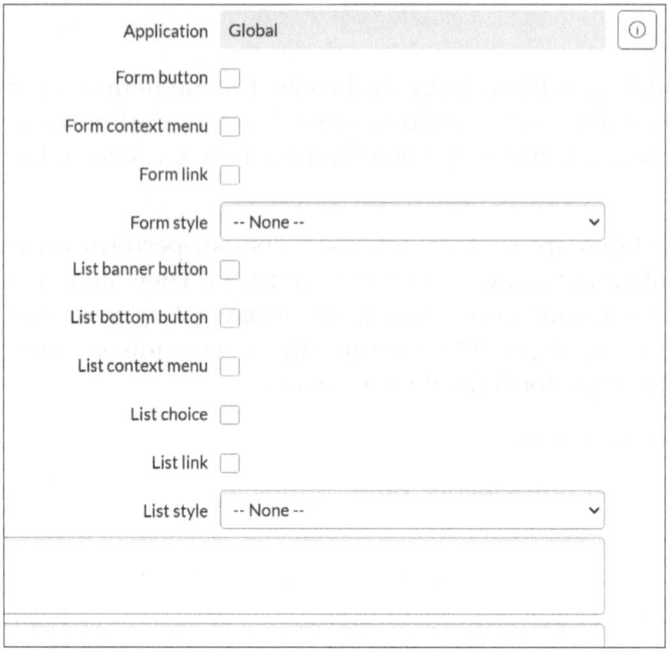

***Figure 6.12**: UI Action form 2*

The advantages of UI action are listed as follows:

- **UI action**: UI actions offer quick access to common ServiceNow functions, making users more efficient.
- **Customizable actions**: They allow administrators to add new functionality to forms and lists without modifying the underlying UI code.
- **Client-side vs. server-side**: UI actions can be configured to run client-side scripts, server-side scripts, or both, allowing for flexible logic execution.

Where they appear:

- **Forms**: UI actions can be added as buttons, links, or context menu items on forms.
- **Lists**: They can also be added to lists, either as buttons in the list header or as context menu items for individual records.

The key configuration options are as follows:

- **Name**: The text that appears on the button or link.
- **Table**: The table on which the UI action is available.
- **Order**: The order in which the UI action appears among other actions.
- **Action name**: A unique name for referencing the UI action in scripts.

- **Client**: Checkbox to enable client-side script execution.
- **Onclick**: Script to execute when the UI action is triggered (client-side).
- **Server**: Script to execute when the UI action is triggered (server-side).
- **Condition**: Optional field to define criteria for when the UI action is visible.

Examples of use cases are provided as follows:

- **Creating a new record**: A button to quickly create a new incident from a problem record.
- **Updating fields**: A button to update the state of an incident to **Resolved**.
- **Navigating to a related record**: A link to open a related change request from an incident.
- **Running custom scripts**: Executing complex logic based on user input or other factors.
- **Adding comments to a record**: A button to add a comment to an incident with a specific message.

A client-side example is provided as follows:

- **Form validation**: Checking if required fields are filled before submitting the form, like ensuring comments are present before **Reopen Incident**.

The server-side example (server) is as follows:

- **Record updates**: Setting a record's state (e.g., "Closed," "Resolved").

Business rules

In ServiceNow, business rules are server-side scripts that execute when specific conditions are met related to database operations like inserting, updating, deleting, or querying records. They are crucial for automating tasks, enforcing data consistency, and improving the user experience.

The key concepts of business rules are as follows:

- **Server-side logic**: Business rules run on the server, unlike client scripts that run in the user's browser, making them suitable for complex operations and data integrity.
- **Conditions and actions**: They are triggered by specific conditions (e.g., when a field changes, when a record is inserted) and execute predefined actions (e.g., updating a field, sending a notification, or preventing an update).
- **Database interactions**: Business rules respond to database operations (insert, update, delete, query) regardless of how the interaction occurs (e.g., through forms, web services, data imports).

The types of business rules are as follows:

- **Before**: Execute logic before the database operation occurs. Useful for modifying field values before they are saved.
- **After**: Execute logic after the database operation completes but before the user sees the updated form.
- **Async**: Run in the background, after the database operation, allowing for faster response times to the user but potentially taking longer to update related records.
- **Display**: Execute when a form is loaded and a record is retrieved from the database. They must finish before the user interacts with the form.
- **Query**: Execute before a database query. Often used to filter or modify the data returned to the user.

The use cases are as follows:

- **Automating tasks**: For example, automatically assigning a task to a user when a specific condition is met.
- **Enforcing data consistency**: Ensuring that certain fields are always populated or that data adheres to specific rules.
- **Customizing the user experience**: Modifying form behavior or displaying specific information based on user roles or data.
- **Integrating with other systems**: Triggering actions in external systems when records are updated.

The best practices are as follows:

- **Enclose scripts in functions**: To avoid conflicts with other scripts.
- **Be specific with conditions**: Define clear conditions for when the business rule should run.
- **Avoid recursion**: Be careful not to create business rules that trigger themselves repeatedly.
- **Consider the impact on performance**: Asynchronous rules can be more efficient for certain tasks.
- Avoid `current.update()` in insert/update business rules because it triggers all business rules again, causing performance issues and potential infinite recursion.

Accessing business rules: Navigate to **System Definition | Business Rules** in the application navigator to view and manage existing business rules.

A business rule is a server-side script that runs when a record is displayed, inserted, deleted, or when a table is queried. Use business rules to automatically change values in form fields when the specified conditions are met.

The following figure shows a **Business Rule**:

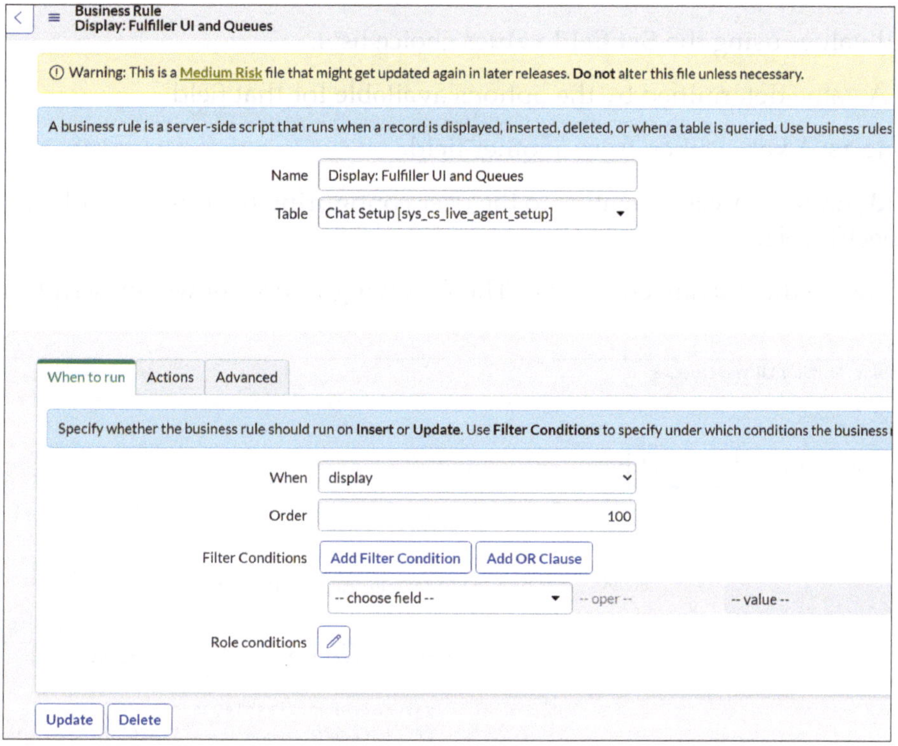

***Figure 6.13**: Business rules*

When to run tab

Specify whether the business rule should run on **Insert** or **Update**. Use **Filter Conditions** to specify under which conditions the business rule should run.

The following figure shows the **Business Rule** configuration:

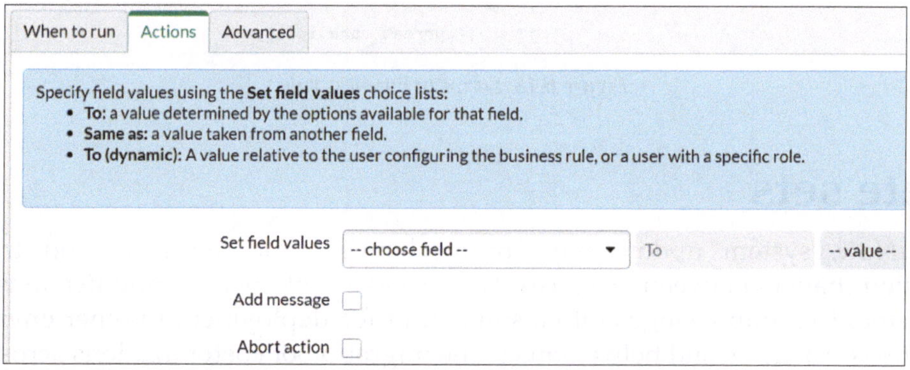

***Figure 6.14**: Business Rule configuration*

Actions

Specify field values using the **Set field values** choice lists:

- **To**: A value determined by the options available for that field.
- **Same as**: A value taken from another field.
- **To (dynamic)**: A value relative to the user configuring the business rule, or a user with a specific role.

Script goes inside the **Advanced** section. The following figure shows the script in a business rule:

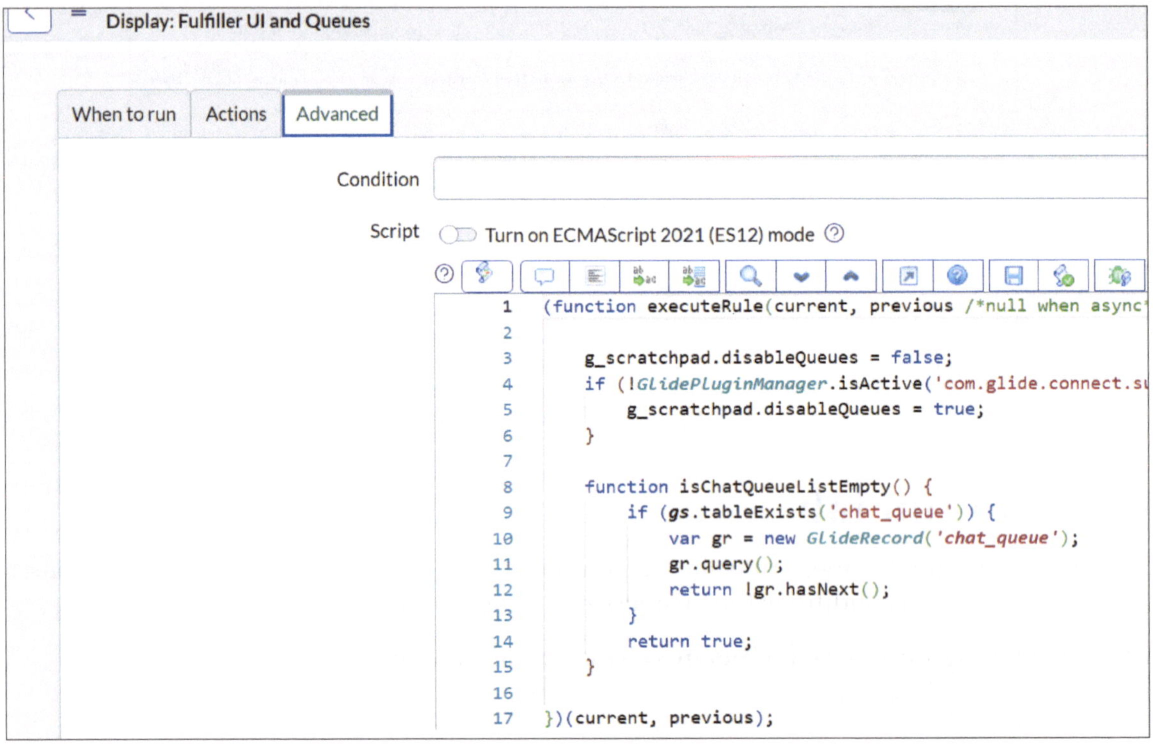

Figure 6.15: Script in business rule

Update sets

In ServiceNow, system update sets are mechanisms for capturing and transferring configuration changes between instances. They act as a container for modifications, allowing administrators to group changes into a single unit for deployment to other environments. This ensures consistency and helps manage the migration of customizations across different instances, like from development to testing and then to production.

An update set in ServiceNow is a group of customizations that can be moved from one instance to another. This includes changes to tables, fields, forms, and scripts, among other things.

An update set is a group of configuration changes that can be moved from one instance to another. This feature allows administrators to group a series of changes into a named set and then move them as a unit to other systems for testing or deployment.

An update set is an XML file that consists of the following:

- A set of record details that uniquely identify the update set.
- A list of configuration changes.
- A state that determines whether another instance can retrieve and apply configuration changes.

In ServiceNow, the primary system table that stores all tracked table changes is the system audit table (**sys_audit**). This table captures audit information whenever a change (insert or update) occurs on tables where auditing is enabled.

The working is as follows:

1. **Auditing enablement**: To track changes for a specific table, the **Audit** checkbox in the dictionary record for that table needs to be set to **true**.
2. **Tracking changes**: Once auditing is enabled, the **sys_audit** table records details about the changes made to fields, including:
    - What was changed (e.g., field values, data).
    - Who made the change (the user or system performing the modification).
    - When the change occurred (date and time).
    - The old and new values for the updated fields.
    - Which record was modified.

Local Update Sets are used within a single instance to capture and organize changes made during development. They serve as a way to track and manage customizations before promoting them to other environments.

To view existing update sets in ServiceNow, navigate to **System Update Sets | Local Update Sets**. This will display a list of all Local Update Sets, including their state (e.g., In Progress, Completed, Loaded, etc.). Then specific update set to view its details and contents can be opened.

Here is a more detailed breakdown:

1. **Navigate to Local Update Sets**: In the application navigator, type `Local Update Sets` in the filter navigator and select **System Update Sets | Local Update Sets**.

2. **Locate the update set**: This will display a list of all Local Update Sets. Then can sort or filter this list to find the specific update set you are interested in.
3. **Open the update set**: Click on the name of the update set to open its form view.
4. **View update set details**: The form view will show information about the update set, such as its state, description, and the user who created it.
5. **View customer updates**: Scroll down to the **Customer Updates** related list to see all the records (e.g., changes to forms, workflows, etc.) captured within that update set.
6. **(Optional) View related links**: Depending on the update set and role, you may see related links like **Show Related Records** or **Live Check**. These can provide further information or tools for managing the update set.

The batching Update Sets are explained as follows:

- Batching allows grouping multiple update sets together, enabling the preview and committing them in bulk.
- It organizes update sets into a parent-child hierarchy to help maintain order and avoid conflicts.
- When the base (parent) update set is committed, the entire batch is committed, simplifying the deployment process.

Dealing with multiple update sets separately can present several challenges and potential problems:

- **Incorrect order of commit**: Committing update sets in the wrong sequence can lead to unexpected behavior and errors, especially if dependencies exist between them.
- **Missing update sets**: It is easy to inadvertently leave out one or more update sets during the migration process, potentially leading to incomplete functionality in the target instance.
- **Conflict resolution complexity**: Managing conflicts across numerous separate update sets can be time-consuming and prone to error, especially when multiple developers are involved.
- **Difficult backouts**: If you need to revert changes, backing out multiple, unrelated Update Sets can be a complex and risky process. Batching allows for backing out specific child update sets or the entire batch.
- **Manual tracking**: Without batching, you might need to manually track the order and relationships between Update Sets, increasing the chance of mistakes.

In summary, batching Update Sets provides a structured and efficient way to manage and deploy changes, mitigating the risks associated with handling multiple update sets individually.

Captured and not captured in update sets

In ServiceNow, update sets primarily capture configuration data such as customizations to tables, fields, forms, and scripts, but they generally do not capture data records like incidents, problems, or change requests. Scheduled jobs, users, groups, and roles are also not automatically included.

What is not captured:

- **Data records**: Tables like incidents, problems, change requests, and any records created by users are not captured.
- **Users, groups, and roles**: These are considered foundation data and are not included in Update Sets.
- **Scheduled jobs**: Scheduled jobs are not automatically captured.
- **Homepages and dashboards**: These are also generally not captured.
- **Certain tables**: Tables without the **update_synch** attribute or those not extending **sys_metadata** are not captured, like the knowledge base table.
- **Unpublished workflows**: Only published workflows are captured in update sets.

Uncaptured data records, users, groups, and roles can be captured using records exported through export to XML from list or form view and then importing XML to another instance.

Instance clone: For moving large numbers of changes and data across the entire instance, the most comprehensive method is to perform a instance clone.

Many administrators leverage a custom **Include in Update Set** or **Force into Update Set** UI action that can be added to forms. If available in your instance, this provides a simple point-and-click way to add a specific record to your current update set from the record's form or list view. This method is used only for specific records and data modifications. Not recommended for large data changes.

Export

To manually export data in ServiceNow, right-click on a column header within a list view and select the **Export** option, then choose the desired file format like **Excel**, **CSV**, **XML**, **JSON**, or **PDF**. Alternatively, export data directly from a URL by crafting a specific URL that includes the instance, table, export format, and any necessary query parameters.

Here is a breakdown of the manual export methods:

1. Exporting from a list view:
   a. Navigate to the desired table's list view (e.g., **Incident | All**).

   b. Right-click on any column header.

   c. Select **Export** and choose the desired file format (**Excel**, **CSV**, **XML**, **JSON**, or **PDF**).

2. Exporting directly from a URL:

   a. This method allows for more dynamic exports, such as from scripts or web services.

   b. Construct a URL with the following components:

      i. **Instance URL**: `https://<instance name>.service-now.com/`

      ii. **Table or list**: For example, `incident_list.do`

      iii. **Export format processor**: ?CSV or ?XML

      iv. **Optional**: Query and sort order using URL parameters: `&sysparm_query=""`

3. **Export sets**:

   a. For more complex scenarios or large datasets, one can configure export sets to manage and automate the export process.

   b. Export sets act as containers for specific table data that one needs to export.

   c. This is helpful for scheduled exports or when dealing with large volumes of data that might exceed the default limits of other export methods.

Creating a new update set

Creating and setting a new update set as current in ServiceNow. To create a new update set and set it as the current working set in ServiceNow, follow these steps:

1. **Create a new update set**:

   a. Navigate to **System Update Sets | Local Update Sets**.

   b. Click **New** to create a new update set.

   c. Provide a descriptive **Name** and an optional **Description** that accurately reflects the purpose of this update set.

2. **Set the update set as current**:

   a. Once the new update set is created, open the record.

   b. Click the **Make This My Current Set Related Link**. This ensures that all subsequent configuration changes made are captured within this specific update set, not the default one.

3. **Begin making changes**:
   a. With the new update set selected as current, any modifications one makes to forms, lists, workflows, business rules, or other configurations will be automatically recorded within it.
   b. Remember to save or submit forms and configurations to ensure they are captured in the update set.

Important points to be noted are as follows:

- If you do not have the update set picker visible in the header, you can enable it by navigating to **System Settings | Developer** and checking the **Show update set picker in header** checkbox.
- Setting an update set as current allows to bundle related changes together for easier tracking and migration between ServiceNow instances, such as from development to testing or production environments.
- Always one should ensure that they are working within the correct update set before making any configuration changes to avoid capturing changes in the wrong set or accidentally using the default set.

Here is how to mark an update set as complete and the risks associated with reopening a completed set:

1. Navigate to **System Update Sets | Local Update Sets** in the development instance.
2. Open the update set wish to be completed.
3. Change the status of the update to **Complete**.

Risks in reopening a completed update set

While it is technically possible to reopen a completed update set by changing its state back to **In Progress**, it is generally discouraged and carries significant risks, especially if the update set has already been retrieved or committed to other instances.

Here is a breakdown of the risks:

- **Inconsistent deployments**: If a completed update set is reopened, modified, and then promoted again, it can lead to inconsistencies in the target instance if the initial version was already deployed or if other changes have been introduced independently.
- **Conflicts and collisions**: Reopening and modifying a completed update set increases the chance of conflicts with other update sets or existing configurations on the target instance.
- **Lost changes and version control issues**: Reopening a completed update set after it has been retrieved by another instance can lead to difficulties in ensuring the latest

changes are captured and deployed correctly, as the retrieved version may not reflect the reopened and updated set.

- **Breach of process and potential for errors**: Reopening a completed update set can violate best practices and potentially disrupt a structured deployment process. It is harder to track changes, especially if multiple developers are involved.
- **Unexpected behavior in target instances**: The changes made to a reopened update set might interact unexpectedly with existing configurations in target instances, leading to bugs or unintended consequences that are harder to troubleshoot.

In short, it is safer and generally considered a better practice to avoid reopening completed Update Sets. If you need to make further changes to a previously completed set of updates, the recommended approach is to create a new update set to capture those new changes and deploy them separately. This helps maintain clear version control, simplifies troubleshooting, and reduces the risk of deployment issues.

To commit an update set in ServiceNow, you need to first preview the update set to identify any potential issues, then resolve those issues, and finally, commit the changes to the target instance.

Here is a more detailed breakdown:

1. **Locate and open the update set**:
   a. Navigate to **Local Update Sets** in the ServiceNow instance.
   b. Find the update set you want to commit and open it.
2. **Preview the update set**:
   a. Click the **Live Check** button to analyze the changes and identify potential problems.
   b. Alternatively, one can click **Run Preview** to perform a more in-depth analysis.
   c. Review the **Update Set Preview Problems** related list for any issues.
3. **Address preview errors**:
   a. If there are errors in the preview, one needs to address them before committing.
   b. This may involve modifying the update set, fixing data issues, or adjusting configurations.
4. **Commit the update set**:
   a. Once the preview is clear of errors, one can commit the update set.
   b. Click **Commit Update Set** to apply all changes in the update set to the instance.
   c. If the update set is very large, the commit process might take some time.

d. The UI action will set the update set state to **Committed**, but the actual process might still be running in the background.

e. Ensure to check the commit progress in the logs to confirm completion.

Important considerations are provided as follows:

- **Preview is crucial**: Always preview an update set before committing to production to avoid unexpected issues.
- **Batching Update Sets**: For multiple update sets, consider creating batches by setting the parent update set to group them together.
- **Performance impact**: Committing large update sets can cause a temporary performance impact due to cache flushes.
- **Version compatibility**: Ensure compatibility when moving update sets between different versions or patches.
- **Domain support**: When using domain support, ensure the correct domain is selected to avoid issues with the commit process.

Scope in update sets

To ensure proper functionality in ServiceNow, particularly when working with scoped applications, it is crucial to verify that the application scope is set to **Global** and the update set is set to **Default [Global]** before continuing. This configuration ensures that changes are captured in the correct context and can be migrated between instances without encountering scope-related errors.

Here is a breakdown of why this is important:

- **Application scope**:
    - o **Global scope**: Represents the base level of the ServiceNow instance and encompasses all applications and configurations. When working with the global scope, making changes affects the entire instance.
    - o **Scoped applications**: These are self-contained units of functionality with their own defined boundaries. They prevent unintended interference with other parts of the system.
    - o **Switching scopes**: When working with scoped applications, it is essential to switch to the correct application scope using the application picker in the header.
- **Update sets**:
    - o **Update sets**: Act as containers for changes made to the instance. They track configuration changes like forms, scripts, and other customizations.

- **Default update set**: Each scope has a default update set (e.g., **Default [Global]** for the global scope).
- **Scope consistency**: When committing Update Sets, it is critical to be in the same scope as the update set, especially when dealing with manually added records, to avoid scope-related errors.
- **Global default update set**: Avoid making significant changes to the global default update set, as it provides system functionality.

- **Best practices**:
  - **Verify scope**: Before making changes, always confirm that the application scope is set to the desired scope (global or a specific scoped application).
  - **Use the update set picker**: Utilize the update set picker to select the correct update set for particular changes.
  - **Scoped ACLs**: Be aware of the potential issues with scoped **access control lists** (**ACLs**) and how they can affect cross-scope access.
  - **Parent update sets**: For complex deployments involving multiple scopes, consider using parent Update Sets to manage the migration of changes

To commit an update set in a higher ServiceNow instance after retrieving it from a lower instance, navigate to **System Update Sets | Retrieved Update Sets**, select the update set, preview it, and then commit it. Ensure the user retrieving the update set has the necessary admin role and that the update source is correctly configured.

Details are provided as follows:

- Change the update set **State** from **In Progress** to **Complete** and save the record in the lower instance.
- Retrieve the update set:
  - **Locate the update source**: In the instance where one wants to commit the update set, they need to navigate to **System Update Sets | Update Sources**. Open the record for the instance from which the update set is retrieved.
  - **Verify user permissions**: Check which user is configured as the update source. Then, verify that this user has the admin role on both the source and target instances.
  - **Retrieving**: Go to **System Update Sets | Retrieved Update Sets** and select the desired update set.
  - **Preview the update set**: Before committing, it is best practice to preview the update set to identify potential conflicts or issues.

Automated Test Framework

The ServiceNow **Automated Test Framework** (**ATF**) is a built-in tool that allows users to automate the testing of applications, customizations, and configurations within the ServiceNow platform. It enables users to create, execute, and manage automated tests directly within ServiceNow, reducing manual testing efforts and improving application quality.

The benefits of using ATF are as follows:

- **Reduces manual testing**: ATF automates repetitive and time-consuming manual testing processes, freeing up resources for more strategic tasks.
- **Improves application quality**: By automating tests, ATF helps ensure that applications and customizations function correctly, reducing the risk of defects and improving overall quality.
- **Accelerates testing**: ATF allows for the rapid execution of tests, speeding up the testing process and enabling faster deployments.
- **Enhances regression testing**: ATF is particularly useful for regression testing, allowing users to quickly verify that new changes or updates have not broken existing functionality.
- **Reduces errors**: Automation reduces the potential for human error, leading to more reliable test results.
- **Enables reusability**: Tests created in ATF can be reused across different environments and after updates, saving time and effort.
- **Facilitates collaboration**: ATF can be used by developers, testers, and even business stakeholders to collaborate on testing efforts.
- **Provides detailed reporting**: ATF generates detailed reports on test results, allowing users to easily identify and address any issues.
- **Supports scheduled testing**: Tests can be scheduled to run at specific times, including during off-peak hours, further streamlining the testing process.
- **Reduces risk**: By identifying potential issues early in the development cycle, ATF helps reduce the risk of deploying faulty applications.
- **Cost-effective**: While custom test frameworks can be expensive, ATF is a built-in tool, making it a cost-effective solution for test automation.
- **Integrates with other tools**: ATF can be integrated with other tools like *Jenkins*, *Selenium*, or *Jira* to enhance testing workflows.

The following figure shows ATF **Tests**:

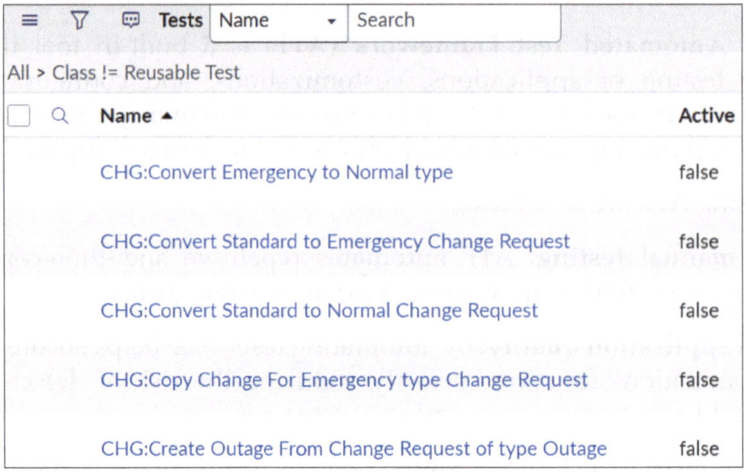

Figure 6.16: ATF Tests

The following figure shows the ATF menu:

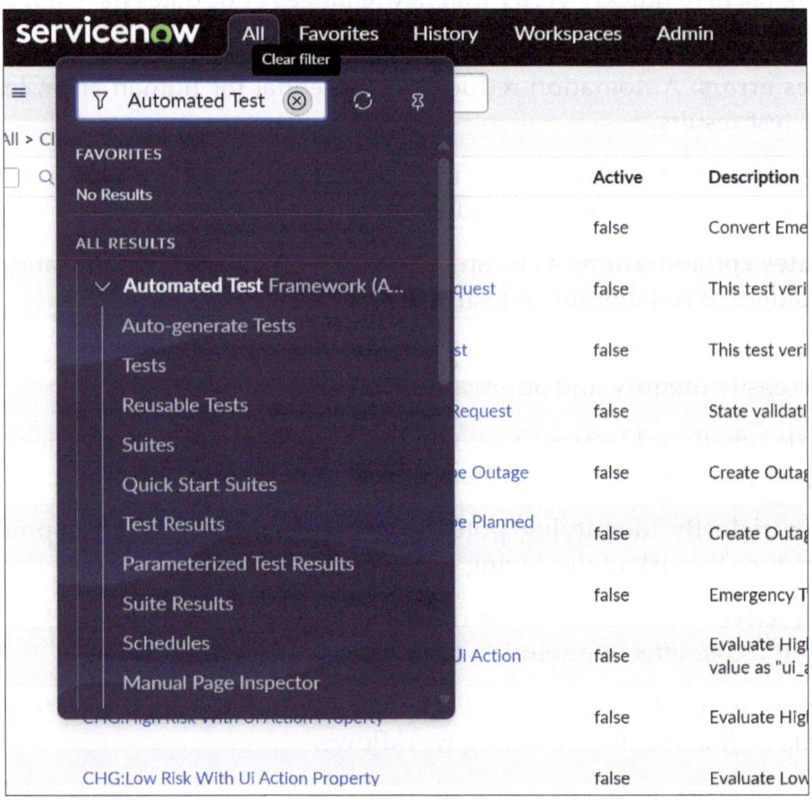

Figure 6.17: ATF menu

Common ATF use cases and examples are as follows:

- **Incident management**: Testing creation, assignment, resolution, and notifications for incidents.
- **Change management**: Validating change requests from creation through approval, implementation, and closure.
- **Service catalog**: Testing order flows, approvals, and fulfillment for requested items.
- **User experience**: Impersonating users to test roles, permissions, and UI interactions.
- **Workflow automation**: Ensuring complex business logic and automated steps execute correctly.

Available suites and modules

ATF can test any module that uses standard ServiceNow UI/logic, including:

- **IT service management (ITSM)**: Incident, problem, change, request, CMDB.
- **Customer service management (CSM)**: Case creation, routing, and resolution.
- **HR Service Delivery (HRSD)**: Employee onboarding, case management.
- **Security operations (SecOps)**: Security incident response, vulnerability response.
- **IT asset management (ITAM)**: Asset lifecycle processes.

Key ATF components are provided as follows:

- **Test suites**: Containers for related tests, often scoped to an application.
- **Tests**: Individual test cases with steps, like "Open Form," "Impersonate," or "Submit".
- **Test steps**: Actions performed within a test, like validating fields or querying records.

App Engine Studio

ServiceNow's **App Engine Studio (AES)** is a low-code development platform that enables users to build and deploy custom applications within the ServiceNow environment. It simplifies and accelerates application development by providing a visual interface, pre-built templates, and automated tools. This allows users, including those with limited technical expertise, to create and customize applications for various needs, such as automating business processes, streamlining workflows, and enhancing user experiences.

The key benefits of AES are as follows:

- **Low-code development**: AES reduces the need for extensive coding, making it accessible to users with varying technical skill levels.
- **Rapid application development**: It provides pre-built templates and a visual interface, enabling users to quickly develop and deploy applications.

- **Flexibility and customization**: AES offers tools for specifying data, experiences (web and mobile), and automation aspects, allowing for tailored application development.
- **Improved user experience**: AES provides tools for building custom user interfaces and workflows, leading to enhanced user experiences.
- **Streamlined workflows**: It allows for the automation of business processes, reducing manual errors and improving efficiency.
- **Enhanced collaboration**: AES facilitates team collaboration during the application development process.
- **Cost reduction**: By simplifying development and enabling automation, AES can help reduce development costs and time.
- **Security and compliance**: AES offers robust security features and supports compliance with industry regulations.
- **Scalability**: AES allows for easy scaling of applications to meet changing traffic demands.
- **Integration capabilities**: AES integrates with various ServiceNow components and external systems, enabling comprehensive solutions.
- **AI-powered tools**: AES incorporates AI-based tools for tasks like incident detection and workflow automation.

To access AES in ServiceNow, log in to the instance and navigate to it through the application navigator or by using the AES application.

The following figure shows **App Engine Studio**:

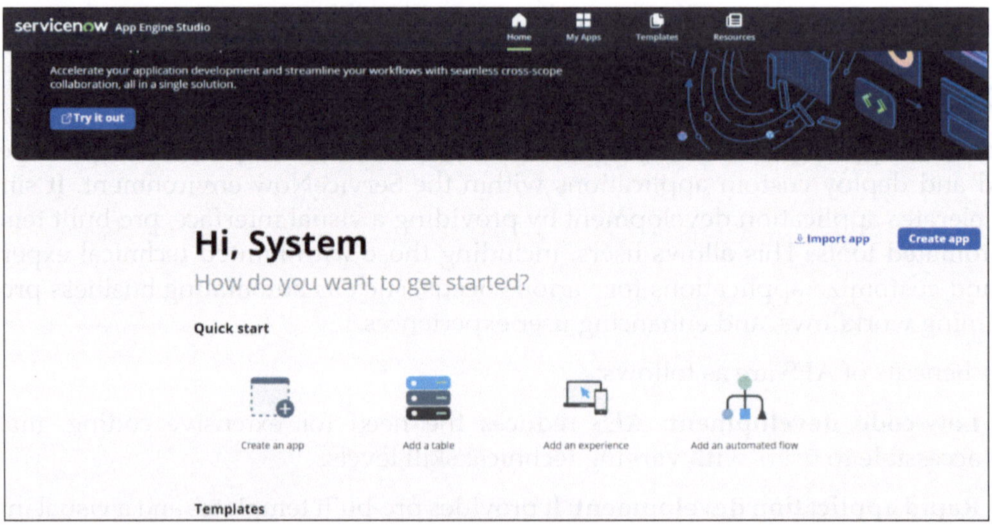

Figure 6.18: AES

The explanation is as follows:

- **Core plugin**: **`com.snc.app-engine-studio`** (AES).
- **Related plugin**: Workspace Builder (for creating workspaces within AES).
- **Installation role**: admin (to install and activate plugins).
- **User roles**:
  - **`admin`** (Full control).
  - **`sn_app_eng_studio.user`** (Standard AES user).

Delegated development

Delegated development is also known as **designated developers** in ServiceNow.

Delegated development in ServiceNow empowers organizations to distribute development and deployment responsibilities without granting full administrative access to all developers. This fosters collaboration and innovation while maintaining control over the ServiceNow platform.

The key concepts are as follows:

- **Delegation**: Allows system administrators or application-specific administrators to designate specific users or groups as delegated developers.
- **Limited privileges**: Delegated developers operate with a reduced set of permissions compared to full administrators, enhancing security and minimizing risk.
- **Application-specific focus**: Permissions are assigned at the application level, granting delegated developers access only to the resources and functionalities relevant to their assigned application.

The benefits are as follows:

- **Increased development agility**: Empowering a broader range of individuals to participate in development accelerates application creation and enhances responsiveness to business needs.
- **Enhanced security**: Administrators can control which application files and functionalities delegated developers can access and modify, limiting the potential impact of errors or malicious activity.
- **Innovation and collaboration**: By decentralizing development, organizations can tap into a wider pool of talent and foster a more collaborative development environment, potentially leading to novel solutions.
- **Reduced backlogs**: Delegated development allows a team to tackle more development tasks concurrently, reducing backlogs and enabling quicker delivery of applications and functionalities.

Permissions and control

Administrators have granular control over the permissions granted to delegated developers. These permissions can include access to specific areas and functionalities within an application.

Examples of access that can be granted include:

- All file types
- Reporting
- Service Catalog
- Service Portal
- Manage ACLs and roles
- Managing other developers
- Integrations
- Workflow
- Flow Designer
- Tables and forms
- Scripting
- Deployment permissions

Through careful configuration of these permissions, administrators can empower development teams while maintaining the security and integrity of the platform.

Example scenario

The safety department example scenario is explained as follows:

1. **The need**: The safety department has a backlog of small improvements for its custom safety application, but IT is busy.
2. **The admin action**: An admin goes to the Safety App's Studio, finds the **Manage Developers** section, and grants *Luke Wilson* (a safety team member) delegated development permissions for only the Safety app.
3. **Luke's new powers**: Luke gets roles allowing him to:
    - Add fields (like a **Project** checkbox) to tables.
    - Design forms and basic layouts.
    - Create reports.
4. **What Luke cannot do**: He cannot touch core system scripts, ACLs, or other global applications, ensuring governance.
5. **Result**: Luke logs in, opens the Safety app in Studio (seeing only that app), adds the checkbox, and saves it, all within minutes, without impacting the broader platform.

Scripting

ServiceNow scripting allows users to extend platform functionality using JavaScript to customize behavior, automate processes, and integrate with other systems. It involves both client-side and server-side scripting, utilizing the Glide API for ServiceNow-specific interactions.

The key concepts in ServiceNow scripting are as follows:

- **Client-side scripting**: Executes in the user's browser and handles user interface interactions, form behavior, and validation. Examples include Client Scripts, UI Policies, and UI actions.
- **Server-side scripting**: Executes on the ServiceNow server and handles business logic, database interactions, and integration with other systems. Examples include business rules, script includes, and scheduled jobs.
- **JavaScript**: The primary scripting language used in ServiceNow, extended with ServiceNow-specific APIs.
- **Glide API**: A collection of ServiceNow classes and methods for interacting with the platform, such as GlideRecord for database manipulation and GlideSystem for system utilities.

Scripting areas in ServiceNow are as follows:

- **Client scripts**: Triggered by user actions (e.g., form load, field changes) and used for actions like showing/hiding fields, adding messages, or showing alerts.
- **UI policies**: Rules that dynamically change form behavior without scripting, often used in conjunction with UI policy actions and scripts.
- **Business rules**: Server-side scripts that execute when records are created, updated, or deleted, often used to automate actions based on record changes.
- **Script includes**: Reusable server-side code that can be called by other scripts, often used for functions or classes.
- **UI actions**: Client-side or server-side scripts that define actions users can take on forms or lists.
- **Scheduled jobs**: Server-side scripts that run at specified times or intervals, often used for automated tasks.

The best practices are as follows:

- Follow technical best practices for writing manageable, efficient, and scalable code.
- Use small, modular components to make code easier to read and maintain.
- Consider the scope of scripts (global or scoped) and whether they are client-side or server-side.
- Utilize the Glide API effectively for interacting with the platform.
- Follow ServiceNow's scripting guidelines and documentation.

In ServiceNow, a client script is a piece of JavaScript code that runs on the client-side, meaning within the user's web browser, rather than on the server. These scripts are used to enhance the user interface by manipulating form elements, validating user input, and automating certain actions based on user interactions.

Here is a more detailed explanation:

- **What it does**:
  - **Form manipulation**: Client scripts can modify the visibility, read-only state, or other properties of form fields or sections based on user actions or data.
  - **Input validation**: They can validate data entered by the user in a field before the form is submitted, ensuring data quality and consistency.
  - **Dynamic updates**: Client scripts can automatically populate fields or trigger actions based on changes in other fields, providing a more responsive and user-friendly experience.
  - **Client-side logic**: They allow for the execution of JavaScript code directly in the browser, enabling real-time interactions and immediate feedback to the user.
- **Types of client scripts**:
  - **onload**: Runs when a form is initially loaded.
  - **onChange**: Runs when the value of a specific field on the form changes.
  - **onSubmit**: Runs when a form is submitted.
  - **OnCellEdit**: Runs when a cell value in a list is edited.
- **Example use cases**:
  - **Auto-populating a field**: When a user selects a category, the subcategory field can be automatically populated with relevant options.
  - **Hiding a field**: If a user is not in a specific role, a field can be hidden from them.
  - **Validating email addresses**: A client script can check if the entered email address has a valid format before the form is submitted.
  - **Showing a message**: When a field value changes, a message can be displayed to the user, providing feedback or guidance.

The key benefits are as follows:

- **Improved user experience**: Client scripts make forms more interactive and responsive, providing immediate feedback to the user.
- **Reduced server load**: By performing validations and updates on the client-side, client scripts reduce the number of requests to the server.

- **Dynamic form behavior** Client scripts enable dynamic form behavior, adapting to user input and data changes.

Some important considerations are as follows:

- **Performance**: While powerful, poorly written client scripts can negatively impact form loading times and overall performance. It is crucial to follow best practices for client scripting.
- **Security**: Client scripts should be carefully designed to avoid security vulnerabilities, especially when dealing with sensitive data.
- **Server-side vs client-side**: Client scripts are for client-side interactions, while server-side scripts (like business rules) handle server-side logic and data processing.

The following figure shows an example of the usage of scripting:

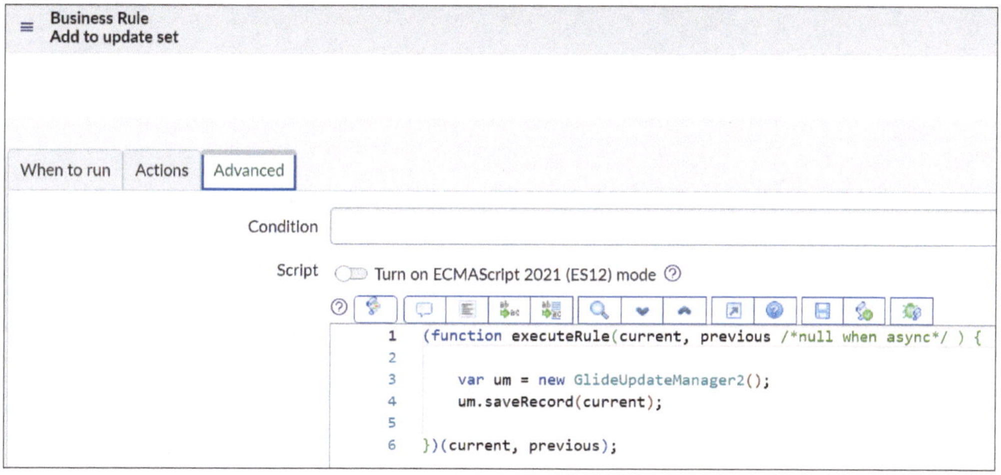

***Figure 6.19**: Scripting example*

In ServiceNow, the Glide API refers to a collection of JavaScript APIs used for scripting and interacting with the platform, primarily for server-side operations. These APIs allow developers to access and manipulate data, interact with the user interface, and automate various processes within the ServiceNow instance.

Conclusion

This chapter covered the concepts of ServiceNow for configuring features of UI policies, business rules, system Update Sets, and scripting. This provided a good understanding of configuring these features.

The next chapter will cover the ServiceNow admins' responsibilities through case studies. These case studies will provide an idea of the work that is performed by admins during the ServiceNow administration.

Chapter 7
Case Studies CSA

Introduction

ServiceNow administrators do the core work of maintaining ServiceNow instances in an organization. This chapter demonstrates ServiceNow admins' responsibilities through case studies.

Structure

The topic covered is as follows:

- Case studies CSA

Objectives

This chapter provides case studies for CSA ServiceNow administrator work and tasks in organizations. ServiceNow admins play a crucial role in the IT operations of the organization. They manage activities including user administration, platform administration, including managing jobs, system upgrade functionalities, monitoring, and maintaining the platform.

Case studies CSA

Let us look at some case studies for CSA, providing an outline of activities performed by them for the organization.

Setup users, roles, and group for a company

In a company, the ServiceNow team has started to setup ServiceNow as admin, ServiceNow users, groups, and roles, focusing on optimizing access and security through best practices like assigning roles to groups instead of individual users.

User groups are created with users aligned together into individual groups. Say Service Desk Tier 1 Group, Service Desk Tier 2 Group, and Service Desk Tier 3 Group.

ServiceNow roles can refer to either the user access roles that define permissions within the platform or the job roles of individuals who manage and develop on the platform. User roles grant specific permissions for tasks like submitting incidents or creating applications, while job roles like system administrator, developer, or business analyst describe a user's function and responsibilities in managing the ServiceNow instance and its various applications.

The user roles are as follows:

- **Standard user**: Can submit and view the status of their own incidents and requests, and access the knowledge base.
- **ITIL user**: Has agent skills and can manage tickets, read problems, and work on changes.
- **Admin**: Has full control over the instance, including user administration, configuration, and system maintenance.

There are predefined built-in roles available from the out-of-the-box ServiceNow.

The following figure shows a sample of predefined **Roles** from out-of-the-box:

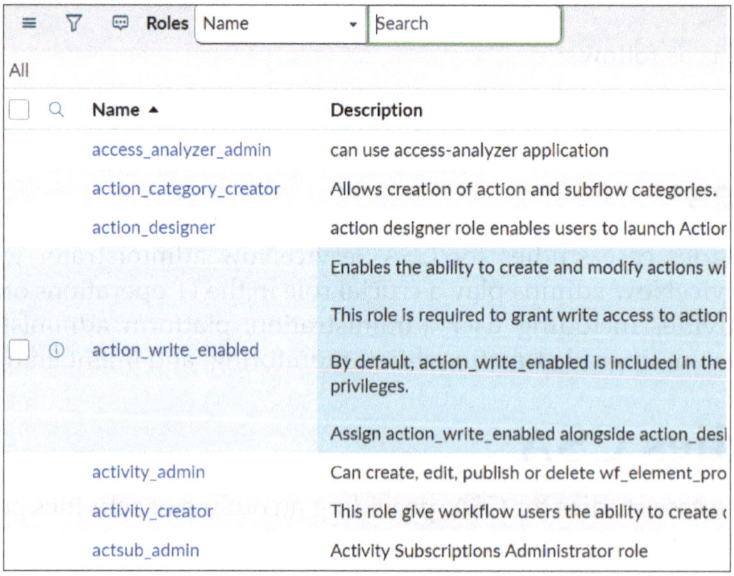

***Figure 7.1**: Role administration*

The job roles are as follows:

- **ServiceNow administrator**: Manages user roles, groups, and permissions. They also perform system maintenance and upgrades.
- **ServiceNow developer**: Builds and customizes applications on the platform, often specializing in a particular module.
- **Business analyst**: Gathers requirements, designs solutions, and bridges the gap between business needs and technical implementation.

- **ServiceNow architect**: Designs the overall structure and strategy of the ServiceNow implementation, ensuring it aligns with business objectives.
- **ServiceNow manager**: Oversees the ServiceNow platform team, strategy, and governance.

They work together in the following manner:

- A user's job role (like developer) might be assigned a collection of user roles (like **admin** and **sn_sb.admin**).
- User roles are collections of permissions, which are granted to a user either directly or through group membership.
- The combination of user and group roles defines a user's persona and determines what applications, tools, and data they can access within the platform.

The following figure shows a sample of **Access Controls** from out-of-the-box:

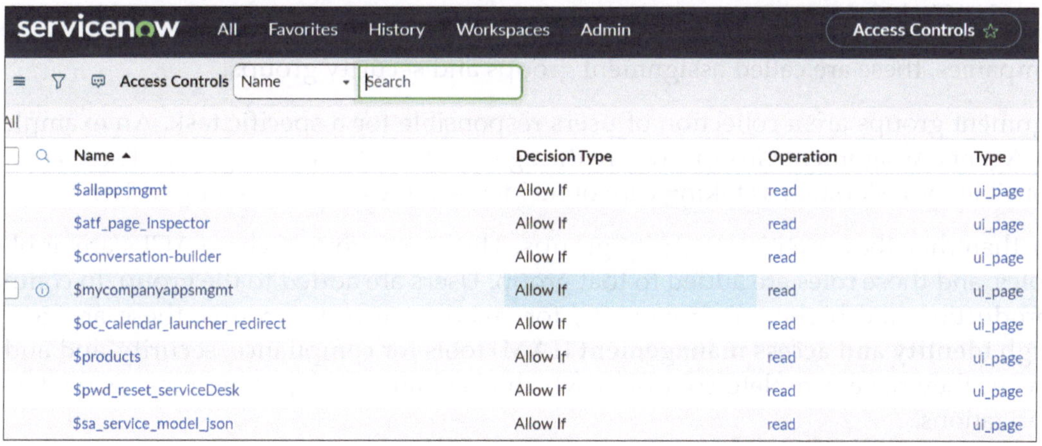

Figure 7.2: Access Controls

The actions are as follows:

1. **Assign permissions to the role:**
   a. You can grant permissions by either adding existing roles to your new role or by creating ACLs.
   b. **Option A**: Add existing roles:
      i. Open the newly created role record.
      ii. Go to the **Contains Roles** or **Roles** tab and click **Edit**.
      iii. Add any existing roles that contain the permissions you need to your custom role.

c. **Option B**: Create ACLs:

   i. Navigate to **System Security | Access Controls**.

   ii. Click **New** and create new ACLs for the tables and operations (e.g., **Create, Read, Write, and Delete** (**CRUD**)) that users with this role should be able to perform.

   iii. In the ACL record, add your new custom role to the **Roles** field.

2. **Assign the role to a user or group**: To a user:

   a. Navigate to **User Administration | Users**.

   b. Open the user record you want to modify.

   c. Go to the **Roles** tab, click **Edit**, select your custom role from the list, and click the arrow to move it to the right-hand list.

   d. Click **Save**.

In companies, these are called assignment groups and security groups.

Assignment groups are a collection of users responsible for a specific task. An example is in Tier 1 Agents Assignment Groups, where the agents are added to this group. These agents are responsible for tasks such as taking care of incidents and cases that belong to Tier 1.

Other than this, they mention security groups. These are groups where ACLs are applied to the roles, and those roles are added to that group. Users are added to the group. In companies for production and higher environments, for creating security groups, these are governed through **identity and access management** (**IAM**) tools for compliance, security, and auditing. This way, they have complete control of which users are given permissions, as well as after authorizations.

Jobs

Scheduled jobs automate tasks in ServiceNow to run at specific times or on recurring intervals, which is necessary for automating routine maintenance, generating reports, and performing actions like sending notifications. They are crucial for streamlining operations, saving administrative time, and ensuring consistency across the platform without manual intervention.

The key needs and use cases are as follows:

- **Automation of routine tasks**: Scheduled jobs run tasks automatically, freeing up administrators from manual, repetitive work.
- **Data processing and maintenance**: They can be used to clean up old records, synchronize data, or perform other maintenance tasks on a defined schedule.

- **Report generation**: Scheduled jobs can be configured to automatically generate and distribute reports at specific times, such as monthly or weekly.
- **Record creation**: They can generate new records from a template on a regular basis, like creating a new incident or change request based on a schedule.
- **Workflow and event management**: They can trigger other business logic, run a business rule, or execute tasks in a script. For example, they can be used to send out email notifications to users.
- **On-demand execution**: Some jobs can be set to run on demand, meaning they can be triggered manually for one-time or ad-hoc tasks, like importing a new spreadsheet of user data.

The following figure shows a sample of **Scheduled Jobs** from out-of-the-box:

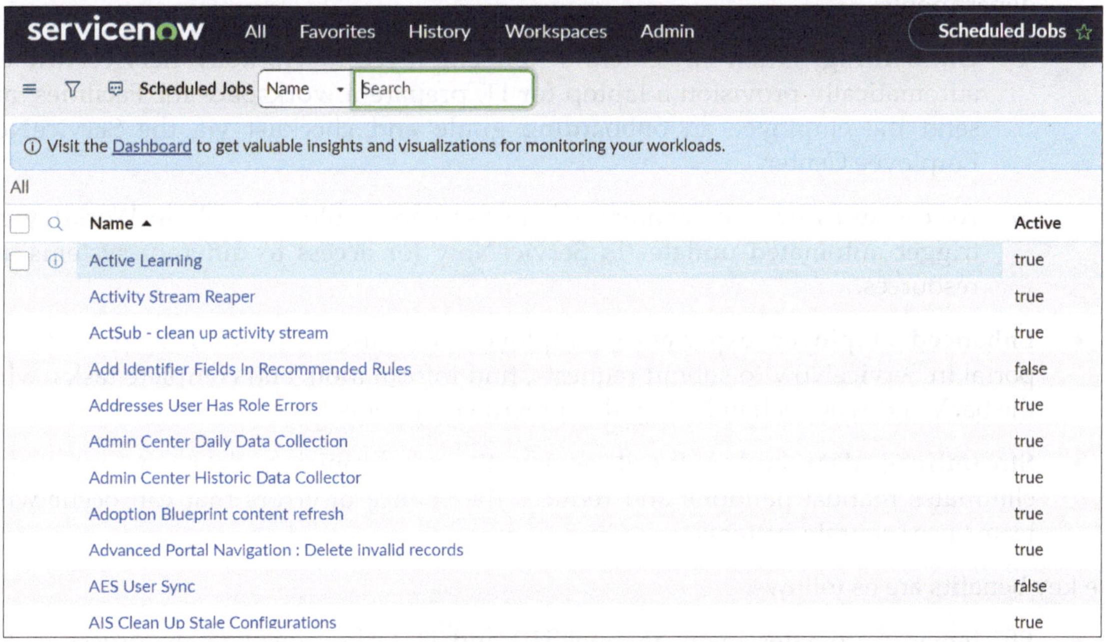

***Figure 7.3**: Scheduled Jobs*

Scheduled jobs in ServiceNow automate repetitive tasks for companies by running scripts or workflows at specific times or on a recurring basis, which reduces manual effort and improves efficiency. In companies, they are used for a wide range of functions, such as generating reports, processing data imports, creating new records, and synchronizing data with other systems.

Companies use jobs for synchronizing data with other systems, such as Workday.

Jobs integrate Workday and ServiceNow HRSD to streamline HR processes. This is achieved by having Workday serve as the system of record for core HR data, while ServiceNow HR Service

Delivery acts as the system of action for employee services and requests. This integration allows Workday to trigger workflows in ServiceNow for tasks like onboarding, employee lifecycle management, and service requests, ensuring data consistency and a more efficient employee experience.

The integration works in the following way:

- **Workday as the source of truth**: Workday manages all core HR data, including employee profiles, compensation, benefits, and hiring information.
- **ServiceNow as the system of action**: When a change occurs in Workday, such as a new hire, this data is sent to ServiceNow. ServiceNow HRSD then uses this information to automate service delivery workflows.
- **Automated workflows**: The integration automates processes across different departments:
    - o **Onboarding**: When HR enters a new employee in Workday, ServiceNow can automatically provision a laptop for IT, prepare a workspace for Facilities, and send the employee an onboarding guide and checklist via the ServiceNow Employee Center.
    - o **Access and role management**: Changes to an employee's role in Workday can trigger automated updates in ServiceNow for access to different systems and resources.
- **Enhanced employee experience**: Employees can use a centralized, personalized portal in ServiceNow to submit requests, find information, and complete tasks, while the back-end work is handled by the integrated systems.
- **Streamlined data and reduced errors**: By synchronizing data, the integration eliminates manual handoffs and reduces the chance of errors that can occur when teams use separate systems.

The key benefits are as follows:

- **Efficiency**: Automates many manual HR and IT tasks, speeding up processes like onboarding and offboarding.
- **Consistency**: Ensures that employee data is consistent across both platforms, reducing discrepancies.
- **Improved employee experience**: Provides a single, user-friendly portal for employees to interact with HR and other departments for their service needs.

As a ServiceNow admin in companies, these scheduled jobs in ServiceNow need to be ensured to run as planned. Alert emails are set, and personnel get notified when they fail so that necessary action can be taken. Ad hoc requests can come to Admins to run jobs in an ad hoc manner.

Plugins, system upgrade

In ServiceNow, a plugin is a set of code that adds specific features and functionalities to an existing application or the platform itself. Unlike a standalone app, which is a complete program, a plugin extends and enhances the platform by providing new capabilities, automating workflows, and integrating with other systems. For example, a plugin could add a new table, script, or automation to streamline a process like change management, or it could be an integration connector to another service.

For every ServiceNow system upgrade, admins will be asked by companies to validate their existing applications against the new plugins. Admins need to work with the respective application development teams so that new plugins can be processed or plugins with new versions can be updated. Admins need to make sure any customization versions need to be updated. Plugin rollback has a lot of limitations.

Issues in production analyzed for root cause

Companies ask the admin to simulate the Prod issues in lower environments. So, for those conditions, Admins need to see logs. **All | System logs** will provide the basic logs. Specific logs are available in email logs and mid-sever logs. job logs menus. These logs will provide a way to understand how logic is working for a particular condition or scenario.

The following figure shows a sample of the **Log** page from out-of-the-box:

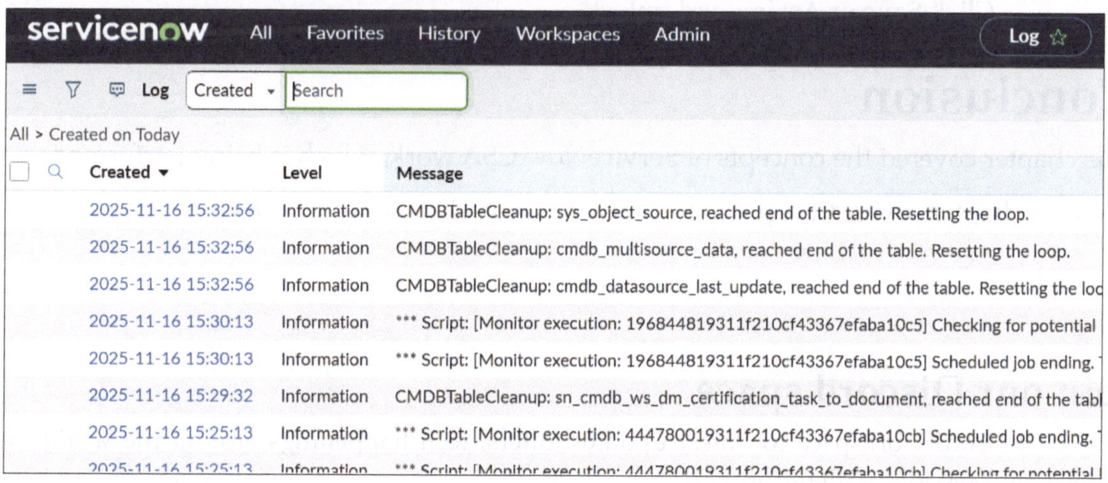

Figure 7.4: Logs

Unlock users

To unlock a user in ServiceNow, navigate to the user record in the **User Administration | Users** module and uncheck the **Locked out** field, then click **Update**. For users locked out of the Now Support portal, go to the portal, select **Manage account and users** from your profile menu, find the user, and click the **Unlock** link or use the toggle switch.

The methods are as follows:

- **Method 1**: Unlock in the ServiceNow instance:
    1. Navigate to **User Administration | Users**.
    2. Search for and open the user's record.
    3. Find the **Locked out** checkbox on the form and uncheck it.
    4. Click **Update**.
- **Method 2**: Unlock in the Now Support portal:
    1. Go to the Now Support portal.
    2. Click your profile icon or name in the top-right corner and select **Manage account and users**.
    3. In the "**Now Support**" tile, click **View all users**.
    4. Find the user in the list.
    5. Click the **Unlock** link next to their name or use the toggle switch to unlock them.
    6. Click **Save** or **Assign** and unlock

Conclusion

This chapter covered the concepts of ServiceNow CSA work, which is being performed.

The next chapter covers CSA practice exams towards CSA exam certification.

Join our Discord space

Join our Discord workspace for latest updates, offers, tech happenings around the world, new releases, and sessions with the authors:

https://discord.bpbonline.com

CHAPTER 8

ServiceNow CSA Practice Exams

Introduction

ServiceNow practice exams refers to the practice questions with answers towards passing the CSA. This covers all the previous chapters discussed in this book.

Structure

This chapter covers the following topics:

- Practice exam questions

Objectives

This chapter provides two sample questions encompassing 120 practice exam questions for the CSA. This will provide an idea of the questions that are to appear in CSA, and practicing towards this provides the right path towards passing CSA.

Practice exam questions

The exam structure of questions is defined in the following section. The exam consists of sixty questions. The formats in which it will appear, according to ServiceNow, are defined here. The passing score is 70 % with 42 questions to be answered correctly.

The types of questions are as follows:

- **Multiple choice (single answer):** For each multiple choice question on the exam, there are at least four possible responses. Select the one response that most accurately answers the question.
- **Multiple select (select all that apply)**: For each multiple select question on the exam, there are at least four possible responses. The question will state how many responses should be selected. Select all responses that accurately answer the question. Partial credit is not provided.

Two sample question papers are provided for practice. Each question is mentioned with the Domain it belongs to, towards the preparation of the exam.

As discussed in other chapters of the book, ServiceNow CSA Certification is divided into six domains, as explained in the following table. The percentage of questions in each domain is listed.

Number of domains	Learning domain	Percent of exam
1	**Platform overview and navigation**: • ServiceNow platform overview. • Platform capabilities and services. • The ServiceNow instance. • Next Experience Unified Navigation.	7%
2	**Instance configuration:** • Installing applications and plugins. • Personalizing/customizing the instance. • Common UIs in the platform.	11%
3	**Configuring applications for collaboration:** • Lists, filters, and tags. • List and form anatomy. • Form configuration. • Form templates and saving options.	20%
4	**Self-service and automation:** • Knowledge Management. • Service Catalog. • Flow Designer. • Virtual Agent.	20%
5	**Database management:** • Data schema. • Application/Access control. • Importing data. • CMDB and CSDM.	27%
6	**Data migration and integration:** • UI policies. • Business rules. • System Update Sets. • Scripting in ServiceNow.	15%

***Table 8.1**: ServiceNow CSA Certification domains*

Sample question paper 1

1. **Which resource would you use to determine if a specific user could contribute to a particular knowledge base?**

   a. User criteria diagnostics
   b. Sn_kb_author role
   c. User criteria job log
   d. Knowledge author group
   e. KB author group

Ans: a

Domain: 4

2. **Which feature allows you to automate business logic for a particular application or process, such as approvals, tasks, notifications, and record operations?**

   a. Flows
   b. Action sequence
   c. Flow diagrams
   d. Action sets
   e. Task flows

Ans: a

Domain: 4

3. **When a flow runs an action, it generates a runtime value, which stays the same for the duration of the flow. What is the name of that runtime value?**

   a. Data pill runtime value
   b. Sequence runtime value
   c. Starting runtime value
   d. Trigger runtime value
   e. Input runtime value

Ans: a

Domain: 4

4. **If a knowledge base has no access details specified. What users are able to read articles in that knowledge base?**

   a. No users
   b. itil users
   c. Users with kb_user role
   d. Any user with an article for permalink
   e. Any active user

Ans: e

Domain: 4

5. **While showing a customer their incident form, they ask to change the priority field title to display their internal terminology, Pvalue. How would you do that? Choose two answers.**

a. Right-click on priority and select configure dictionary
b. Right-click on priority and select configure label
c. Right-click on priority and select configure display settings
d. Right-click on priority and select configure column

Ans: a, b

Domain: 3

6. **What access does a user need to be able to import articles to a knowledge base?**

a. Sn_Knowledge_import
b. Sn_knowledge_contribute
c. can contribute
d. sn_knowledge_write
e. can write
f. can import

Ans: c

Domain: 4

7. **What controls the publishing and retiring process for knowledge articles?**

a. Workflow designer
b. Workflows
c. State life cycle
d. Approval policies
e. Approval definitions

Ans: b

Domain: 4

8. **Which field (or fields) is used as a unique key during imports?**

a. Sys IDs
b. Match fields
c. Coalesce fields
d. Key fields

Ans: c

Domain: 5

9. **What module enables an administrator to define destinations for imported data on any ServiceNow table?**

a. Field transform
b. Schema map
c. Import map
d. Transform map

Ans: d

Domain: 5

10. **What do you click when you have made modifications to your report, and you want to see the results without saving?**

a. Run
b. Execute
c. Test
d. Preview
e. Try it

Ans: a

Domain: 3

11. **What section on the notes tab shows the history of the work documented on the record?**

a. Journal
b. Activity
c. Timeline
d. audit log
e. diary

Ans: b

Domain: 1

12. **What type of rules specify which user groups are responsible for working on different types of tasks?**

a. On call
b. Assignment
c. Routing
d. Calendar
e. Escalation

Ans: b

Domain: 2

13. **Which component of a table contains a piece of data for one record?**

a. Field
b. Factor
c. Data point
d. Item
e. Element

Ans: a

Domain: 5

14. **ServiceNow contains over 25 different report types. What are some of the types? Choose five answers.**

a. Semi-donut
b. Speedometer
c. Donut
d. Thermometer
e. Pie
f. Horizontal Bar
g. Odometer

Ans: a,b,c,e,f

Domain: 3

15. **Of the CI tables, which is a base table of the CMDB hierarchy?**

a) ECMDB

b) Cmdb_rel_ci

c) Cmdb_ci

d) cmdb

e) Ecmdb_rel_ci

f) Ecmdb_ci

Ans: d

Domain: 5

16. **Your customer wants to update a notification, so it is sent to the caller and also to the manager of the caller. How would you approach this requirement?**

a. Set who will receive the subscription

b. On the send to tab, add the caller field, dot walk to the caller's manager to add the manager

c. Create a workflow and include a notification in the workflow

d. On who will receive the tab, select the copy manager checkbox

e. On who will receive the tab, add the caller field, dot walk to the caller's manager to add managers

Ans: e

Domain: 2

17. **An IT user calls the service desk because they need to work on task records. All they can see is the self-service on their homepage when they log into the service now instance. What issue could explain this? Choose two answers.**

a. Their user record was not approved by their managers

b. That user account does not belong to any group that contains the ITIL role

c. Their user account is not logged in properly

d. Their user account does not have the ITIL role

e. That user account failed LDAP authentication

Ans: b, d

Domain: 2

18. **When looking at a long list of records, you want to quickly filter to show only those that have a category of hardware. What is the best option below to filter and show those values?**

    a. On breadcrumbs, click on icon, type hardware, and click enter
    b. Right click on the magnifier, type hardware, and click enter
    c. Click the funnel icon, type hardware and click enter.
    d. On the list, locate and right-click on the value hardware, select show matching
    e. On the category column header, right-click and select show I hardware

Ans: d

Domain: 1

19. **What is the best way to learn about Performance Analytics?**

    a. Use the ServiceNow wiki
    b. Schedule a demo with the ServiceNow sales team
    c. Take a service now Performance Analytics course on now learning
    d. Activate the plugin on your production environment and start the default data collectors

Ans: c

Domain: 3

20. **What module do you use to access the reports that are available to you?**

    a. Self-service > my reports
    b. Reports > overview
    c. Report's > home page
    d. Report's > view/run
    e. Self-service > my dashboards

Ans: d

Domain: 4

21. **Why is it recommended that you limit Update Sets to a maximum of 100 records? Choose two answers.**

    a. Comply with ISO audit requirements
    b. Smaller Update Sets can be imported to production during business hours
    c. Reduce potential conflicts
    d. Improve the ability to troubleshoot issues with the default update set
    e. Make it easier to identify and review changes
    f. Keeps updating set logs shorter
    g. Make it easier for developers to organize their work

Ans: c, e

Domain: 6

22. **Which flow components allow you to specify when a flow should be run?**

    a. Trigger and condition
    b. Trigger and condition pill
    c. Condition and table
    d. Scope and trigger condition
    e. Trigger criteria and clock

Ans: a

Domain: 4

23. **A customer has asked for the following updates to a form:**

    - **Make resolution code mandatory**
    - **When the state is changed to resolved**
    - **Hide major incident checkbox**
    - **Unless logged-in user has major incident manager role**

    What type of rules would you use to implement this requirement?

    a. Field lipper
    b. UI policy and actions
    c. UI design
    d. Dictionary design
    e. Form constraint

Ans: b

Domain: 6

24. **What is a set of conditions applied to a table list to show as a subset of the data?**

    a. Mask
    b. Divisor
    c. Filter
    d. Funnel
    e. Query

Ans: c

Domain: 2

25. **Which admin role is required to make changes to high security settings?**

    a. Ad_admin
    b. High_sec_admin
    c. Sn_ad_admin
    d. Admin
    e. Security_admin

Ans: e

Domain: 2

26. **What process allows a user to create, categorize, review, approve, and browse important information in a centralized location that is shared by the entire organization?**

a. Self-service management
b. Knowledge-centered management
c. Knowledge Management
d. Business information management
e. Information portal management

Ans: c

Domain: 1

27. **Which role can manage multiple knowledge bases?**

a. Sn_kb_admin
b. Kb_Admin
c. Knowledge_admin
d. Knowledge_base_admin

Ans: c

Domain: 2

28. **Which storefront is a single location for accessing prebuilt spokes to quickly integrate with third-party services to build and share content?**

a. Integration portal
b. Integration store
c. ServiceNow spoke store
d. Integration one stop
e. ServiceNow Store
f. Integration spoke hub
g. Spoke store

Ans: c

Domain: 1

29. **You are creating a catalog item for ordering a new desktop computer. The computer has these options:**

- **Color: Black or silver**
- **Ram: 32 MB or 64 MB**
- **Keyboard: Standard or economic**
- **Monitor: 24 inch or 32 inch**

How would you add this option to the catalog item form?

a. Add choices
b. Add UI options
c. Add variables
d. Add fields

Ans: c

Domain: 4

30. **To quickly return to the homepage you were using five minutes ago, which item would you click?**

   a. Gear icon
   b. Homepage icon
   c. History menu
   d. Start icon

Ans: c

Domain: 1

31. **What is the most important thing to remember about activating a plugin?**

   a. Install dependent plugins first
   b. Tick the box for adding demo data
   c. Plugins, once installed, cannot be uninstalled
   d. Submit an HI ticket to get Authorization
   e. Plugins are prohibited in personal developer instances

Ans: c

Domain: 2

32. **What are the steps to commit an update set?**

   a. Retrieve, preview, and commit
   b. Check, retire, and apply
   c. Verify, check, and commit
   d. Test, validate, and commit

Ans: a

Domain: 6

33. **What is captured in Update Set?**

   a. Groups users
   b. Scheduled jobs
   c. CI data
   d. Workflow

Ans: d

Domain: 6

34. **Where is the data stored?**

   a. List
   b. Table
   c. Record
   d. Form

Ans: b

Domain: 5

35. Which table does user data get stored in?

a. sys_user_group
b. sys_user_has_role
c. sys_user
d. sys_user_certificate

Ans: c

Domain: 5

36. When will knowledge articles be visible to users?

a. Approved
b. Published
c. Retired
d. Checkout

Ans: b

Domain: 4

37. In application form menus and modules, which one of the following users will be used when needed to access quickly or often?

a. Favorite
b. Bookmark
c. Tag
d. Breadcrumbs

Ans: a

Domain: 1

38. What is at the start of the flow?

a. Actions
b. Error handler
c. Triggers

Ans: c

Domain: 4

39. What are the main types of triggers in Flow Designer?

a. Record based, date based, application based
b. Record based, scope based, application based
c. Record based, data based, scope based
d. Record based, scope based, application based

Ans: a

Domain: 4

40. **Which one of the following applications is available to all users?**

a. Incident

b. Change

c. Problem

d. Self-service

Ans: d

Domain: 4

41. **Multiple choice, Single Line, and Single Line Text are what type of elements in ServiceNow?**

a. Related lists

b. Variable types

c. Order guides

d. Request types

Ans: b

Domain: 1

42. **Can only production instances of ServiceNow be cloned?**

a. True

b. False

Ans: b

Domain: 2

43. **Will changing the list layout by clicking the gear icon impact all users?**

a. False

b. True

Ans: a

Domain: 2

44. **Which of the following is correct regarding data stored in the table?**

a. Row represents a record, and column represents a field

b. Row represents a field, and column represents a record

Ans: a

Domain: 5

45. **What is ServiceNow's default search engine?**

a. Zing

b. SearchNow

c. GoogleNow

Ans: a

Domain: 1

46. **Which of the following operations can be done via the user menu? Select 3.**

a. Elevate privileges
b. Impersonate
c. Logout
d. Send notifications

Ans: a, b, c

Domain: 1

47. **Which of the following are states in workflow?**

a. Published
b. UnPublished
c. Checked Out
d. Checked In

Ans: a,c

Domain: 1

48. **What are the steps to commit an update set?**

a. Retrieve, preview and commit
b. Check, review and commit
c. Verify, validate and commit

Ans: a

Domain: 6

49. **In Incident form, which of the following is best to use for hiding a field or making a file mandatory?**

a. Business rule
b. UI policy
c. UI action
d. Script

Ans: b

Domain: 6

50. **Which one of the following is captured in the update set?**

a. Workflow
b. Groups, users
c. Scheduled jobs
d. CI data

Ans: a

Domain: 6

51. **In which of the following data is stored?**

a. Form
b. List
c. Column
d. Table

Ans: d

Domain: 3

52. Which one of the following is an order guide?

a. Can create an individual request for each item

b. Users can submit all requests in a single request

Ans: b

Domain: 2

53. When an admin creates a new table, which one of the following is an appropriate table name?

a. task_cde

b. d_cde

c. u_cde

Ans: c

Domain: 5

54. Which table does user data get stored in?

a. sys_user

b. user

c. user data

Ans: a

Domain: 5

55. Which one of the following correctly defines workflow?

a. Workflow cannot be captured in the update set

b. Workflow can be checked out so that two users are not editing the workflow at the same time

Ans: b

Domain: 6

56. Which one of the following base modules is used to load data in ServiceNow?

a. Incident

b. Change

c. Import set

Ans: c

Domain: 5

57. Where can the applications, modules, or tables be stored which is used frequently?

a. Favourites

b. Bookmarks

c. Applications

d. Header bar

Ans: a

Domain: 1

58. **Where can the ServiceNow's current version of the instance be found?**

    a. System Diagnostics I Stats
    b. System logs
    c. Memory Stats
    d. System.upgraded

Ans: a

Domain: 1

59. **Which one of the following correctly defines System Dictionary in ServiceNow?**

    a. The system dictionary is itself a table that holds definitions for every other table and field in the ServiceNow instance.
    b. This is a script
    c. This is a data schema

Ans: a

Domain: 5

60. **What is the first step to import spreadsheet data into ServiceNow?**

    a. Define data source
    b. Load data
    c. Transform map

Ans: a

Domain: 5

Sample question paper 2

1. **The employee onboarding team has asked for a way for managers to order computers, monitors, business cards, and cell phones for new employees. How would you proceed to meet this requirement?**

    a. Create requested item
    b. Create order guide
    c. Create record producer
    d. Create on boarding bot

Ans: b

Domain: 2

2. **From the form designer, how would you define a section so that it displays as a tab?**

   a. Name the section
   b. Click the gear and check the tab option
   c. Click context menu and select configure tabs
   d. Add .tab to the end of the section name
   e. Add _tap to the end of the section name

Ans: a

Domain: 3

3. **What module do you use to access the reports that are available to you?**

   a. self-service | my reports
   b. reports | overview
   c. reports | view/run
   d. reports | home page
   e. self-service | my dashboards

Ans: c

Domain: 4

4. **Which flow components allow you to specify when a flow should be run?**

   a. Trigger and condition pill
   b. Condition and table
   c. Trigger and condition
   d. Scope and trigger condition
   e. Trigger criteria and clock

Ans: c

Domain: 4

5. **A customer has asked for the following updates to a form: make resolution code mandatory, when the state is changed to resolved, hide the major incident checkbox, unless logged-in user has the major incident manager role. What type of rules would you use to implement this requirement?**

   a. Field lipper
   b. UI design
   c. UI policy and actions
   d. Dictionary design
   e. Form constraint

Ans: c

Domain: 2

6. A new employee joins the IT department and needs to perform work assigned to the network and Hardware groups. How would you setup their access? Choose three answers.

a. Add user account to hardware group
b. Add a user account to ACL
c. Add a user account to itil group
d. Create a user account
e. Add user account to IT knowledge base
f. Add user account to network group

Ans: a, d, f

Domain: 2

7. What is the language used for scripting in ServiceNow?

a. Perl
b. Python
c. JavaScript
d. C++
e. PHP
f. Glide

Ans: c

Domain: 1

8. Which script can run when a record is displayed, inserted, updated, deleted, or when a table is queried?

a. client script
b. business rule
c. UI script
d. scheduled job
e. record

Ans: b

Domain: 6

9. Which ServiceNow resource can be used as a blueprint to map your IT services to the ServiceNow?

a. **Configuration management database** (**CMDB**)
b. Now learning
c. Service now wiki
d. Service mapping guided setup
e. **Common Services Data Model** (**CSDM**)
f. IT

Ans: e

Domain: 5

10. **What are the steps for importing data using an import set?**
    a. Identify source; import transform map; run transformer; verify import
    b. Load the data; create a transform map; transform data; clean up import table
    c. Select source file; run auto map; transform data; clean up target table
    d. Setup LDAP; run auto map; transform data; clean up target table

Ans: b

Domain: 5

11. **When importing data, what happens to imported rows if no coalesce field is specified?**
    a. All rows are treated as new records, but errors will be flagged in the import log
    b. Duplicate rows are rejected from the import
    c. All rows are treated as new records. No existing records were updated
    d. All rows were rejected from the import, as the coalesce field is required

Ans: c

Domain: 5

12. **Within the report library, there are many baseline reports that can be used for learning about reports. What could you search for to locate ITIL best practice indicator reports?**
    a. KPI
    b. ITSM
    c. ITIL
    d. PA
    e. Sn_itil

Ans: a

Domain: 3

13. **What are examples of core tables in the ServiceNow platform?**
    a. Team, party, awards
    b. Work, caller, timecard
    c. User, task, incident
    d. Base configuration item, configuration item, base task

Ans: c

Domain: 3

14. **A manager is complaining that they cannot get the data that they need for a report, because the data resides in two different tables. This data is used for many different reports in their department. You have checked to see if dot walking will meet the requirement, and it is not possible. What else might you try to help this manager?**

   a. Create a report source
   b. Create a database view
   c. Create a custom table
   d. Export the tables to spreadsheet
   e. Create a report template

Ans: b

Domain: 5

15. **What are the advantages of using Flow Designer? Choose three answers.**

   a. Supports legacy workflows
   b. Less manual scripting
   c. Enables complicated scripting
   d. Reduces technical debt
   e. Supports advanced developers
   f. Compliments the integration store
   g. Smooth integration with third-party systems

Ans: b, d, g

Domain: 4

16. **What policies are applied to all data entered into the platform via form (UI), import sets, or web services?**

   a. Data submission policies
   b. Data quality policies
   c. Write policies
   d. Data integrity policies
   e. Data policies

Ans: e

Domain: 6

17. **What catalog tool would you use to create a catalog item or record producer?**

   a. Catalog formatter
   b. Catalog flow builder
   c. Catalog designer
   d. Catalog builder
   e. Variable designer
   f. Form designer
   g. Workflow designer

Ans: d

Domain: 4

18. **What are the different types of data sources that may be imported into the service now? Choose four answers.**

a. Implementation spoke
b. JDBC connection
c. DataHub
d. Network server
e. LDAP connection
f. Local sources (i.e., XML, CSV, Excel)

Ans: b, c, e, f

Domain: 5

19. **What are the examples of UI actions relating to forms? Choose three answers.**

a. Form context menu
b. Form columns
c. Form links
d. Form buttons
e. Form view

Ans: a, c, d

Domain: 5

20. **What feature allows us to limit users' ability to contribute or read knowledge within a knowledge base?**

a. User criteria
b. Roles
c. Categories
d. Groups

Ans: a

Domain: 4

21. **How to navigate to the schema map for a table?**

a. System dictionary | show schema map and select table
b. System definitions | tables and select table. Go to related links and click show schema map
c. System definition | dictionary and select table. Go to related links and click show schema map
d. System definition> show schema map. select table

Ans: a

Domain: 5

22. **What type of entities can receive task assignments in ServiceNow? Choose two answers.**

a. Users
b. Groups
c. Departments
d. Teams

Ans: a, b

Domain: 2

23. **Which capability allows the user to create dashboards with big widgets to visualize data over time to identify areas of improvement?**

a. Reporting
b. Analytics reports
c. Scheduled reports
d. Performance Analytics

Ans: d

Domain: 3

24. **Which would you follow when testing a catalogue item that has a manager approval flow? Choose three answers.**

a. Use the instance Incognito settings to quickly toggle between the requester and approval
b. Use your admin account, so you can approve the items quickly
c. Impersonate the requester to ensure the form works
d. Make sure the requester's user record as manager is specified
e. Create and select your testing update set before starting the test cases
f. Make sure the latest flows are activated

Ans: b, c, d

Domain: 2

25. **When designing a flow, how do you reference data from a record in that flow?**

a. Drag the data pill onto the flow definition
b. Add the table reference using the slush bucket
c. Specify the source table on the data pill related list
d. Drag the table icon onto the flow definition
e. Use the condition builder to specify the desired values

Ans: a

Domain: 4

26. **Access controls are evaluated in this order:**

- **Match object against table ACL.**
- **Match the object against field ACL.**

Within step one above, win hat order are the table ACLs evaluated?

a. General to specific: table ACL, table.field ACL, parent table. field ACL
b. Specific to general: table.field ACL, parent table.field ACL, * Field ACL
c. Top to bottom: wildcard table ACL, parent table ACL, table ACL
d. Bottom to top: table ACL, table. field ACL, parent table. field ACL
e. Specific to general: table ACL, parent table ACL, wildcard(*) ACL

Ans: a

Domain: 5

27. **After finishing your work in a high security setting, what is a possible way to return to normal admin security levels?**

a. End impersonation
b. Use system administration> normal security module
c. Select normal role
d. Logout and back in
e. Select global update set

Ans: d

Domain: 6

28. **When selecting the target table for an import, which table can be selected? Choose three answers.**

a. Related tables, using dot walk
b. Tables within the existing application scope
c. Tables within the global scope
d. Tables which allow write access to other applications
e. Tables outside of servicenow

Ans: b,c,d

Domain: 4

29. **Which statement correctly describes the difference between a client script and a business rule?**

   a. A client script executes on the server, and a business rule executes on the client

   b. A client script executes before a record is loaded, and a business rule executes after a record is updated

   c. A client script executes on the client, and a business rule executes on the server

   d. Client scripting executes before a record is loaded, and a business rule executes after a record is loaded

Ans: c

Domain: 6

30. **How would you distinguish between a base class table and a parent class table?**

   a. Extended tables can be extended from parent tables or base tables, but they cannot be extended from both

   b. Base class table is not extended from another table. Parent class tables may be extended from another table

   c. Extended tables are always extended from parent tables. Extended tables are usually extended from base tables

   d. Base class tables always have tables extended from them. Parent tables do not have tables extended from them

Ans: b

Domain: 5

31. **Many actions are included with the Flow Designer. What are some frequently used core-actions? Choose four answers.**

   a. Wait for the condition
   b. Create record
   c. Look up record
   d. Ask for approval
   e. Wait for match
   f. Look for update

Ans: a, b, c, d

Domain: 4

32. **On a filter condition, which component is always a choice list?**

   a. Filter criteria
   b. Match criteria
   c. Operator
   d. Operation

Ans: c

Domain: 2

33. **Which is the most efficient way to move a large amount of data between instances?**

    a. Export to zip
    b. Update sets
    c. Export to data package
    d. Export to XML

Ans: b

Domain: 6

34. **Which ServiceNow utility gives a service desk agent the ability to trace from a service having an issue, to see which CIs supporting that service have active issues?**

    a. Event management homepage
    b. Service dashboard
    c. CI Dependency View
    d. CI health dashboard

Ans: d

Domain: 5

35. **When managing tags, you can adjust who is able to see them. What are the visibility options? Choose three answers.**

    a. Admins
    b. Everyone
    c. Groups and users
    d. Me
    e. Roles and permissions

Ans: b, c, d

Domain: 2

36. **Which modules allow the creation of a new table? Choose two answers.**

    a. Tables
    b. Tables and columns
    c. Dictionary
    d. Schema map

Ans: a,b

Domain: 5

37. **A task worker asks how they can monitor any updates occurring to records assigned to them, like responses from customers. What can be suggested?**

    a. On my work list, select the Activity Stream icon to show a frame with live updates
    b. Select service desk | my work dashboard
    c. Open an Agent Workspace tab for each record he wants to monitor
    d. Click on the eyeglass icon to expand the monitor frame

Ans: a

Domain: 1

38. **What are the advantages of using spokes for integration? Choose three answers.**

    a. Reduces the need for code

    b. Features scale and control mechanism

    c. Ensures discoverability and reuse

    d. Automated event management

    e. Free spokes are available in the ServiceNow Store

Ans: a, d, e

Domain: 1

39. **What icon is used to change the label on your favorite?**

    a. Triangle

    b. Star

    c. Pencil

    d. Clock

Ans: c

Domain: 1

40. **What is the result of the order in which access controls are evaluated?**

    a. Ensures the user has access to the fields in a table before considering their access to the table

    b. Ensures the user has access to the application before evaluating access to a module within the application

    c. Ensures the user has access to a table before evaluating access to a field in the table

    d. Ensures the user can get to work as quickly as possible

Ans: c

Domain: 2

41. **Group records are stored in which table?**

    a. Group[s_sys_group]

    b. Group[sys_user_group]

    c. Group[u_sys_group]

    d. Group[sn_sys_group

Ans: b

Domain: 5

42. **An IT manager is responsible for the network and hardware assignment groups; each group contains 5 team members. These team members are working on many tasks, but the manager cannot see any tasks on the service desk | My Groups Work List. What could explain this?**

   a. The assignment group manager field is empty
   b. The manager is not a member of the network and hardware groups
   c. The manager is not a member of the service desk group
   d. The manager does not have the ITIL role

Ans: b

Domain: 2

43. **What do you activate when you want to add applications or functionality within your development instance?**

   a. App updated set
   b. Patch
   c. App package
   d. Plugin
   e. Updated pack

Ans: d

Domain: 1

44. **What is an Order Guide?**

   a. A collection of related catalog items grouped together
   b. A single catalog item
   c. A Catalog form

Ans: a

Domain: 2

45. **The employee onboarding team has asked for a way for managers to order computers, monitors, business cards, and cell phones for new employees. How to proceed to meet this requirement?**

   a. Create an onboarding bot
   b. Create order guide
   c. Create the requested item
   d. Create a record producer

Ans: b

Domain: 2

46. **For a customer's inventory application, several inventory application fields are needed on a needed-on inventory ticket. This ticket will be assigned to the inventory support team members. How to start implementing this requirement?**

   a. Create an inventory table with the inventory specification fields. In the create view between the inventory and task table

   b. Create the inventory table with the inventory specification fields. Then, create many-to-many relationships between the inventory and the task table

   c. Create an inventory table as an extended table from the task table. Then add the inventory specification fields, as needed

   d. Create an inventory table as a new base table. Then add inventory specification fields as needed

Ans: c

Domain: 5

47. **What utility enables process owners to access other cross-enterprise workflows within a single unified process?**

   a. Floor designer
   b. Flow editor
   c. Workflow manager
   d. Process owner dashboard
   e. Process workflow designer
   f. Process flow manager
   g. Process automation designer

Ans: g

Domain: 4

48. **The time for the end user is based on the round-trip between the client and the server. What activities are included in the round-trip?**

   a. Submit+ query
   b. Request+ response
   c. Insert+ verify
   d. Save+ update
   e. Write+ read

Ans: b

Domain: 1

49. **Here is an example of the criteria set for a knowledge base: Companies: ACME North America, Department: HR, Groups: ACME MANAGERS, Match all: yes. In this example, what user would have access to this knowledge base?**

a. Members of the ACME managers group and the HR department, regardless of geography

b. Employees of ACME North America who are members of the HR department or the ACME managers group

c. Users who are members of either ACME North America, the HR department, or the ACME Managers group

d. Members of the ACME Manager group, who are also members of HR departments and part of ACME North America

Ans: d

Domain: 2

50. **Which type of field allows you to enter freely using letters, numbers, and special characters?**

a. Multi line text

b. Single line text

c. Text

d. Open text

e. String

Ans: e

Domain: 5

51. **A manager wants to run a report showing how many service requests have been fulfilled for business cards since the beginning of the year. What table would they select for building this report?**

a. request[sc_req]

b. task[task]

c. catalog item[sc_cat_item]

d. catalog task[sc_task]

e. requested item[sc_req_item]

f. service catalog[sc_catalog]

Ans: e

Domain: 5

52. **When moving a homepage or dashboard between instances, what must you remember?**

a. They are automatically added to the updates set

b. Create a separate update set for them

c. They can be moved using zip files

d. Manually add them to the update set

e. They cannot be moved via XML

f. They cannot be moved via updates set

Ans: d

Domain: 6

53. **When adding a related list to a form, you choose the related list from the list collector. What is an example of a related list one might see on the list collector? Choose three answers.**

a. problem == parent

b. release phase == parent

c. outages > task number

d. catalog task > parent

e. HR case > parent

Ans: c, d, e

Domain: 3

54. **In Flow Designer, where is the data from an action stored so it can be used in subsequent actions in the flow?**

a. Field value

b. Data pill

c. Data trigger

d. Data element

e. Field icon

Ans: b

Domain: 4

55. **Which module would you use to create a new automation of business logic, such as approvals, tasks, and notifications?**

a. Process automation | active flows

b. Process automation | flow designer

c. Process automation | flow administration

d. Process automation | process flow

e. Process automation | workflow editor

Ans: b

Domain: 4

56. **When a custom table is created, which access control rules are automatically created? Choose four answers.**

a. Execute
b. Create
c. Update
d. Read
e. Delete
f. Write

Ans: b, d, e, f

Domain: 5

57. **When you set a policy that is applied to all data entered into the platform (UI, import sets, or web services). Where does this policy require the default?**

a. Server
b. Client
c. Browser
d. Network

Ans: b

Domain: 6

58. **What capability allows users to create dashboards with big widgets to visualize data over time to identify areas of improvement?**

a. Analytics Reports
b. Performance Analytics
c. Reporting
d. Scheduled Reports

Ans: b

Domain: 3

59. **After finishing your work on high security settings, what is a possible way to return to normal admin security levels?**

a. Select global update set
b. End impersonation
c. Use system administration | normal security module
d. Logout and back in
e. Select normal role

Ans: d

Domain: 1

60. **A user wants to create a set of filter conditions, where they want to show records that satisfy two conditions:**

- **Incidents where the state is closed**
- **Incidents where the assignment group is a network**

After clicking the funnel icon, what should the user do?

a. Define the first condition; click the AND button; define the second condition; click run
b. Define the first condition; click I icon on the breadcrumb, define the second condition; press enter
c. Define the first condition; click I icon on breadcrumb, define second condition; click run
d. Define the first condition; click the AND button; define the second condition; press enter

Ans: a

Domain: 3

61. **When selecting the target table for an import, which table can one select? Choose three answers. (Additional)**

a. Tables within the existing application scope
b. Tables within the global scope
c. Tables that allow write access to other applications
d. Related tables, using dot walk
e. Tables outside of ServiceNow

Ans: a, b, c

Domain: 5

62. **What ServiceNow feature allows you to include data from a secondary related table on a report? (Additional)**

a. Dot walking
b. Outer join
c. Joins
d. SQL

Ans: a

Domain: 3

63. **Which ServiceNow feature provides assistance to help users obtain information, make decisions, and perform common work tasks via a messaging interface? (Additional)**

a. Virtual Agent
b. Now support
c. Chat box
d. Knowledge chat

Ans: a

Domain: 4

Conclusion

This chapter provided the practice questions with answers for passing the CSA certification. The idea is that if these concepts are understood, it will enable the passing of the CSA Certification. Further, this will enable us to apply these concepts practically towards implementation.

The next chapter will provide a brief idea of future trends in ServiceNow towards system administration. The next chapter will show the impact of **artificial intelligence** (**AI**) in ServiceNow.

Join our Discord space

Join our Discord workspace for latest updates, offers, tech happenings around the world, new releases, and sessions with the authors:

https://discord.bpbonline.com

CHAPTER 9
Summing Up and Future Trends

Introduction

ServiceNow enters into a more exciting phase of use of **artificial intelligence** (**AI**) in 2026 and beyond. This applies to CSA work for ServiceNow Administration as well. Most of the products of ServiceNow are built with Now Assist, a tool for AI. Automation with workflows done by ServiceNow using Flow Designer is further augmented by a visual, drag-and-drop, low-code/no-code palette. Details of these future trends are discussed in this chapter.

Structure

The chapter covers the following topics:

- Summing up and future trends
- Generative and agentic AI in ServiceNow

Objectives

This chapter provides insights into the summation of this book and provides details of future trends in ServiceNow technology towards ServiceNow administration.

Summing up and future trends

ServiceNow's future is defined by its evolution from a service management tool to an AI-first enterprise operating system that orchestrates work across an entire organization. This strategy is built on embedding AI into its platform, expanding its suite of workflow-focused products, and moving into new markets and industries.

ServiceNow CSA future trends revolve around the platform's expanding use of AI-driven automation, the demand for low-code/no-code development, and the creation of user-centric workflows across various business functions. With ServiceNow's focus on digital transformation, the leverage is to use new tools like Now Assist and understand the implications of integrating AI, promoting scalable and cost-effective solutions, and staying competitive and advancing careers.

The key trends are as follows:

- The integration of AI is a primary driver for innovation, with tools like Now Assist enabling predictive insights, automated task management, and enhanced decision-making across all departments.
- ServiceNow's App Engine and Creator Studio facilitate citizen development, allowing users with business expertise to build custom applications and workflows with minimal coding, increasing efficiency and reducing development costs.
- A focus on seamless user experiences and user-centric design is crucial for eliminating bottlenecks and providing real-time visibility across integrated systems.
- Organizations are seeking scalable, cost-efficient solutions to manage complex operations and reduce redundant systems, a trend ServiceNow aims to address with its platform.

The AI Now Assist capability is in every module, where it can do more automations in tasks.

Now Assist is ServiceNow's generative AI offering, integrated into the Now Platform to help users work more efficiently by automating tasks like summarizing incident records, drafting knowledge articles, and generating plain-language answers to questions. It provides AI-powered assistance for administrators, developers, agents, and employees across various ServiceNow products, increasing productivity and accelerating time to value by reducing manual work and providing personalized, AI-guided recommendations.

Now Assist utilizes **large language models** (**LLMs**) and is built on the ServiceNow AI Platform. An LLM is a statistical language model, trained on a massive amount of data, that can be used to generate and translate text and other content, and perform other **natural language processing** (**NLP**) tasks.

Now Assist can do the following:

- Instantly summarizes complex information from exhaustive notes in incident and case records.
- Draft knowledge articles from case descriptions and generate responses to employee inquiries.
- Helps automate routine tasks and provides proactive, AI-guided recommendations for workflows.
- Delivers faster and more relevant answers by providing better context for searches.
- Generates code and business logic to help developers create applications more quickly.
- Enhances self-service capabilities for employees by providing quick access to information and support.

The benefits for users are as follows:

- Reduces time spent on manual tasks like searching and re-explaining, freeing up time for problem-solving.
- Speeds up processes and helps resolve issues faster.
- Accelerates the benefits users get from the platform by making AI-powered tools readily available.
- Offers a personalized experience with AI-guided recommendations and easy access to workflows.

Generative AI is a type of AI that learns from vast amounts of data to create new, original content, such as text, images, music, and code, in response to prompts. Unlike traditional AI, which often follows predefined rules or identifies patterns, generative AI models use deep learning techniques like transformer architectures and LLMs to generate statistically probable outputs that are similar but not identical to the data they were trained on.

ServiceNow embeds this technology into its platform through Now Assist, a suite of tools that leverages LLMs via the generative AI controller to automate tasks, enhance agent productivity, improve employee experiences, and generate valuable content like knowledge articles and code.

The key aspects of generative AI in ServiceNow are as follows:

- Assist the user-facing experience and the primary way users interact with ServiceNow's generative AI capabilities.
- Generative AI Controller is the foundational layer that connects ServiceNow to powerful external LLMs from providers like *OpenAI*, *Azure OpenAI*, and *Google Gemini*.
- ServiceNow also has its own LLM, trained on domain-specific data, to provide enterprise-grade, conversational AI experiences within the platform.
- Generative AI creates original content, including summarizing long texts, generating knowledge base articles, suggesting code for developers, and providing contextual responses for customer service.
- It helps automate routine tasks, saving time and resources for employees.
- By assisting with tasks like content creation and data analysis, generative AI allows employees to focus on more complex, meaningful work.
- It enables more intelligent chatbots and provides agents with the information and tools they need to resolve issues faster and more effectively.
- Generative AI can also assist developers by helping to generate code and even entire low-code applications.

Agentic AI is a form of AI where AI agents can observe systems, make decisions, and initiate workflows autonomously, requiring minimal human intervention for repetitive processes.

Key differences between generative AI and agentic AI are defined as follows:

- **Focus**: Generative AI is about creation, while agentic AI is about action.
- **Nature**: Generative AI is reactive, responding to prompts; agentic AI is proactive, pursuing goals autonomously.

Agentic AI is proactive, goal-driven, and capable of handling complex workflows beyond simple content creation independently. This can be designed to insert manual decision-making in needed actions for careful monitoring and execution of workflows.

AI Agents can make decisions from Topics and the Flow Designer in ServiceNow. This is done by leveraging generative AI with Now Assist to interpret user intent and context, then execute the necessary, pre-defined automated processes built using Virtual Agent topics and Flow Designer.

Generative and agentic AI in ServiceNow

The promise: AI will run IT operations end-to-end with minimal human input.

The reality: Generative AI is no longer a side experiment; it is mainstream. ServiceNow's generative AI features are being deployed for the following:

- **Incident triage**: Automatically categorizing and prioritizing tickets.
- **Summarization**: Turning lengthy tickets into short action items for agents.
- **Virtual Agents**: Handling FAQs and basic IT queries.

However, the real step-change in 2025 is Agentic AI. Instead of waiting for instructions, AI agents can now observe systems, make decisions, and trigger workflows autonomously.

Example: A large company deployed ServiceNow AI agents to monitor recurring outage tickets. The system automatically correlated incidents with faulty routers, cross-checked dependencies in the CMDB, and initiated a workflow to schedule replacements.

Result: 35% reduction in **mean time to response** (**MTTR**) and improved **service level agreement** (**SLA**) compliance.

The hype: Believing AI can replace entire IT teams. In reality, agentic AI still requires governance, observability, and human-in-the-loop oversight. Left unchecked, it can misclassify critical incidents or trigger workflows with unintended consequences.

AI is moving from pilot to production, but needs to be implemented with governance.

Virtual Agent automations in the future will use targeted, purpose-built LLMs to recognize, summarize, translate, predict, and respond to natural language inputs.

As ServiceNow grows, employee demand grows as well. Employees expect services and quick responses when needs arise. Service agents are avoiding manual and repetitive tasks, which is improving productivity.

However, requests require information either for the employee seeking to solve a problem or for the agent working to find a resolution. And information is not always easy to access, distill, and share, especially in a growing enterprise. More personalization, shortening the time it takes to find answers, and simplifying the complexity of our information ecosystem for all users are expected.

Experience the benefits of ServiceNow products, which are more sophisticated and feature-rich for customers. One of the main solutions is the Virtual Agent with Now Assist. This AI-powered chatbot provides anytime self-service to our employees, helping them complete routine tasks and answer questions using natural language processing.

The second piece is AI Search, which connects employees to answers. AI Search brings in data from internal and external sources and uses machine learning capabilities to improve over time.

Now Assist use cases include summarizing incident and chat data, automatically generating resolution notes and knowledge articles, and providing AI-powered automation for IT, HR, and customer service tasks. It supports various industries like manufacturing, financial services, and healthcare by streamlining operations, improving customer experiences, and ensuring compliance.

In ServiceNow, AI agents were introduced. AI agents are autonomous software programs that use machine learning and natural language processing to automate tasks, make decisions, and provide insights. They act as digital teammates that can handle everything from simple requests, like resetting a password, to complex workflows by analyzing data, interacting with users, and executing actions across various ServiceNow products. They are used to improve productivity and efficiency in areas like IT service management, HR, and customer service.

With the AI Agent Studio, you can build your own AI agents without writing a single line of code. You only need to describe what you want your AI agents to achieve using simple, natural language prompts. AI agents can make decisions based on topics and flows.

A long-term goal is to achieve highly autonomous operations where AI agents can manage and resolve complex issues and processes with minimal human intervention.

The following is a sample of questions that may appear in CSA in the future regarding this topic:

1. Which ServiceNow feature uses generative AI capabilities to summarize content or generate new content, such as draft responses for agents?
   a. **Configuration management database (CMDB)**
   b. Flow Designer
   c. Performance Analytics
   d. Now Assist

   Answer: d. Now Assist

2. What is the primary purpose of AI features embedded within the ServiceNow platform, such as predictive intelligence?
   a. To replace all human administrators with autonomous agents.
   b. To automate code development for new applications.
   c. To provide machine learning solutions that categorize and route work, predict performance, and identify major incidents without explicit programming.
   d. To generate realistic images and marketing content for the service catalog.

   Answer: c. To provide machine learning solutions that categorize and route work, predict performance, and identify major incidents without explicit programming.

Conclusion

This chapter covered the concepts of ServiceNow CSA future trends and the summation of this book towards CSA certification. This book thus provides the needed concepts of ServiceNow administration for passing the certification, as well as applying practically the same, focusing on the success of the individual and the organization.

Join our Discord space

Join our Discord workspace for latest updates, offers, tech happenings around the world, new releases, and sessions with the authors:

https://discord.bpbonline.com

Index

U

V

W